With my sincerest thanks for your
guidance and encouragement, which
made this book possible.

Townsend Wilhelm Bowling

STUDIES ON VOLTAIRE
AND THE
EIGHTEENTH CENTURY

〰〰

196

General editor

HAYDN MASON
School of European Studies
University of East Anglia
Norwich, England

TOWNSEND WHELEN BOWLING

THE LIFE, WORKS, AND LITERARY CAREER OF LOAISEL DE TRÉOGATE

THE VOLTAIRE FOUNDATION

AT THE

TAYLOR INSTITUTION, OXFORD

1981

ISSN 0435-2866

ISBN 0 7294 0261 4

Printed in England by Cheney & Sons Ltd,
Banbury, Oxfordshire

Contents

~~~~~~~~

Acknowledgements		9
Abbreviations and sigla		10
Introduction		13

I. Biography and literary career   31

1. Biography
   - i. Bretagne: pays natal   33
   - ii. Gendarme du roi   38
   - iii. Paris   45

2. Literary career   51
   - i. Triste élève d'Apollon: le genre sombre   52
   - ii. Savant: le bien public   75
   - iii. Homme de lettres: le mélodrame   86
   - Chronological chart of play performances   87

II. Annotated listing of the works of Loaisel de Tréogate   99

1. Scope, sources, and procedures
   - i. Scope and concept   101
   - ii. Sources consulted   101
     - a. Periodicals and literary correspondences   104
     - b. Bibliographies, *répertoires*, reference works, and sale catalogues   106
     - c. Library collections and catalogues   108
   - iii. Bibliographical procedures and format   110
     - a. Organisation   110
     - b. Definitions   111
     - c. Problems of attribution and unlocated editions   112
     - d. Format of play performance histories   113
     - e. Format of publication histories   114
     - f. Note on library and source citations   116

5

2. Novels   117
3. Plays   148
4. Poems   185
5. Miscellaneous works   187

Appendices   191

   A. Chronology of Loaisel de Tréogate   193
   B. Chronological list of editions and translations   196
   C. *A monsieur le chevalier de Parny* and *Réponse*   200
   D. Descriptive summaries of the novels   202
   E. Descriptive summaries of the plays   214

Works consulted

   A. Biographical sources   229
      1. Archives   229
      2. Additional biographical sources   230
   B. Bibliographical sources   231
      1. Periodicals and literary correspondences   231
      2. Bibliographies, *répertoires,* reference works, and sale catalogues   233
      3. Library catalogues   240
   C. Other works   241

Index   245

'Malheureux qui raisonne toujours, et ne sent
jamais que les défauts.'

Mercure de France, 26 février 1780,
review of *La Comtesse d'Alibre*

Acknowledgements

THE author owes a considerable debt of gratitude to the Interlibrary Loan Office of Sterling Memorial Library at Yale University. Their continued assistance over a period of many months was instrumental in laying the bibliographical groundwork for this study. The additional co-operation of a number of European and American libraries has also been extremely helpful, especially the personal attention provided by mr Chalmoine and mr G. Nigay of the Bibliothèque universitaire de Rennes, mr R. Laslier of the Bibliothèque municipale de Reims, mr G. Hoyoux of the Bibliothèque générale de l'Université de Liège, mrs I. F. Grigorieva of the Saltykov-Shchedrin State Public Library in Leningrad, dr Heinz Gittig of the Deutsche Staatsbibliothek, and Harriet Jameson of the Library of the University of Michigan at Ann Arbor. Mrs Felkay of the Archives départementales de la Seine and the personnel of the Archives départementales du Moribihan provided valuable guidance during the phase of archival research. Mr Jacques-Yves de Sallier Dupin of the Bibliothèque municipale de Nantes and mr F. Dousset of the Archives nationales aided in performing additional biographical research. Julia Przybos assisted with the study of the supposedly plagiarised Polish original of *La Bisarrerie de la fortune*. As is evident throughout the Listing, a great deal of highly significant bibliographical information – including the discovery in 1974 of a copy of the long lost novel *Valrose* – has been supplied by professors Richard Frautschi, Angus Martin, and Vivienne Mylne from their *Bibliographie du genre romanesque français, 1751-1800*. The author wishes to express his sincerest appreciation for their generosity in sharing the results of their research prior to the publication of the *Bibliographie* and for the time and effort they devoted to answering the continuous barrage of queries about Loaisel's novels. This study would not have materialised without the initial and continued encouragement and advice of professor Georges May in preparing an earlier version. His suggestions have proved both challenging and fruitful, and his scholarship has served as an inspiration and ideal. Final thanks go to the University of Richmond for a Faculty Summer Research Fellowship, which made possible the completion of the study in its present form.

Abbreviations and sigla

A. D.: Archives départementales

Ainsi finissent: Loaisel, *Ainsi finissent les grandes passions* (1788)

A. N.: Archives nationales

Arnault: *Biographie nouvelle des contemporains* (1820-1825)

Arras, *Cat*: *Catalogue de la Bibliothèque d'Arras* (1885-1889)

Ars: Bibliothèque de l'Arsenal

Ars, *BL*: Arsenal, Ancien fonds, *Belles lettres* (ms catalogue)

Ars, *Rondel*: Arsenal, Fonds Rondel, *Théâtre français, Révolution* 2: vol.xi of *Catalogue mss. de la Bibliothèque Rondel* (ms)

Assézat-Tourneux: ed., Diderot, *Œuvres complètes* (1875-1877)

Aux âmes sensibles: Loaisel, *Aux âmes sensibles, élégie* (1780)

Babault: *Annales dramatiques* (1809-1812)

Barbier: *Dictionnaire des ouvrages anonymes* (1872-1882)

Barroux: 'Loaisel de Tréogate', *Dictionnaire des lettres françaises: le XVIIIe siècle* (1960)

BL: British Library

BL, *Cat*: British museum, *General catalogue of printed books* (1959-1966)

BN: Bibliothèque nationale

BN, *Cat*: Bibliothèque nationale, *Catalogue général des livres imprimés* (1897-   )

Bousquet: *Anthologie du dix-huitième siècle romantique* (1972)

Brenner: *Bibliographical list of plays* (1947)

Cioranescu, *Bibl*: *Bibliographie de al littérature française du dix-huitième siècle* (1969)

CLU: Library of University of California at Los Angeles

Cohen, 3rd ed [– 6th ed]: *Guide de l'amateur de livres* (1876 [-1912])

Comtesse d'Alibre: Loaisel, *Comtesse d'Alibre* (1779)

CtY: Library of Yale University

Delandine: *Bibliographie dramatique*

Delcro: *Dictionnaire des romans* (ms)

Desessarts, *Dict*: *Nouveau dictionnaire bibliographique* (1804)

Desessarts, *Siècles litts*: *Siècles littéraires* (1800-1803)

Didier: *Littérature française, 1778-1820* (1976)

DLC: United States Library of Congress

Dolbreuse: Loaisel, *Dolbreuse* (1783)

Douay, *Rép Paris*: *Répertoire de pièces représentées sur les théâtres de Paris* (ms)

Douay, *Rép prov*: *Répertoire de pièces représentées sur les théâtres de province* (ms)

Dufrenoy, ii: *L'Orient romanesque, bibliographie* (1947)

Duval: *Dictionnaire des ouvrages dramatiques* (ms)

Ersch, *Fr lit*: *La France litéraire* (1797-1798)

Ersch, suppl: *La France litéraire, supplement* (1802)

Ersch, sec suppl: *La France litéraire, second supplement* (1806)

Etienne: *Genre romanesque* (1922)

Fantin des Odoards: *Tableau des écrivains français* (1809)

'fiches Lecomte': Lecomte, collection of *fiches*, Bibliothèque de l'Arsenal (ms)

Florello: Loaisel, *Florello* (1776) [see listing pp.114-15 and no.29 for explanation of page references]

Fromm: *Bibliographie des traductions allemandes* (1950-1953)

FU: Library of University of Florida

Gay: *Bibliographie des ouvrages relatifs à l'amour* (1894-1900)

Y. Giraud: *Bibliographie du roman épistolaire* (1977)

Godenne, *Nouvelle: Histoire de la nouvelle française* (1970)

Goizet, *Dict: Dictionnaire du théâtre* (1867)

Grieder, *Trans: Translations of French sentimental prose fiction* (1975)

Hill: *American plays* (1934)

Hoefer: *Nouvelle biographie générale* (1853-1866)

Horn-Monval: *Répertoire des traductions du théâtre étranger* (1858-1867)

IaU: Library of University of Iowa

ICN: Newberry Library, Chicago

ICU: Library of University of Chicago

IEN: Library of Northwestern University

InU: Library of Indiana University, Bloomington

Krauss and Fontius: *Französische Drücke des 18. Jahrhunderts* (1970)

Lacroix, *Bibl Pixerécourt: Bibliothèque de Pixerécourt* (1838)

Lacroix, *Bibl Soleinne: Bibliothèque dramatique de Soleinne* (1843-1845)

Laporte, *Nouv suppl:* [Guiot], *Nouveau supplément à la France littéraire* (1784)

Laporte, *Suppl: Supplément à la France littéraire* (1778)

Lefilleul: *Catalogue mensuel de la librairie Lefilleul* (mars 1877)

Le Mans, *Cat: Catalogue de la Bibliothèque du Mans, Belles-lettres* (1880)

Leningrad: Saltykov-Shchedrin State Public Library, Leningrad

Levot: *Biographie bretonne* (1852-1867)

Lewine: *Bibliography of eighteenth-century art books* (1898)

Liège: Bibliothèque générale de l'Université de Liège

LNHT: Library of Tulane University

Lorenz: *Catalogue général de la librairie française* (1867-1945)

Marc: *Dictionnaire des romans* (1819)

Martin, 'First listing, 1784-1788': 'First listing of new French prose fiction, 1784-1788' (1967)

MB: Boston Public Library

MH: Library of Harvard University

Michaud: *Biographie universelle* (1811-1828)

MiU: Library of University of Michigan, Ann Arbor

MMF: Martin, Mylne, and Frautschi, *Bibliographie du genre romanesque français, 1751-1800* (1977)

Monglond, *Fr rév: France révolutionnaire, bibliographie méthodique* (1930-1963)

Morabito: *Uno scrittore sconosciuto: Loaisel de Tréogate* (1975)

Mornet ed, *Nouvelle Héloïse*, i: 'Introduction' to *Nouvelle Héloïse*, by Rousseau (1925)

Mornet, *Sentiment de la nature: Sentiment de la nature* (1907)

MWA: American Antiquarian Society, Worchester, Massachusetts

NIC: Library of Cornell University

Nicoll: *History of English drama* (1952-1967)

NN: New York Public Library

NNC: Library of Columbia University

NPV: Library of Vassar College

NUC: National union catalogue: pre-1956 imprints (1968-   )

Nyon, *Cat La Vallière: Catalogue de la bibliothèque de La Vallière, seconde partie* (1784)

OCIW: Library of Case Western Reserve University

OO: Library of Oberlin College

Opéra: Bibliothèque de l'Opéra, Paris

Pigoreau: *Petite bibliographie biographico-romancière* (1821)

Pixerécourt, 'Tableau chronologique': 'Tableau chronologique de mes pièces' (1841)

PU: Library of University of Pennsylvania, Philadelphia

Quérard, *Fr litt: La France littéraire* (1827-1864)

Quérard, *Supercheries: Supercheries littéraires dévoilées* (1869-1870)

Rabany: *Kotzebue* (1893)

Rabbe: *Biographie universelle* (1836)

Rennes: Bibliothèque universitaire de Rennes

Rondel, 'Conférence bibliographie dramatique': 'Conférence sur la bibliographie dramatique' (1913)

RPB: Library of Brown University

Sabin: *Bibliotheca américana* (1868-1936)

Saulnays: Loaisel de Saulnays, *Un méconnu: Loaisel de Tréogate* (1930)

Slatkine: Librairie Slatkine, Catalogue no.274 (1968)

Soirées de mélancolie: Loaisel, *Soirées de mélancolie* (1777)

SteG: Bibliothèque Sainte Geneviève, Paris

Summers: *Gothic bibliography* (1941)

Taylor, *Bibl* ms: *Catalogue des pièces de théâtre de la collection Taylor* (ms)

Thieme-Becker: *Allgemeines Lexikon der bildenden Künstler* (1907-1950)

Tourneux: *Bibliographie de l'histoire de Paris* (1890-1913)

Troyes, *Cat: Catalogue de la Bibliothèque de Troyes* (1883)

Valmore: Loaisel, *Valmore* (1776)

Valrose: Loaisel, *Valrose* (An VIII)

Versini: *Laclos et la tradition* (1968)

Virely: *Guilbert de Pixerécourt* (1909)

Wegelin: *Early American plays* (1905)

Weller: *Dictionnaire des ouvrages français portant de fausses indications des lieux d'impression* (1864)

Wicks and Schweitzer: *Parisian stage* (1950-1957)

Worp: *Geschiedenis van het drama en vat het tooneel in Nederland* (1904-1908)

*: Duplicate series of pagination preceding the series numbering the main body of the text.

**: Duplicate series of pagination following the series numbering the main body of the text.

†: All copies of the work under consideration which exist in the library so marked have been examined by this writer.

‡: The (a) copy of the work under consideration which exists in the library so marked served as the basis of the bibliographical description.

Introduction

LOAISEL de Tréogate has been described as everything from 'gibier de l'hôpital'[1] to the source of inspiration for Chateaubriand, Lamartine, and Hugo. By his own admission, 'd'un sombre qui effaroucheroit le Docteur Young lui-même' (*Florello*, p.8*), Loaisel also wrote some of the finest prose descriptions of nature prior to the romantics. Pursuing *le genre sombre* in emulation of Baculard d'Arnaud, he created a number of plays that earned him the title 'un des pères du mélodrame'.[2] As a moralistic disciple of Rousseau, he set out in his novels to 'remettre en honneur parmi nous l'amour conjugal' (*Dolbreuse*, i.ix) while at the same time amusing his readers with highly explicit scenes of *amour sensuel*. Since the time he was 'discovered' by Fernand Baldensperger and Daniel Mornet at the beginning of this century, Loaisel has become known as one of the most curious of the minor 'préromantiques'.

Besides presenting such a variety of interests, Loaisel's *œuvre* spans one of the most problematical periods of French literary history, his first novel appearing in 1776 and his last play in 1804. The concept of 'préromantisme', in which Loaisel has figured from the outset, has created considerable controversy among literary historians. A 1972 colloquium designed to tackle the question 'Le Préromantisme: hypo-thèque ou hypothèse?' failed to resolve the controversy.[3] Béatrice Didier opened her recent volume in the Arthaud *Littérature française* series with an impassioned plea for re-examining the authors of this period on their own right and not in the teleological shadow of 'ceux qui attendront pour naître que le siècle ait deux ans':

Ces hommes qui ont écrit entre 1778 et 1820 ne sont pas de faibles con-tinuateurs des Philosophes, torturés par quelques pressentiments de mystique romantique. Ils ont, chacun avec sa personnalité, exprimé une pensée souvent forte, exigeante, dans une langue qui, mis à part quelques débordements

---

[1] Charles Monselet *Les Oubliés et les dédaignés: figures littéraires de la fin du XVIIIe siècle* (Paris 1859), p.295. The new edition of 1876 drops the mention of Loaisel.

[2] Paul Ginisty, *Le Mélodrame* (Paris 1910), p.24.

[3] *Le Préromantisme: hypothèque ou hypothèse?*, Colloque, 29-30 juin 1972, Clermont-Ferrand, ed. Paul Viallaneix (Paris 1975).

d'éloquence et de phraséologie révolutionnaires, est d'une rare qualité de pureté, de précision et d'harmonie.[4]

Recent re-evaluations of the significance of melodrama have created considerable interest in further study of the genre.[5] The long awaited *Bibliographie du genre romanesque français, 1751-1800*, published finally in 1977, provides at last the research tool necessary to facilitate a more accurate determination of the true status of the novel during this confusing period.[6] The programme of study outlined by such renewed interest and redefined emphasis requires a foundation of the type of literary history Werner Krauss referred to as embracing 'la totalité des réalisations et des aspirations d'une époque'. It seems appropriate to reiterate his call for 'l'étude des écrivains obscurs', which he applied to the study of the Enlightenment, to apply it now to these reassessments currently in progress.[7] Loaisel de Tréogate, who has long figured in the ranks of the wilfully neglected *obscurs*, is certainly one of the most appropriate candidates, since his works are by both their nature and their timing of prime importance. An examination of the existing research and criticism on Loaisel reveals that much remains to be discovered and studied.

Charles Monselet reflects the attitude of the nineteenth century towards Loaisel when he dismisses him in one sentence: 'Puis encore, tout-à-fait dans le fond du tableau, Loaisel de Tréogate, gibier de l'hôpital, auteur de Dolbreuse ou l'homme du siècle' (pp.294-95). The nineteenth-century biographies which treat Loaisel offer no critical comment of any significance.[8] Most of the extended critical treatment of Loaisel has centred either on his novels or on his melodramatic plays, while

---

[4] tome xi: *Le XVIIIe siècle*, vol.3: *1778-1820* (Paris 1976), p.7.

[5] see for example Jean-Marie Thomasseau, *Le Mélodrame sur les scènes parisiennes de Coelina à l'Auberge des Adrets (1800-1823)* (Lille 1973); Peter Brooks, *The Melodramatic imagination: Balzac, Henry James, melodrama, and the mode of excess* (New Haven, London 1976); *Le Mélodrame*, special issue of *Revue des sciences humaines* (avril-juin 1976), no.162.

[6] Angus Martin, Vivienne G. Mylne, and Richard Frautschi (London, Paris 1977).

[7] 'L'étude des écrivains obscurs du siècle des lumières', *Studies on Voltaire* 26 (1963), pp.1019-24.

[8] Antoine Vincent Arnault *et al*, *Biographie nouvelle des contemporains* (Paris 1820-1825), xii.63; Jean Chrétien Ferdinand Hoefer, *Nouvelle biographie générale* (Paris 1853-1866), xxxi.414-15; Prosper Jean Levot, *Biographie bretonne* (Vannes, Paris 1852-1857), ii.349-50; [Joseph François Michaud], *Biographie universelle, ancienne et moderne* (Paris 1811-1828), xxiv.594-95; Alphonse Rabbe, *Biographie universelle et portative des contemporains* (Paris 1836), iii.318-19.

little if any notice has been taken of the poems or comedies. Certainly the novels have received the most attention.

The very first serious critical notice of Loaisel came in 1901, when Fernand Baldensperger published an article demonstrating resemblances between Loaisel's *Florello* and Chateaubriand's *Atala* and *Natchez*.[9] Although Baldensperger made no claims that *Florello* was a 'source' later critics were to do so using the flimsiest of evidence. Baldensperger was undoubtedly unaware at the time of the vast extent of literature exploiting American exotic themes. As later demonstrated, especially in the work of Gilbert Chinard, there are many other much more probable 'sources' of Chateaubriand's works.[10]

Nobody has written more widely on Loaisel than Daniel Mornet, and it is certainly he who has most heavily influenced modern attitudes toward the novels. In his 1907 dissertation, *Le Sentiment de la nature en France de J.-J. Rousseau à Bernardin de Saint-Pierre: essai sur les rapports de la littérature et des mœurs*, he uses Loaisel's works repeatedly to illustrate the literary expression of nature themes.[11] The analyses are accurate and revealing. Mornet finds Loaisel one of the most adept of the writers who followed Rousseau in using descriptions of nature to reflect inner sentimental states (pp.316-24). He concludes also that Loaisel's sense of the *pittoresque* is the most original and exceptional to be found along the line of its development from Rousseau to Bernardin (p.432). These value judgements are of course subjective and open to question. Much more questionable, however, is the accuracy of Mornet's conclusions regarding the degree to which the literary works he has selected to analyse – including Loaisel's – are indicative of public taste. This point serves to illustrate the importance of accurate, detailed bibliographical data as a basis for valid literary history or cultural history as reflected by literary taste. Mornet explains, 'Si l'on ne tient pas compte des *Liaisons dangereuses*, de 1761 à la Révolution, *les romans les plus lus* s'inspirent très précisément de la *Nouvelle Héloïse*. Dorat, Léonard, Loaisel de Tréogate ou d'Arnaud sont évidemment ses disciples fidèles'. In a note to this passage he continues, 'Notre *Index* indique, comme pour les autres ouvrages, le nombre de leurs éditions. *Aucun*

9 'Un prédécesseur de René en Amérique', *Revue de philologie française* 15 (1901), pp.229-34.

10 see particularly his *L'Amérique et le rêve exotique dans la littérature française au XVIIe et au XVIIIe siècle* (Paris 1913) and *L'Exotisme américain dans l'œuvre de Chateaubriand* (Paris 1918).

11 Paris 1907. All quotations are taken from the reprint edition (New York 1971).

autre roman n'a atteint, croyons-nous, les mêmes chiffres' (p.302; emphasis in original). The inaccuracy of the statistics in Mornet's 'Index' becomes evident when they are compared to those published more recently by Angus Martin in 'Romans et romanciers à succès de 1751 à la Révolution d'après les rééditions'.[12] One finds not only that Mornet's figures fall short of those now known for the novels of Dorat, Léonard, and Baculard d'Arnaud (his figure of four editions of Loaisel's *Dolbreuse* was, however, correct) but also that many other novels attained much higher numbers of editions. He seems particularly to have overstated the popularity of Loaisel and Léonard and thus their representativeness vis-à-vis public taste or contemporary writers. In fact, his conclusions might be more valid were he to have emphasised instead the importance of these writers as *exceptions*.

In 1909, Mornet published an article on the *Soirées de mélancolie*, a work omitted from his *Sentiment de la nature* probably not by choice but because he had not at that time located a copy.[13] This article established Loaisel's reputation as one of the most striking of the French preromantics. While most of the analysis of preromantic themes is quite valid, Mornet's hypothesis that the *Soirées de mélancolie* abound with 'confidences personnelles' presents a problem. He quotes as proof a few lines from the 'Avertissement', which he very questionably interprets an an admission of 'le goût de l'auteur pour la confession'. Mornet offers no further justification for this claim other than an implied trust in his own intuitive critical sense: 'La vie de Loaisel n'a pas tenté les biographes dédaigneux et nous sommes mal renseignés sur les années que vécut en Bretagne ou à Paris cet homme de lettres. *Pourtant nul doute pour le lecteur* que ce soit bien souvent lui-même qu'il raconte et que l'émotion de son récit soit celle d'un souvenir et d'une confidence' (p.497; emphasis added).

Edmond Estève, perhaps inspired by a passing remark in Mornet's article implying a similarity between a passage in the *Soirées de mélancolie* and Lamartine's *Milly*, wrote in 1912 an article enlarging on this

[12] *Revue des sciences humaines* 35 (1970), pp.383-89.
[13] 'Un "préromantique"': les *Soirées de mélancolie* de Loaisel de Tréogate', *Revue d'histoire littéraire de la France* 16 (1909), pp.491-500. Mornet recounts his problems of locating copies as follows: 'L'opuscule est assez rare et nous l'avions vainement cherché à Paris. La bibliothèque de Troyes et celle de l'Arsenal où il se dissimule par une erreur de catalogue (les œuvres sont toutes rangées régulièrement à *Loaisel de Tréogate,* sauf les *Soirées* inscrites à Tréogate [Mornet's note]) nous en ont fourni deux exemplaires' (pp. 491-92).

comparison.[14] Estève demonstrates convincingly that the sentiments and images expressed in passages of *Milly* and *L'Isolement* closely parallel – but are by no means necessarily inspired or influenced by – *Le Port* and *A ma Julie* in Loaisel's *Soirées de mélancolie,* thus adding to the prestige of this work as an example of preromanticism. Estève's sensible critical judgement, which prevents him from talking of 'sources', unfortunately does not carry over into his unquestioning acceptance of Mornet's unproven hypothesis of 'confidences personnelles'.

Loaisel is one of the chief authors discussed in Mornet's *Le Romantisme en France au XVIIIe siècle,* written in 1912.[15] The remarks concerning representativeness of Loaisel and other authors are questionable for the same reasons as in his *Sentiment de la nature,* but again the thematic analysis of Loaisel's works is certainly most enlightening (*Romantisme,* p.125). Since all the novels except *Valmore* are treated here, this study has served to enlarge considerably the image of Loaisel as preromantic. Unfortunately, Mornet also enlarges the search for 'confidences personnelles' and further beclouds this issue (pp.169-72). His theoretical explanation, now raised to the level of a general rule, relies again more on intuition than on reason: 'Le lyrisme est né du jour où les écrivains se proposèrent non de raisonner, mais d'attendrir, non d'être vrais, mais de troubler. Les "délassements de l'homme sensible" devaient être, *par une loi nécessaire,* ses Confidences ou ses Confessions' (p.154; emphasis added).

The most extensive study of Loaisel's novels remains that done in 1922 by Servais Etienne in his *Le Genre romanesque en France depuis l'apparition de la 'Nouvelle Héloïse' jusqu'aux approches de la Révolution.*[16] He deals again with Lamartinian parallels, the sense of landscape, and certain elements of the preromantic psychology. He is the first to discuss the sensual element, so characteristic of Loaisel's novels, although this discussion is dominated by highly subjective disapproval (p.370):

Je ne veux pas savoir de Victor Hugo, de Vigny, de Lamartine, si leur limon a contenu l'ardeur concupiscente d'un Loaisel; il me suffit de constater qu'ils

[14] 'Dix-huitième siècle et romantisme', *Revue d'histoire littéraire de la France* 19 (1912), pp.75-84. Mornet's remark, 'et dans un "instant de calme, au retour de la campagne d'un de ses amis", il évoque son Milly, son foyer natal' (p.499), refers to a passage in *Le Port* (*Soirées de mélancolie,* pp.151-52).

[15] Paris 1912. All quotations are taken from the reprint of the 1925, second edition (New York 1971).

[16] (Brussels 1922), pp.326-84 and *passim.*

ne m'ont offert que les fleurs admirables et qu'ils ont eu la pudeur de cacher la pourriture où peut-être elles ont poussé. De pauvres fleurs sont éparses sur la pourriture qu'étale Loaisel aux yeux de tous. La suprême volupté d'après lui est le plaisir charnel.

In his attempts to define what he likes about Loaisel – and he is indeed Loaisel's most partisan supporter – Etienne seems unable to find a valid, precise critical explanation, preferring instead a highly dramatic and rhetorical comparison of Loaisel to Chateaubriand. He rightly seems uneasy about accepting fully the 'confidences personnelles' hypothesis. But his alternative interpretation that Loaisel's inspiration is based on a mixture of reality and imagination is hardly a profound insight (pp.378-79).

In the 'Introduction' to his edition of *La Nouvelle Héloïse*, Mornet outlines the influence of Rousseau's novel on 'les romanciers disciples de Rousseau', among whom he includes Loaisel.[17] He repeats his conclusions from his *Sentiment de la nature*, first, that Rousseau definitely inspired Loaisel's use of descriptions of nature to reflect emotional and sentimental states and, second, that Rousseau's influence on Loaisel was minimal concerning the motif of the 'idylle rustique', which was already popular before the publication of *La Nouvelle Héloïse* (pp.284, 286). He returns to the notion of 'confidences personnelles' in what may be construed as the apotheosis of the hypothesis – still undemonstrated – to state that Loaisel is the only disciple to follow Rousseau along the path of the 'roman personnel' (pp.285-86). Like Etienne, Mornet passes along his personal regrets that Loaisel, among other disciples, resorts to sensuality, a regrettable tendency even when practised by the master, Jean-Jacques (p.283).

Reference is rarely made to Mornet's discussion of *Dolbreuse* in his early article 'L'influence de la *Nouvelle Héloïse* sur le roman français de 1761 à 1787'.[18] He bases this article on eight novels which evoke *La Nouvelle Héloïse* in their titles and on *Dolbreuse*, included because 'il est tout plein de Rousseau' (p.307). *Dolbreuse* and Léonard's *Lettres de deux amants* turn out to be those most closely influenced by Rousseau according to Mornet's analysis, which is repeated largely in the 'Introduction' to his edition of *La Nouvelle Héloïse*. Another article by Mornet, 'L'influence de Jean-Jacques Rousseau au XVIIIᵉ siècle', repeats essentially what he has said before elsewhere about Loaisel.[19]

[17] (Paris 1925), i.268-86.   [18] *Revue universitaire* 14 (1905), pp.306-18.
[19] *Annales de la Société Jean-Jacques Rousseau* 8 (1912), pp.33-67.

Mornet is primarily responsible for establishing Loaisel's reputation as a disciple of Rousseau, but Pierre-Maurice Masson provides additional evidence of the religious influence in *La Religion de Jean-Jacques Rousseau*.[20]

Although both Mornet and Etienne spoke in passing of similarities between Baculard d'Arnaud and Loaisel, the question of direct influence by Loaisel's senior remained to be treated. Inklaar's 1925 thesis on Baculard adds little to this important question since most of the seven pages devoted to it merely gather together what has been said before.[21] However, Inklaar does raise a new question concerning a possible connection between *Dolbreuse* and Baculard's *Germeuil*, published earlier.

A short chapter on Loaisel in Emile Henriot's *Romanesques et romantiques* does little more than summarise what was said earlier by Mornet and Baldensperger on the *Soirées de mélancolie* and *Florello* and add curtailed résumés of *Valmore* and *Dolbreuse*.[22] André Monglond treats Loaisel's novels very briefly in *Le Préromantisme français*. His analysis of *Dolbreuse* as 'un René Louis XVI' has contributed substantially to the reputation of that novel.[23]

Loaisel's plays have not stimulated as much interest as his novels. The melodramatic productions have, nevertheless, attracted some attention as being significant works in the early evolution, perhaps even the birth, of the melodrama. The pioneering studies of the melodrama in France are Paul Ginisty's *Le Mélodrame*, written in 1910, and an article by Alexis Pitou, 'Les origines du mélodrame français à la fin du XVIIIe siècle', published in 1911.[24] Ginisty baptises Loaisel 'un des pères du mélodrame' for his *Château du Diable*, a title which few have disputed since (p.24). He summarises this play along with *La Forêt périlleuse* and *Roland de Monglave*. Although there are few critical comments, the space devoted to Loaisel emphasises the importance accorded to his role in the early history of the melodrama. Pitou's article is concerned with demonstrating the thesis that the melodrama

---

[20] (Paris 1916), iii *passim*.

[21] Derk Inklaar, *François-Thomas Baculard d'Arnaud, ses imitateurs en Hollande et dans d'autres pays* (Paris 1925), pp.155-61.

[22] (Paris 1930), pp.1-9.

[23] originally published as *Histoire intérieure du préromantisme français de l'abbé Prévost à Joubert* (Grenoble 1929). In the new edition (Paris 1965-1966), Loaisel is discussed on the following pages: i.73, 81-84 (*Dolbreuse*), 226, 232, 241; ii.331.

[24] *Revue d'histoire littéraire de la France* 18 (1911), pp.256-96.

developed out of the 'pantomime héroïque'. He sees *Le Château du Diable* as a key work in this evolutionary process and *La Forêt périlleuse* as another. Among the very few early studies of the melodrama, the only other one to deal with the origins is that written by Eise Carel van Bellen in 1927, entitled *Les Origines du mélodrame* (Utrecht 1927). Bellen discusses the same three plays chosen by Ginisty and presents some enlightening ideas on how certain elements fit into different stage and literary traditions.

Thus by 1930, Loaisel had an established but very limited reputation among literary historians.[25] The study *Un méconnu: Loaisel de Tréogate (1752-1812), monographie littéraire* published in 1930 (Alger) by an indirect descendant, Henry Loaisel de Saulnays, contains some new biographical data, mostly undocumented, along with the first modern attempt to assemble a complete bibliography. Most bibliographical data and some of the biography seem based on nineteenth-century biographies. Saulnays copies and compounds former errors and questions nothing, but at least he compiles much data previously scattered throughout many old sources. The critical portion of his monograph is merely a reprint of the articles by Baldensperger, Mornet (*Soirées de mélancolie*), and Henriot. Any remarks of a critical nature in the introduction by Saulnays are based on these articles. Mornet's hypothesis of 'confidences personnelles' has been distorted by Saulnays to the point that, without so indicating, he has drawn a large part of the biographical data from the novels. That *Florello* served as a 'source' for Chateaubriand is now taken to be a demonstrated fact. These two perpetually distorted *idées reçues* of Loaisel criticism are finally put in proper perspective three years later by Georges Collas in a most sensible article, 'Un préromantique breton: Loaisel de Tréogate, 1752-1812'.[26] Collas reviews previous studies of Loaisel's novels, and although he provides no new ideas, his objective and well reasoned summing up befits the last comprehensive appraisal of the novels for over thirty years. Kurt Wais makes repeated use of isolated quotations from the novels as illustrations of *Das Antiphilosophische Weltbild des französischen Sturm und Drang, 1760-1789*, but Loaisel is just one of many sources used to demonstrate his thesis (Berlin 1934).

[25] Pierre Trahard, who seems not to rate Loaisel as a true 'maître', mentions him only in passing, in the introduction and the conclusion to *Les Maîtres de la sensibilité française au XVIIIe siècle (1715-1789)* (Paris 1931-1933), i.21 and iv.265.

[26] *Mémoires de la Société d'histoire et d'archéologie de Bretagne* 14 (1933), pp.297-319.

For the twenty-five years following Wais's book, Loaisel receives hardly any attention at all except for the years 1951 and 1952. Pierre Sage briefly mentions two of the novels in his study of 'le bon prêtre'. He also analyses *Le Fils naturel* as part of Loaisel's *œuvre*, although that attribution now appears highly doubtful.[27] Armand Hoog, in two very significant articles on preromanticism, 'rediscovers' Loaisel and further reveals his 'âme romantique', particularly the signs of a 'mal du siècle' in the *Soirées de mélancolie*.[28] He also redirects attention to *Florello* as an illustration of 'The Romantic spirit and the American "elsewhere" '.[29] Hubert Fabureau published a short article on *Dolbreuse* in the *Mercure de France*, but his autobiographical interpretation of the novel is little more than conjecture.[30]

Starting in 1960, Loaisel's novels appear more and more frequently as part of the bank of sources examined in large syntheses treating the ideas, themes, and literary techniques of the eighteenth century.[31] In these studies, scrutiny of Loaisel's writing rarely rises above the level of an isolated sentence or paragraph cited in the context of the central argument of the synthesis. In Robert Mauzi's article 'Les maladies de l'âme au XVIIIe siècle', the analysis of portions of the *Soirées de mélancolie* reveals even further the strange imagination that infuses the work.[32] Robert Barroux provides a few new items of biography and a fairly accurate bibliography but no critical comments in his article on Loaisel in the *Dictionnaire des lettres françaises: le XVIIIe siècle*.[33] In 1967 appears the first comprehensive study of the novels since Collas, this

[27] *Le 'Bon prêtre' dans la littérature française d'*Amadis de Gaule *au* Génie du Christianisme (Geneva, Lille 1951).

[28] 'L'âme préromantique et les instincts de mort', *Bulletin de la Faculté des lettres de Strasbourg* 31 (1952), pp.123-33, 149-60; 'Un cas d'angoisse préromantique', *Revue des sciences humaines* 17 (1952), pp.181-97.

[29] *Yale French studies* 10 (1952), pp.16-17.

[30] 'Loaisel de Tréogate', *Mercure de France* 314 (1952), pp.370-73.

[31] Dorothy M. McGhee, *The Cult of the 'conte moral': the moral tale in France – its emergence and progress* (Menasha, Wisconsin 1960); Robert Mauzi, *L'Idée du bonheur dans la littérature et la pensée françaises au XVIIIe siècle* (Paris 1967); Paul Van Tieghem, *Le Sentiment de la nature dans le préromantisme européen* (Paris 1960); Laurent Versini, *Laclos et la tradition: essai sur les sources et la technique des 'Liaisons dangereuses'* (Paris 1968); René Godenne, *Histoire de la nouvelle française aux XVIIe et XVIIIe siècles* (Genève 1970); Pierre Fauchery, *La Destinée féminine dans le roman européen du dix-huitième siècle, 1713-1807: essai de gynécomythie romanesque* (Paris 1972); Robert Favre, *La Mort dans la littérature et la pensée françaises au siècle des lumières* (Lyon 1978).

[32] *Revue des sciences humaines* 25 (1960), pp.459-93.   [33] (Paris 1960), ii.132.

one by Henri Coulet in *Le Roman jusqu'à la Révolution.*[34] Coulet finds Loaisel's principal merit in 'certaines de ses notations morales et psychologiques' (p.440). Jacques Vier's *Histoire de la littérature française: XVIIIe siècle* presents a discussion of three of the novels, along with others by Dorat, Baculard d'Arnaud, and Mouhy, in a thematic essay on psychological and moral aspects of what he calls 'le pathétique de la vertu'.[35] In his *Anthologie du dix-huitième siècle romantique*, Jacques Bousquet presents a summary of the known biographical and bibliographical facts followed by several excerpts from the novels. Bousquet's thoughtful selection of texts provides a good indication of some of Loaisel's most curious and fascinating qualities.[36] Béatrice Didier devotes a very small amount of space to Loaisel in her 1976 volume in the Arthaud *Littérature française* series (pp.164, 326). Her assessment of Loaisel, based on Monglond's description of *Dolbreuse*, is far from enthusiastic.

Pasquale Morabito's *Uno Scrittore sconosciuto: Joseph-Marie Loaisel de Tréogate*, the first monograph since the one prepared by Saulnays, is limited in scope since it was designed only to serve as a text for a university course in 1975-1976.[37] It contains, in addition to the complete texts of *La Forêt périlleuse* and *Aux âmes sensibles*, a very brief sketch of the life and works, drawn mostly from Michaud, Rabbe, and the listing of the works in the catalogue of the Bibliothèque nationale. Morabito suggests that Loaisel's modesty, professed in the novel prefaces, is perhaps a sincere recognition of his limited capabilities. The introduction also includes a basic explication of *La Forêt périlleuse*, but there is no mention of the concept of melodrama. A short general analysis of the novels and the *élégie* concludes the commentary. This analysis, which treats primarily the themes of sentiment (*sentiment, sensibilité*) and nature and compares Loaisel to his contemporaries, is based largely on Servais Etienne, Mornet's *Romantisme en France au XVIIIe siècle*, and Van Tieghem's *Sentiment de la nature dans le préromantisme européen*.

Attention has recently been focused again on Loaisel's theatre, particularly *Le Château du Diable* and *La Forêt périlleuse*, thanks in part to the important work being done on the melodrama. The two

[34] (Paris 1967), i.439-42. [35] (Paris 1970), ii.529-42.
[36] (Paris 1972), pp.411-31.
[37] Università degli studi, Facoltà di magistero, Messina, Testi universitari, Sezione di lingue romanze (Reggio, Calabria 1975).

works continue to be mentioned as among the first examples of the melo-drama formula in France.[38] Frank Rahill cites *Le Château du Diable* as providing the 'successful début' of the comic character as a 'popular accessory'.[39] Aspects of a 'poétique de la ruine' in the decor of the same play are analysed by Pierre Frantz in a discussion of 'l'espace dramatique'.[40] The influence of *La Forêt périlleuse* on Victor Hugo's *Lucrèce Borgia* is discounted by Anne Ubersfeld.[41] However, Richard Fargher demonstrates convincingly that *Le Château du Diable* served as a source – in the true sense of the word – for Hugo's first dramatic work, under the same title.[42] Finally, *La Forêt périlleuse* has been included in *Le Théâtre de la Révolution et de l'Empire*, a microfiche collection of 132 plays 'particulièrement représentatives du double point de vue du témoignage historique et de l'évolution des genres'.[43]

The 1970s have yielded several important studies of individual novels. René Godenne finally lays to rest the question of any possible 'influence' of *Florello* on Chateaubriand by concluding his investigation with the remark, 'Il est à peu près sûr que Chateaubriand n'a jamais songé à *Florello* en composant *Les Natchez*.'[44] *Dolbreuse*, which seems to be regarded currently as Loaisel's masterpiece, has been analysed in depth by Jolita Kavaliunas in a study of passion, guilt, and happiness in selected eighteenth-century novels[45] and by Janine Rossard, who examines the problem of *la pudeur*.[46] Finally, Michel Delon, in what is

[38] Brooks, p.87; Anne Ubersfeld, 'Les bons et les méchants', *Revue des sciences humaines* 41 (1976), p.193.

[39] Frank Rahill, *The World of melodrama* (University Park, Pennsylvania and London 1967), p.26.

[40] 'L'espace dramatique de *La Brouette du vinaigrier* à *Coelina*', *Revue des sciences humaines* 41 (1976), p.158.

[41] Anne Ubersfeld, *Le Roi et le bouffon: étude sur le théâtre de Hugo de 1830 à 1839* (Paris 1974), p.164, n.27.

[42] 'Victor Hugo's first melodrama', *Balzac and the nineteenth century: studies in French literature presented to Hubert J. Hunt by pupils, colleagues and friends*, ed. D. C. Charlton, J. Gaudon, and Anthony R. Pugh (Leicester University Press 1972).

[43] *Le Théâtre de la Révolution et de l'Empire, 132 pièces de théâtre sélectionées et présentées par Marc Régaldo*, Microéditions Hachette (Paris 1975), p.6 of accompanying (printed) descriptive catalogue.

[44] 'Loaisel de Tréogate et Chateaubriand', in *La Bretagne littéraire au XVIIIe siècle*, Colloque Duclos, 6-8 avril 1973, Rennes, *Annales de Bretagne et des pays de l'Ouest* 83 (1976), p.844.

[45] 'Passions and the search for happiness: the concepts of passions and guilt in their relationship to happiness, as manifested in certain French novels of the eighteenth century', Ph.D. dissertation, Case Western Reserve University 1972.

[46] *Une clef du romantisme: la pudeur* (Paris 1974).

to date the most penetrating study of Loaisel's thought, seeks to evalu-
tate the synthesis announced by the subtitle of *Dolbreuse: l'homme du
siècle ramené à la vérité par le sentiment et par la raison.*[47]

This brief survey of research and criticism devoted to Loaisel shows
that a few of his individual works, especially *Dolbreuse* and the melodramas, are finally beginning to receive close examination based on their
own merits. However, no thorough comprehensive critical treatments
of either the novels or the plays has yet appeared, nor has any attempt
been made to analyse the *œuvre* as a whole.[48] Most lacking of all are
studies to supply the basic foundation for valid critical analysis. Mornet's
remark in 1909 that 'La vie de Loaisel n'a pas tenté les biographes
dédaigneux' remains still true today (*Sentiment de la nature*, p.497).
There never has been a serious effort to determine the corpus of the
works. Some old misconceptions, particularly concerning the 'confidences personnelles' in the novels, continue to survive unchallenged.
In short, there is a strong need to establish an accurate record, as complete as possible, of the facts surrounding Loaisel's life and works. The
present study is designed to do just that.

Of the little that has been written about Loaisel's life, much is either
inaccurate or undocumented.[49] Some of the more significant mistakes

[47] 'Vision du monde "préromantique" dans *Dolbreuse* de Loaisel de Tréogate', in *La
Bretagne littéraire au XVIIIe siècle*, Colloque Duclos, 6-8 avril 1973, Rennes, *Annales de
Bretagne et des Pays de l'Ouest* 83 (1976), pp.829-38. This article is discussed below on
pp.78-79.

[48] René Godenne in his article 'Loaisel de Tréogate et Chateaubriand' refers to a
'mémoire inédit de licence en philologie romane de l'Université de Liège' by Jean Wéris
entitled 'Loaisel de Tréogate romancier et dramaturge' (p.845, n.1), This work could not
be obtained, nor was any information discovered about its eventual publication.

[49] the nineteenth-century biographies of Michaud, Arnault, Rabbe, Hoefer, and Levot
give date and place of birth and death and mention Loaisel's profession as *gendarme* but
say nothing more of significance (see note 8 above). The few details of Loaisel's family and
early life set forth in the monograph by Henry Loaisel de Saulnays are mostly erroneous,
and none is documented (pp.8-10). The article by Georges Collas provides a few new items
of interest but with no documentation other than acknowledgement of the colleagues who
communicated the information (pp.298-99, 315-16). The one-sentence biography in
Robert Barroux's article in the *Dictionnaire des lettres françaises* adds a few more details
concerning Loaisel's wives and children. He evidently obtained this information from
documents in the Archives départementales de la Seine, of which he was *conservateur*, but
even so there is an error in the one date given, and the name of the first wife is misspelled.
Hubert Fabureau's remarks on Loaisel's military career are drawn almost entirely from
the fiction of *Dolbreuse*. (pp.370-71). Jacques Bousquet basically repeats Barroux's data
and adds a remark about an unhappy love affair in Paris, a 'fact' most probably based on
the plot of *Ainsi finissent* (pp.411-12).

of detail in these existing biographical accounts will be pointed out at appropriate moments in the biography in Part I, ch.I, but otherwise they do not warrant serious consideration. Given the dearth of existing biographical information in secondary sources, a return to original documents was absolutely essential. Research conducted in the Archives départementales du Morbihan, the Archives départementales de la Seine, the Minutier des notaires at the Archives nationales, and the Service historique de l'armée at the Château de Vincennes has made it possible to establish with confirmed accuracy a significant number of facts surrounding Loaisel's personal life.[50]

Much of the biographical information presented in Part I, ch.I is based on documented fact. Documents are rare, however, concerning some of the most important moments in Loaisel's life. To fill in the record in these areas, special consideration has been given to some of the more probable autobiographical revelations in the novels. Although they do not provide definitive answers, they do offer hypothetical explanations suggestive of directions for future research. Furthermore, since so much has been written about these so-called 'confidences personnelles' in the novels, it is essential to examine this question in order to establish the useful limits of such speculation. A very important passage dealing with Loaisel's military career appears in the 'Lettre à m. Coll', the preface to *Florello*, in which Loaisel is clearly speaking in his own voice. Some highly suggestive information about both the military career and the activities before 1788 is found in the first chapter of the newly discovered novel *Valrose*. The passage in question contains enough verifiable autobiography to warrant considering the remainder as possible autobiography. A few additional passages from the *Soirées de mélancolie* are also discussed even though their autobiographical content is in no way verifiable.

To date, no satisfactory bibliography of Loaisel's works has been published. Existing sources contain a large amount of data that are conflicting, unconfirmed, and incomplete.[51] Consequently a major

[50] a manuscript genealogy of the Saulnays branch of the Loaisel family, drawn up in the nineteen-fifties, is held in the Archives départementales du Morbihan (Loaisel de Saulnays (famille de la région de Sérent), 385. T13). It is quite helpful for leads, but some of the information it contains is based on sources of questionable accuracy, including the monograph by Loaisel de Saulnays.

[51] bibliographies contained in the nineteenth-century biographies of Michaud, Arnault, Rabbe, Hoefer, and Levot were found to vary considerably as to completeness and to disagree on specifics of many common entries. The modern attempts at complete bibliographies in Saulnays, Barroux, Cioranescu (Alexandre Cioranescu, *Bibliographie de la*

project of bibliographical research was undertaken to establish for the first time the complete, authentic corpus of Loaisel's works. Surpassing the limits of a normal bibliography, the annotated listing presented in Part II is actually a comprehensive documentation of the histories of the individual works. It includes discussions of all works ever attributed to Loaisel. In addition to publication histories of all the texts it also gives performance histories of the plays. The scope and concept of the listing are discussed in detail in the introductory section of Part II.

One of the major efforts involved in preparing the annotated listing was the selection of research sources. During this selection process as well as during the actual research, it became apparent that a considerable amount of time could have been saved were more information available concerning the utility of these sources. It is hoped that the discussion of methods and sources in Part II, will help to remedy this situation by providing a useful guide for similar research projects involving late eighteenth-century French literature, specifically concerning the novel during the period 1776-1812 and the theatre during the period 1788-1812. Bibliographical sources have been listed under 'Works consulted' according to the categories of the discussion in Part II, ch.1.ii, to facilitate consultation.

Loaisel's literary career has never been seriously considered in its entirety. Most studies have centred on individual works or have dealt separately either with his novels or his melodramas. Very little thought has ever been given to the general, overall direction of his evolution as a writer. The survey of Loaisel's literary career presented in Part I, ch.2 is intended precisely to remedy this situation. Based on analysis of information from the biography, the listing, contemporary periodical reviews, and the novel prefaces, this survey examines the evolution of his

littérature française du dix-huitième siècle (Paris 1969), ii.1134-35), Bousquet, and Morabito failed to resolve the many discrepancies or to assure completeness, and eighteenth-century sources only compounded the problems. The one notable exception, limited however to the novels published prior to 1801, is the Martin *et al Bibliographie du genre romanesque français, 1751-1800*, a model of thorough, detailed, and accurate scholarship. A detailed discussion of these sources is found in the 'Sources consulted' section of the annotated listing in Part II. There is a certain amount of duplication of information in the *Bibliographie* and in the listing presented here in Part II inasmuch as the authors of the *Bibliographie* and this writer have shared results of research on the novels in question. However, the scope and aims of the two studies differ considerably. The listing is designed to contain more comprehensive and detailed data than the *Bibliographie* as well as to treat matters the *Bibliographie* does not consider.

literary career taking all his works into consideration. The focus is on Loaisel himself: his hopes and ambitions, his successes, and his failures.

The starting point for an analysis of any writer's literary career is of course the literary production itself. Each individual work is treated in Part I, ch.2, but the discussion is restricted to tracing the broad outlines of the *œuvre*.[52] Particular emphasis is given, however, to the highly important novel prefaces.

Loaisel has willed to posterity an impassioned but clear and coherent picture of the wide-ranging aspirations and successive disappointments of his literary career. As will be seen in the biography, the novel prefaces contain a limited amount of verified autobiography. When Loaisel shifts from talking of his personal life to speak of his 'professional' life, one might expect to find a certain amount of rhetorical posturing by an author seeking to sound like his peers. There is definitely no small amount of this sort of publicity aimed toward the contemporary reading public and, even beyond, toward posterity. However, certain statements in the prefaces take on added significance and veracity when seen in the larger context of his overall literary production and the reception of his works by his contemporaries. When these prefaces are viewed together as a series and analysed on a deeper level, they reveal a definite evolution in Loaisel's ambitions and interests. The story of his literary career as Loaisel tells it himself in the novel prefaces is one of the most interesting facets of his *œuvre*.

Loaisel's successes and failures as determined by the public's reception of his works can be judged with a fair degree of accuracy from publication histories of the texts and performance histories of the plays. Publication histories do present some difficulties of interpretation, which must be kept in mind. The significance of total numbers of editions and re-editions of a given work is affected by such unknown factors as the number of copies printed, the number of copies left unsold, and indeed whether or not those copies sold were actually read. However, the fact that a work was re-edited at all signifies at least that

[52] although a detailed knowledge of Loaisel's *œuvre* is not essential for an understanding of Part I, ch.2, basic familiarity with the individual texts would be helpful. The descriptive summaries in appendices D and E have been designed to provide the necessary background for those readers who are not familiar with the works. Only two texts are currently available on the market: *La Forêt périlleuse* and *Aux âmes sensibles*. Both are reproduced in Morabito's monograph, and the former is available in the Microédition Hachette collection. Excerpts of *Florello*, *La Comtesse d'Alibre*, *Dolbreuse*, *Ainsi finissent*, and *Aux âmes sensibles* appear in Bousquet (pp.413-31).

it was not a complete failure on the market. The dates of re-editions, whether they immediately followed the first edition or came later, their groupings, and the overall time period during which they appeared are all indications that help to ascertain roughly the degree, duration, and fluctuation of the work's popularity. Translations, which are subject to the same restrictions of interpretation as re-editions, can provide similar information concerning a work's geographical appeal.[53] In the case of plays, performance histories are a much more significant index of public reaction than are publication histories of the texts. Although interpretation of performance statistics is complicated by the unknown factor of the size of audiences, the number and frequency of performances provide a good indication of degree of popularity. Dates of concentrated groupings of performances indicate duration and fluctuations in popularity.

Additional insights into contemporary reactions to both printed works and play performances are provided in the reviews contained in periodicals. Their reliability as an index to influence, popularity, or public taste is a somewhat debatable point.[54] A review does reflect, however, the opinions of a contemporary observer who was in a position to influence a certain public's opinion and receptiveness in regard to the work under consideration. Reviews of plays at times provide significant information on audience reactions. Most important of all perhaps is that critical comments in reviews indicate not only what the public was

[53] these problems of interpreting various aspects of publication histories are discussed briefly in the following: Roger Laufer, 'La bibliographie matérielle dans ses rapports avec la critique textuelle, l'histoire littéraire et la formalisation', *Revue d'histoire littéraire de la France* 70 (1970), p.781; Angus Martin, 'Romans et romanciers à succès de 1751 à la Révolution d'après les rééditions', *Revue des sciences humaines* 35 (1970), p.383; and Daniel Mornet, 'Les enseignements des bibliothèques privées (1750-1780)', *Revue d'histoire littéraire de la France* 17 (1910), pp.450-51, 471.

[54] Mornet's 'Enseignements des bibliothèques privées' shows little correlation between the selection of books reviewed in the *Mercure* from 1750 to 1760 and the frequency with which these same books are listed in the private library catalogues he had surveyed (pp.471-73). In a highly lucid review of the quantitative study of eighteenth-century culture, Robert Darnton recalls Mornet's cautions and points out further how the failure to take into account the journalists' biases and special fields of interest when interpreting the statistics of book reviews can lead to false conclusions regarding the taste of the general public ('Reading, writing, and publishing in eighteenth-century France: a case study in the sociology of literature', *Daedalus* 100 (1971), pp.221-22). In addition, it is important to note that some periodicals attempted comprehensive reviewing, especially in the case of first performances of plays, so that the mere appearance of a review in these journals has no significance whatsoever as to popularity.

being advised to think about these works but also what the author was being forced to think about himself. Loaisel's sensitivity to the reviews of his novels is evident in the novel prefaces and seems to have influenced markedly the nature of his literary production and the direction of his career. For this reason alone, the reviews warrant very close consideration.

If the analysis of Loaisel's literary career raises more questions than it answers about the works themselves, then it will have functioned as had been hoped. For it has been designed, in addition to providing a biographical and bibliographical background, to serve as a stimulus and inspiration to future studies involving detailed literary analyses of the individual works and eventually a comprehensive evaluation of Loaisel's entire *œuvre*.

I
Biography and literary career

I

Biography

i. Bretagne: pays natal

JOSEPH Marie Loaisel was born on 17 August 1752 in the parish of Saint Guyomard, a picturesque rural area about 25 kilometres northeast of Vannes on the route to Ploermel.[1] He was the fourth of five children born to Vincent Joseph Loaisel and Anne Marie de La Cour, both of whom were from families of the same general region.[2] Vincent Joseph, like his father, Anselm Loaisel, was an *avocat* and an officer in the system of seigneurial justice.[3] Anselm was 'greffier de la jurisdiction de Malestroit' and 'avocat au Parlement'.[4] He was perhaps at one time *sénéchal* of Sérent.[5] Vincent Joseph was 'Sénéchal de la Baronnie de Molac'.[6] He thus held the highest grade in the seigneurial judicial system but in one of the less powerful jurisdictions.[7] This office can

[1] A. D. Morbihan, E. Suppl., 611, Etat civil, Paroisse de St Guyomard, baptême, 18 août 1752.

[2] A. D. Morbihan, Etat civil, Paroisse de Sérent: mariage, 24 novembre 1744, Vincent Joseph Loaisel – Anne Marie de la Cour; baptême, 4 septembre 1745, Françoise Mathurine Marie Loaisel; baptême, 16 octobre 1746, Alexandre Marie Loaisel; baptême, 2 décembre 1747, Gobrien Mathurin Joseph Loaisel. A. D. Morbihan, E. Suppl. 611, Etat civil, Paroisse de St Guyomard: ondoyé, 18 avril 1754, Emilie Judith Loaisel; baptême, 17 septembre 1754, Emilie Judith Loaisel.

[3] both Anselm and Vincent are referred to by the title 'maître' on all documents in which they are mentioned. Anselm appears only on the marriage record of Vincent, cited above in note 2.

[4] unconfirmed notations appearing on the genealogical chart of the Loaisel de Saulnays family (A. D. Morbihan, Loaisel de Saulnays (famille de la région de Sérent), 385. T13 [prepared in the 1950s]).

[5] according to another unconfirmed notation on the Saulnays genealogy, Anselm 'dirige à Serent le duché de ce nom'. Georges Collas maintains that Anselm was actually *sénéchal* of Sérent, but again this could not be confirmed ('Un préromantique breton: Loaisel de Tréogate: 1752-1812', *Mémoires de la Société d'histoire et d'archéologie de Bretagne* 14 (1933), p.2, n.2).

[6] he is referred to thus on the baptismal records of his first three children, cited above in note 2.

[7] Molac was not one of the nine *baronnies* of Brittany having 'droit de présidence' at the Etats de Bretagne (André Giffard, *Les Justices seigneuriales en Bretagne au XVIIe et au XVIIIe siècle, 1661-1791* (Paris 1903), p.53, n.6).

33

hardly be considered a high distinction, since there were some 2500 seigneurial jurisdictions in Brittany just before the Revolution (Giffard, p.42). It was not a lucrative office either. The *sénéchal* was not salaried by the seigneur in Brittany as he was elsewhere but received remuneration only through payments from the litigants in the cases he handled (Giffard, pp.87-88).

Loaisel de Saulnays's remark that Loaisel de Tréogate's father was 'ingénieur dans la maison du roi' has no foundation whatsoever in fact (Saulnays, p.9). It is most probably based on verbally transmitted family history and thus suffers from the inevitable accumulation of inaccuracies. The confusion seems to be explained by a document in the Archives départementales de la Seine, which document also explains two more inaccuracies in Saulnays's biography: that Loaisel 'eut une sœur mariée à M. de Miramont' and that the Tréogate branch died out with Loaisel's death in 1812 (Saulnays, p.9). The document in question is the 'décès' of Alexandre Prosper Loaisel de Tréogate, the son of Joseph Marie.[8] Alexandre Prosper is listed on the document as '*ingenieur* civil', and the death was witnessed by, among others, 'Pierre Marie Louis Antidore *Miramont* [. . .] *gendre* du défunt'. A confusion seems to have grown into the traditional family history whereby Joseph Marie was mistakenly thought to have been the son of Alexandre Prosper instead of vice versa. This explains all three of the inaccuracies mentioned above. This confusion plus the embellishments 'ingénieur *de la maison du Roi*' and 'M. *de* Miramont' are ample warnings of the unreliable nature of Loaisel de Saulnays's biographical information.

Joseph Marie spent his early years in the Château de Bovrel, just outside the village of Saint Guyomard. It is not certain that he was born here, as most of the biographies claim, but the family was living at Bovrel when his sister Emilie Judith was born in 1754.[9] The site of the present 'Cour de Bovrel', a small country manor, certainly comes as close to the idyllic – literary or real – as is possible. Located in a small clearing on the side of a wooded hill, Bovrel is completely isolated from the outside world. Just how much of the present structure on this site dates from the eighteenth century could not be determined, but there is

[8] A. D. Seine, Etat civil, décès, 5 février 1849, Alexandre Prosper Loaisel de Tréogate.

[9] Loaisel's baptismal record, cited above in note 1, gives no indication of the family residence, although the baptism was carried out in the parish of St Guyomard. But Emilie Judith's baptismal record, cited above in note 2, lists the parents as 'demeurants au chateau de bauvrel [*sic*]'.

no resemblance between the structure existing today and a 'château'. The term 'château' is indeed used in one of the documents examined,[10] but this could well have been an inflation in terminology similar to that of the titles of nobility used – or misused – by *roturiers* during the same period to acquire status.[11] Whatever the case, Loaisel could certainly have acquired from life at Bovrel a large measure of the inspiration behind his descriptions of country life and of nature, both idyllic and 'farouche'.

Sometime after 1754, Loasel's father appears to have acquired the title seigneur Du Paty.[12] The eldest son, Alexandre Marie, is referred to around 1771, after the father's death, as sieur Du Paty.[13] Whether these titles are more than honorific and might indicate possession and inheritance of land is not known at present. Loaisel de Saulnays's claim that Joseph Marie 'prit le nom TRÉOGATE de la terre que son père eut en partage' could be neither confirmed nor disproven.[14]

Indeed the origin of the name Tréogate and the reason for Loaisel's having adopted it remain a mystery. The name 'Tréogat', without a final 'e', was attached to a 'ferme et pont sur le ruisseau de la Vallée-Sainte-Anne, commune d'Augan', an area located about 12 kilometers due east of Ploermel.[15] 'Tréogat' also seems to have been the name of a parish in the diocese of Quimper.[16] No other geographical locations of this name were discovered, nor could these two be connected in any way with the Loaisel family. A notarial act concerning a 'rectification de ses noms' was drawn up for Loaisel in Paris but unfortunately in the

[10] 'Baptême', Emilie Judith, cited in note 2 above.

[11] for a discussion of this inflation in titles of nobility, see Jean Meyer, *La Noblesse bretonne* (Paris 1966), ii.1121.

[12] the title 'seigneur Du Paty' was not listed on any of the records cited in note 2 above, the latest dating from 1754, but appears on both the 'promesse de mariage' (A. D. Seine, Etat civil, mariage, 21 juillet 1783, Joseph Marie Loaisel – Marie Opportune Prout [listed under LOISEL in the card catalogue]) and the 'contrat de mariage' (A. N., Minutier des notaires, Etude x (Gobin), 777, 21 juillet 1788) of Loaisel's first marriage.

[13] 'Baptême', Gabriel Alexandre Marie Gobrien Hervé, A. D. Morbihan, E. Suppl. 590, Etat civil, Paroisse de Malestroit, 7 décembre 1771.

[14] Saulnays, p.9. Further research remains to be done on these problems, since time did not permit a thorough examination of the many unindexed documents in the A. D. Morbihan relating to acquisition of real estate.

[15] M. Rosenzseig, *Dictionnaire topographique du Département du Morbihan comprenant les noms de lieu anciens et modernes* (Paris 1870), p.274.

[16] A. D. Morbihan, B. 3084.

form of a 'brevet' so that no record was kept of the contents.[17] There does, in fact, seem to have been some problem concerning the use of the name 'Tréogate' for legal purposes. It first appears in the records of the Gendarmerie as 'Loaisel de Tréogate'.[18] But of the fourteen other legal documents discovered that concern the period after 1788, all but four use only the name 'Loaisel'. The political pressure to drop the particle of nobility 'de' probably accounts for publishing under the name 'Loaisel Tréogate' after the Revolution. But political considerations do not seem a satisfactory explanation for the complete dropping of the name 'Tréogate' on legal documents, nor could they have had any influence on the two marriage documents drawn up in 1788, which give only the name 'Loaisel'.[19] The 1789 and 1790 baptismal records of Loaisel's two children carry the name 'Loaisel-Tréogate',[20] but a definite indication of a question of legality is indicated in the 1800 death certificate of his first wife, which lists the name as 'Loaisel *dit* Tréogate'.[21] The act of 'rectification de ses noms' was drawn up at the time of the second marriage, as one of a number of documents designed to get Loaisel's legal house in order as a preliminary step to setting up the marriage contract.[22] That contract and all later documents carry only the name 'Loaisel', leading one to conclude that the name 'Tréogate' had no legal status.[23] An 'Etat des meubles appartenant à Madame Loaisel de Tréogate', which was written in 1809 in Loaisel's own hand,

---

[17] A. N., Minutier des notaires, Etude xliv (Hua), Répertoire 13, 3e jour complémentaire an xii, 'Notoriété passée en brevet, Constatant le Deces des ayeux de Mr Loaisel et au rectification de ses noms'.

[18] Service historique de l'Armée (Château de Vincennes), Yb 73, Contrôle des officiers, Maison du Roi, Gendarmes d'ordonnance, 1775, Compagnie des Gendarmes de la Reine.

[19] 'Promesse de mariage' and 'Contrat de mariage', cited above in note 12.

[20] A. D. Seine: Etat civil, baptême, 5 juillet 1789, Alexandre Prosper Loaisel Tréogate; Etat civil, baptême, 29 mai 1790, Angélique Eulalie Loaisel Tréogate.

[21] A. D. Seine, Etat civil, acte de décès, 16 février 1800, Marie Opportune Prout.

[22] the others were A. N. Minutier des notaires, Etude xliv (Hua): 737, 3e jour complémentaire an xii, 'Procès verbal de Carence après le décès de Made Loaisel [Prout]'; Répertoire 13, 5 vendémiaire an xiii, 'Notoriété passée en brevet, Après le décès des ayeux de Joseph Marie Threogate Loaisel [*sic*]'. The latter reference containing mistaken spelling and incorrect order of the last two names is only an entry in a *répertoire* and not an official notarial act.

[23] A. N., Minutier des notaires, Etude xliv (Hua), 738, 18 vendémiaire an xiii, contrat de mariage, Joseph Marie Loaisel – Jeanne Sophie Delaville. A. D. Seine: Etat civil, décès, 12 octobre 1812, Joseph Marie Loaisel; D4 U1 51 No.535, Description après décès de Joseph Marie Loaisel, 12 octobre 1812; D2390 Q7, Déclaration des mutations par décès de Joseph Marie Loaisel, 3 mai 1813.

is signed by him as 'Joseph Marie Loaisel de Tréogate'.[24] However, this document was an 'acte sous seing privé' and not as official as a notarised act or a public record. Loaisel was thus free to sign as he pleased. And it is thus by this name that posterity should remember him. Indeed, his son Alexandre Prosper died in 1849 using the name 'Loaisel de Tréogate'.[25]

Gobrien Mathurin Joseph Loaisel, one of Loaisel's older brothers, became *recteur* of Redon in 1777, the position formerly held by their paternal uncle, Julien Alexandre Loaisel.[26] Gobrien was deputy to the Etats généraux in 1789 and emigrated to Jersey in 1792. After returning to Redon, he resumed the cure, which he finally resigned in 1816.[27] A younger sister, Emilie Judith, died unmarried in 1781 at the age of 27.[28] The older sister, Françoise Mathurine Marie, married a lawyer, who was 'avocat en Parlement, subdélégué, procureur fiscal de l'ancienne baronie de Malestroit'.[29] Practically nothing is known about Alexandre Marie, Loaisel's oldest brother. The most illustrious among in-laws and godparents of the family seems to have been the husband of Emilie's godmother, 'haut et puissant messire Jan René Bonin, chef de nom et d'armes, Chevalier Seigneur Comte de la ville Bouquais, Vicomte de Trégranteur, Baron de Château Merlet, et autres biens, Conseiller Originaire au Parlement de Bretagne'.[30] The Loaisel family and closest friends are thus principally judicial officers and clergymen.

It is not possible to say at the present time which if any members of the immediate family were actually of true nobility. The references to '*noble* Maître Vincent Joseph Loaisel' in the Archives départementales du Morbihan are by no means proof of nobility,[31] since such titles were commonly usurped by *roturiers* at that time, leading to the inflation of

[24] A. D. Seine, included with the 'Description après décès' cited in the preceding note.
[25] 'Décès' Alexandre Prosper, cited above in note 8.
[26] Julien Alexandre is listed as 'Recteur de Redon' on the Saulnays genealogy. He is identified as 'prestre' on the baptismal record of Alexandre Marie, cited above in note 2.
[27] Régis Marie Joseph de L'Estourbeillon de la Garnache, *Les Familles françaises à Jersey pendant la Révolution* (Nantes 1886), p.406.
[28] this fact was taken from the Saulnays genealogy. The date of death is noted as having been taken from the 'régistre [paroissial] de Redon (Ille et Vilaine)', without specifying whether the *régistre* is located in the church or in the A. D. Ille et Vilaine.
[29] A. D. Morbihan, E. Suppl. 590, Etat civil, Paroisse de Malestroit, mariage, 15 janvier 1771, Joseph François Hervé – Françoise Mathurine Marie Loaisel.
[30] 'Baptême', Emilie Judith Loaisel, cited above in note 2.
[31] all documents cited above in notes 1 and 2 except the 'baptême' of Alexandre Marie Loaisel refer to Vincent Joseph as 'noble maître' etc.

titles mentioned above. Loaisel's military record states specifically 'Etat du père – noble'.[32] But some doubt has been cast upon the authenticity of this claim, which could have been made without proof. A recently discovered reference to an as yet unlocated document concerning Loaisel's candidacy for the Gendarmerie evokes this very problem, stating that Loaisel was of a 'bonne famillie *bourgeoise* alliée à plusieures gentilshommes'. Until the original document is located, the doubt remains.[33] And certainly, much further genealogical research is required before it will be possible to confirm claims by Loaisel de Saulnays and the Saulnays genealogy concerning the direct descent of this particular Loaisel family from such notables in Brittany's history as 'Robin de Loaysel, Seigneur du Coudray, nommé dans l'association de nobles de [Bretagne], pour la défense du Duché, en 1374' or Jean Loaisel, whose heroism was mentioned 'dans une charte de l'An 1170, d'Alain de Dinan, pour Marmoutiers'.[34]

ii. Gendarme du roi

Nothing at all is known of Loaisel's early life. Sometime between 1754 and 1771, both of his parents died.[35] Whether or not he was during this time raised by 'un vieux gentilhomme de la Maison du Roi, son parent', as maintained by Loaisel de Saulnays, it is impossible to say, nor is it even possible to guess who this 'vieux gentilhomme' might be (p.9). All trace is lost of Loaisel's oldest brother, Alexandre Marie, after

[32] Service historique de l'Armée, document cited above in note 18.

[33] the document in question is a manuscript *fiche* forming part of a large collection of notes gathered together by René Kerviler in preparation for a projected *Répertoire général de bio-bibliographie bretonne*. Publication stopped after 17 volumes (Rennes 1886-1907) with the name 'Guépin'. The notes for the remainder of the work are now located in the Bibliothèque municipale de Nantes. The *fiche* in question was provided by m. Jacques-Yves de Sallier Dupin, Conservateur-adjoint, in reply to a query. It came from *liasse* 112 or 113. It has not yet been possible to decipher the references on the *fiche* which might provide a clue to the origin of the information.

[34] Saulnays, p.809. The description of Robin de Loaysel is from one of Saulnays's listed sources: François Alexandre Aubert de la Chesnaye-Desbois, *Dictionnaire de noblesse*, 3rd ed., rev. (Paris 1863-1876), xii.216. Gaps, inaccuracies, and unconfirmed information in the family genealogy at the A. D. Morbihan do not permit accurate tracing of the family line any further than has been outlined above.

[35] they were both alive in 1753 as testified to by the birth of Emilie Judith in early 1754. They are not mentioned again in any document so far discovered until the 'mariage' of Françoise Mathurine in 1771 (document cited in note 29 above), which lists them as deceased.

1771. Joseph Marie and his other brother, Gobrien, went the way of so many *cadets* – one to the military and one to the church.

On 31 May 1773, at the age of 21, Joseph Marie entered the Gendarmerie d'ordonnance of the Maison du roi. At that time he appears to have had an income of '300 livres de rente',[36] the minimum sum required for admission to the Gendarmerie.[37] The Maison du roi was composed of several *corps d'élite* gathered around the throne for both ceremony and security. Besides the ten companies of the Gendarmerie, the Maison du roi included such other renowned corps as the Mousquetaires and the Cent-Suisses. The Gendarmerie was the oldest of the corps, being directly descended from the first permanent army of the French monarchy. Although the Maison du roi had served brilliantly in the wars of Louis xiv, the battle of Fontenoy in 1745 was its last moment of glory. In the second half of the eighteenth century, it became a refuge for a privileged elite interested mainly in pleasure, dissipation, and court intrigue. The Gendarmes had resided at the Château de Lunéville since 1767, so that Loaisel would presumably have passed much of his military service there.[38] He was attached to the Compagnie des Gendarmes de la reine, in which he served almost two full years. On 10 April 1775 he received a 'congé de retraite'.[39] The dates Loaisel entered and left the Gendarmerie and the name of his company are the only facts obtainable from official documents concerning his military career. There is not even an indication of his grade. These facts do, however, serve to confirm some of the apparently autobiographical passages in the novels, thus justifying consideration of the other information contained in these same passages for clues to fill out the story of this period of Loaisel's life.

The most important event in Loaisel's military career is his 'congé de retraite'. The novels reflect, in those autobiographical passages dealing with this period, a tremendous sense of disappointment, disillusionment, and despair at not having been able to continue the career

[36] information contained on the Kerviler fiche cited above in note 33.

[37] P. Fr. d'Isnard, *La Gendarmerie de France: son origine, son rang, ses prérogatives et son service* (Paris 1781), p.67.

[38] this information is taken from Léon Mention's short but highly informative chapter on the Maison du roi in his *L'Armée de l'ancien régime de Louis XIV à la Révolution* (Paris n.d.), pp.111-12, 128-33.

[39] 'Contrôle des officiers' cited above in note 18. The *prénoms* are given as 'Louis Marie'. However, the age listed combined with the parents' names prove that this could only have been 'Joseph Marie'.

in the Gendarmerie. They lead one to conclude that Loaisel did not leave voluntarily but was forced out, or suspended, and forbidden to return. At times he seems bitter and resentful, appearing to place the blame on exterior circumstances, and yet in other passages he sounds repentant and apologetic, leaving the impression that he was somehow responsible for the unhappy turn of events that closed him off from the military life forever. The definitive answer is not to be found, but a limited number of hypothetical explanations can be drawn up.

The longest and surely most authentically autobiographical passage treating the military career appears in the 'Lettre à m. Coll', the preface to *Florello*. The letter is dated '3 Mars 1776', less than a year after the 'congé de retraite', and is addressed to a 'M. Coll, Officier dans le Régiment de Walsch'. Whether or not m. Coll is a fiction, Loaisel demonstrates the esteem with which he regards the military by directing this disguised dedication to an officer.[40] The following passage from the 'Lettre à m. Coll', while packed with rhetoric and a pretence of modesty vis-à-vis his literary talents, reveals Loaisel's love of the pomp and glory of the military life he has left behind (*Florello*, pp.9*-10*):

Il fut un temps où mon esprit pétilloit comme le Champagne, où j'étois fou comme une vieille amoureuse; mais de Disciple joyeux de Mars que j'étois alors, je suis devenu le triste Eleve d'Apollon. Autrefois je marchois fier, intrépide, hérissé de piques étincelantes, au bruit belliqueux des fanfares; aujourd'hui je marche hérissé de vers, de phrases & de grands mots, aux sons rauques & mal cadencés d'une lyre brisée. Autrefois, monté sur un beau cheval, que je nommois le *Superbe*, dont le regard de feu, la magnifique encolure répondoient merveilleusement à son nom, j'aimois à le voir écumant, caracoler & s'élancer rapidement dans la plaine; j'aimois à me voir enveloppé d'un noble tourbillon de poussiere, au milieu d'un brillant Escadron; maintenant à l'ombre d'un manteau Platonicien, courbé sous la besace philosophique, je marche d'un pas lent & timide dans les sombres détours qui précedent les avenues du Temple de Mémoire.

A note to this passage provides the few definite clues that do exist as to the circumstances of the 'congé de retraite'. One gets a hint of the reason when Loaisel states, 'que ne puis-je oublier l'évenement malheureux qui me fit renoncer pour un temps à une Profession faite pour

[40] it would appear that m. Coll was a colleague from the service, but the following 'Contrôles des officiers' in the archives of the Service historique de l'Armée revealed no officier named 'Coll' in the 'Régiment de Walsch' (known earlier under the name of 'Régiment de Rothe'): YB 227, Corps de Troupe, Régiment de Rothe (irlandais), 1763; YB 361, Corps de Troupe, Régiment de Walsh [*sic*] (irlandais), 1776.

produire l'enthousiasme des vertus!' (p.10*, note). The term 'évenement malheureux' hardly helps to establish responsibility, but perhaps the very mention of 'l'enthousiasme des vertus' as the guiding principle of the 'Profession' reveals that failure to live up to that principle might have been the reason for having to renounce the profession. The words 'pour un temps' suggest that it was perhaps a question of suspension rather than irrevocable dismissal. The use of the conditional in the following apostrophe to his commander supports the idea of a suspension: 'Mon cœur est plein de mille sentimens de respect, de reconnoissance & d'admiration pour vous; que ne puis-je l'épancher comme je le desirerois?' Loaisel names the marquis de Castries in a note to the note as the one to whom the apostrophe is addressed (p.10*, note to note). Around the time of Loaisel's service, the marquis de Castries was indeed commander of the Gendarmerie (Isnard, pp.6, 66-67, 81). As the apostrophe continues, Loaisel seems to be indicating that a personal relationship existed between the two – no small honour for Loaisel, since the marquis de Castries would become Maréchal de France in 1783 – and that it was the marquis de Castries who was responsible for Loaisel's suspension and the failure to reinstate him: 'Pourquoi eûtes-vous à vous plaindre de moi? . . . Vous m'honorâtes de votre protection. Mais . . . je ne sers plus vos ordres. Voila [l]a plus amere de toutes mes douleurs' (pp.10*-11*, note).

Leaving for a moment the sure footing of documents and certain autobiography, it is time to venture temporarily into the area of probable or possible autobiography. A passage and note from *A ma Julie* in the *Soirées de mélancolie* (pp.145-46) appear to support the hypotheses of a close relationship between Loaisel and the marquis de Castries and of an 'unvirtuous' act on the part of Loaisel as the reason for the 'congé de retraite':

Quand de faux amis & des parens crédules m'abandonnerent; quand des protecteurs, autrefois bienfaisants, mais devenus inflexibles, s'éleverent avec trop de rigueur* contre les écarts excusables d'une jeunesse inconsidérée; quand mon orgueil humilié reçut d'eux des reproches accablants [. . .]

* Vous qui sçavez à qui s'adressent ces plaintes légitimes; vous qui me comblâtes de vos bienfaits, & que je réverai comme le plus loyal et le plus généreux des hommes; c'est à votre sévérité constante que je dois la plus grande partie de mes chagrins. Depuis que votre oreille s'est fermée aux gémissemens de mon sincere repentir, je porte en tous lieux un trait déchirant, dont la mort seule pourra me délivrer. Si la vertu est dans votre cœur, comme

elle parôit dans la simplicité de vos discours, vous aurez à jamais à vous faire
le reproche cruel d'avoir enlevé, à la societé, un jeune homme qui auroit pu
prétendre au noble privilège de servir ses semblables, & que ses longs ennuis
ont dégoûté de tout.

The term 'protecteurs' recalls the words 'votre protection' of the
apostrophe to the Marquis in *Florello*. It is evident from the words 'le
plus loyal et le plus généreux des hommes', in the note, that Loaisel
is in fact addressing only one person, at least in that note. The marquis
de Castries was singled out in the apostrophe in *Florello* as the one
responsible for preventing Loaisel's future service in the military, just
as here, the person to whom the note is addressed has barred Loaisel
from the 'noble privilège de servir ses semblables'. It no longer seems,
however, as in *Florello*, that Loaisel foresees even the slightest possibility of his reinstatement; rather, he now accepts his separation from
the Gendarmerie as permanent. The cause for the 'congé de retraite'
is here more obviously than in *Florello* an act of reprehensible behaviour
on Loaisel's part, as evident in the words 'les écarts excusables d'une
jeunesse inconsidérée' and the reference to 'gémissemens de mon sincere
repentir'. However, even though his conduct may have been reprehensible in the eyes of others – whence the 'sincere repentir' designed
to cater to their point of view and return into their good graces – for
Loaisel, the 'écarts' were 'excusables' because acts of a 'jeunesse inconsidérée' and not of a corrupt spirit. In fact, he very obviously feels that
the reaction against him was of an unwarranted severity, as is revealed in
the accusation that his 'protecteurs' not only had become 'inflexibles'
but also 's'éleverent avec trop de rigueur'. This feeling of unjustified
persecution was already apparent in the opening lines of the main body
of the 'anecdote' *Florello*, when in a series of apostrophes invoking his
various sources of inspiration, Loaisel speaks of himself as 'victime
assidue de la persécution' and addresses his persecutor as 'O vous qui
prêtâtes une oreille de fer aux cris de ma jeunesse délaisée, & qui me
fermâtes l'asyle sacré de la bienfaisance' (*Florello*, p.2). Throughout
these passages, there is also evidence of no small amount of bitterness.

　　Further evidence of the moral distinctions surrounding the cause of
Loaisel's 'congé de retraite' are found in the first chapter of *Valrose*,
where, in a seemingly autobiographically inspired passage, Loaisel has
Valrose speak of 'l'événement malheureux dont les circonstances vous
sont connues, et qui, bien qu'honorables pour votre jeune ami [Valrose
himself], le forcèrent de quitter la carrière militaire qu'il commençoit de

parcourir avec distinction' (*Valrose*, i.24-25). Here are the identical words of the passage in *Florello* – 'l'événement malheureux' – only now the circumstances are qualified as 'honorables' for Valrose-Loaisel. The moral argumentation whereby honour is preserved in the face of seemingly immoral acts abounds throughout Loaisel's works and accompanies many of the amatory episodes. In what might well be an autobiographically inspired passage, at least in so far as the moral argumentation is concerned, the author *Le Port* in the *Soirées de mélancolie* imagines how those who have pardoned 'les folies de mon jeune âge' reasoned in arriving at that pardon: 'Vous avez dit: "dans le riant printemps de l'âge, dans la saison des amours, qui peut résister aux secousses du desir? Le sang qui coule dans nos veines, ne peut être souillé: c'est un jeune homme qui a été foible, & non pas méchant; *son honneur est intact:* il faut rendre la consolation à son ame abattue" ' (*Soirées de mélancolie*, p.155: emphasis added). The wording of this passage is extremely important because the concept of honour is involved linking it, conceptually at least, to the passage from *Valrose* just cited. Finally, returning from the realm of hypothetical supposition based on seemingly autobiographical references back to the surer ground of the 'Lettre à m. Coll', one finds in a note to the 'héroïde' to his mistress – fictional or real – exactly the same argument: 'Censeurs atrabilaires, qui condamnez ces douces peintures, répondez-moi! Vit-on jamais le crime faire des heureux? Vous me direz que non sans doute. Eh bien, jamais bonheur ne fut plus vif & plus pur que celui que j'ai goûté dans les bras de ma Maîtresse. La vertu peut donc sourire à l'amour, & goûter quelquefois ses plaisirs. Voilà un argument sans réplique' (*Florello*, p.13*).

That is as far as one can profitably venture into autobiographical extractions from the novels so far as the military career is concerned. Further hypothesising would encounter too much vagueness, ambiguity, and open contradiction among the different texts to serve any useful purpose at all in contributing to Loaisel's biography. In fact, one is already on somewhat uncertain footing in venturing this far. The whole question of youthful loves is open to a variety of interpretations: the mysterious mistress could have existed in Brittany, in Paris, or at Lunéville, where the Gendarmerie was garrisoned; she could have been faithful and a paragon of virtue or untrue and deceitful; the obstacle to their happiness could have been parents, Loaisel's commander, too great a difference in class, or a combination of these factors. But perhaps most important of all, one should realise that Loaisel's mistresses, and particularly his 'Julie', were most probably fashioned in his imagination. After all, Loaisel was an acknowledged disciple of the creator of the century's most famous 'Julie'.

Another tricky point of autobiographical extractions from the novels concerns Loaisel's ambitions of glory and power and his bitterness at not having been able to fulfil them. Some passages, especially in *Le Songe* and *Le Romords* in the *Soirées de mélancolie,* would seem to suggest that lack of social position or wealth may have figured in his failure to realise those ambitions. Whereas these suggestions are entirely too vague to warrant close consideration of the passages, the ideas should be kept in mind as points to be verified in future research. It is entirely possible that Loaisel's poverty did indeed keep him from obtaining a *charge* in the Gendarmerie, since these *charges* could be obtained only by buying them for substantial sums.[41]

During 1775-1776, the new Secrétaire d'état de la guerre, the comte de Saint-Germain, undertook a reform of the Gendarmerie as well as all the rest of the military establishment. The marquis de Castries, head of the Gendarmerie at this time, was in charge of carrying out the reforms, but he fought vigorously to save his command from the planned reductions. Among the reforms actually carried out was the abolishment of two companies of Gendarmes, although not Loaisel's, and a restructuring of the remaining companies. Of the excess personnel, the 'gendarmes', as opposed to officers with 'charges', were to be given 'congés pour se retirer chez eux'. It would be tempting to see these reforms as a possible explanation for Loaisel's plight, and they could very well have affected his not having been reinstated, given the general policy of reduction of forces. But Saint-Germain came into power in October 1775, and the royal ordonnance setting out the reforms is dated 24 February 1776, whereas Loaisel's 'congé de retraite' was effective 10 April 1775.[42]

Loaisel continued for a long while to consider himself as primarily of the military profession. A long footnote in *Dolbreuse* lauding the

[41] Mention, *L'Armée de l'ancien régime,* p.131.

[42] the 'Ordonnance du Roi, Concernant la Gendarmerie, Du 24 février 1776' is reprinted in its entirety in Isnard (pp.68 ff.). See particularly Articles 1-4, concerning the reorganisation, and Articles 27 and 32, concerning disposition of the excess personnel. The reform of the Gendarmerie by Saint-Germain is discussed both in Isnard and in Léon Mention, *Le Comte de Saint-Germain et ses réformes (1775-1777) d'après les Archives du dépôt de la guerre* (Paris 1884), pp.42-46.

Gendarmerie testifies to the strong feelings he retained still in 1783 (i.55, note). The documents relating to his first marriage, in July 1788, both give his profession as 'officier de cavalerie'.[43] Perhaps this was because of the limitations that the ancien régime placed on the proper professions of the nobility, or perhaps it reveals Loaisel's continued clinging to shattered dreams. It is certain, however, that Loaisel was not an 'officier de cavalerie' at the time.[44]

iii. Paris

Loaisel's whereabouts and activities between the 'congé de retraite', on 10 April 1775, and his first marriage, in Paris on 21 July 1788, cannot be established with any great certainty. The fact that he still considered himself as belonging to the military profession right up to the time of the marriage indicates probably no more than his unwillingness to abandon the distinctive label of his former occupation. He certainly could not be considered a retired officer after only two years of service. Furthermore, there is no record of his having received any pension from the Gendarmerie. It is possible that he was attempting to support himself by his writing as a supplement to his '300 livres de rente'.[45] This is the period when he wrote most of the novels. In 1777, he announced a plan to publish a series of *anecdotes* on a regular basis, a project similar to Baculard d'Arnaud's *Epreuves du sentiment* (*Soirées de mélancolie*, pp.xii, 158). This project, discussed more fully below (see pp.63-64) could have brought him something in the way of a regular income, but it never materialised. There are unconfirmed references to his having written anonymous contributions for periodicals and to his having collaborated with Delisle de Sales on the *Histoire des hommes*, which would have occurred at this time.[46] However, judging from his total confirmed literary production for this thirteen-year period – five novels, one collection of short stories, and two short poems – it seems doubtful

[43] 'promesse de mariage' and 'contrat de mariage', cited above in note 12.

[44] in 1863, the Ministère de la guerre, in response to a query from Loaisel's daughter for information on her father's military service, conducted a search of all applicable records but found no trace of Loaisel's having served at the time in question in any unit of which a member might have been designated as 'officier de cavalerie' (Service historique de l'Armée, Classement alphabétique, 1791-1847, Loaisel).

[45] information contained on the Kerviler fiche (see note 33 above).

[46] see discussion of these problems in the listing under 'Miscellaneous works'.

that any income it may have brought could have contributed significantly to his support.

Should one choose to take as autobiographically inspired the broad outlines of the first chapter of *Valrose* – and there is reason to do so since many facts of the early life of Valrose parallel the known facts of Loaisel's early life – it appears possible that during these years 1775-1788, Loaisel's income was derived at least partially from the proceeds of the sale of the family home in Brittany, following which sale he moved to Paris. The passage quoted earlier that evokes the 'événement malheureux' which brought to a close Valrose's military career continues as follows (*Valrose*, i.25):

Je revins dans mon pays natal. Mon père, ma mère étoient morts depuis quelques années; et par une fatalité aussi étrange que cruelle, une sœur chérie, le seul être au monde qui me fît espérer des consolations, venoit aussi de descendre au tombeau, à la fleur de son âge. Le cœur gros de ces pertes douloureuses, frappé de la tristesse de ces lieux, témoins autrefois du bonheur de mon enfance, et transformés depuis peu, en une effrayante solitude, je réglai mes comptes avec mes fermiers; j'arrangeai d'autres affaires de famille; et malgré quelques vieux amis de la maison, qui me conseilloient sagement de conserver l'héritage de mes pères, je le convertis en une somme d'argent, que je plaçai dans une maison de banque à Paris, et j'abandonnai le séjour de la province. C'étoit en 1779; j'avois alors vingt-deux ans.

The early deaths of Loaisel's parents have been fully verified as well as the death of his sister Emile Judith in 1781. The chronology described in *Valrose* does not correspond exactly to the facts of Loaisel's life (Valrose joins the military at age 17, Loaisel at age 22; Valrose's sister dies before 1779, Loaisel's in 1781), but such embroidery on autobiography is what autobiographical fiction is made of.[47]

The 'Avertissement' of the *Soirées de mélancolie* places Loaisel in the country at least during the period of their composition, which was before 1777: 'J'étois à la campagne quand j'écrivis ces petits Contes Moraux' (*Soirées de mélancolie*, p.i). In the section 'Au lecteur', at the end of the book, he speaks of 'un assez long voyage' which delayed him from carrying out the projected series of *anecdotes* announced in

---

[47] as pointed out above (note 14), no records were found in the A. D. Morbihan of either the inheritance or the sale of land by Loaisel. But since the search was far from exhaustive, this scenario of Loaisel's early life provides an interesting hypothesis for future research and verification.

the 'Avertissement'.[48] According to the preface of *La Comtesse d'Alibre*, published around September 1779, it was Loaisel's return to Paris that caused him to take up writing again: 'Un incident me ramene à Paris, & la maudite influence du sol me remet la plume à la main' (*Comtesse d'Alibre*, p.vi). There is no further explanation of the nature of the incident or of the duration of the stay in Paris. When these statements are co-ordinated with the information provided in the passage just quoted from *Valrose*, it would appear that the 1779 stay in Paris referred to in *La Comtesse d'Alibre* was not the final move to the city, since Loaisel's sister Emile Judith was still living then and that move did not come until after her death.

Loaisel's first wife, Marie Opportune Prout, was daughter of a 'négotiant'. Their marriage took place on 21 July 1788,[49] just one day before the opening performance of his first play, *L'Amour arrange tout*. They had two children in rapid succession – first a son, Alexandre Prosper, born 5 July 1789, and then a daughter, Angélique Eulalie, born 29 May 1790.[50] Loaisel de Saulnays's indication that the Tréogate branch of the Loaisel family was 'éteinte' in 1812 with the death of Joseph Marie is thus wholly inaccurate (Saulnays, p.9). Just how much farther into the future the branch did extend is not fully known with certainty, but no trace has been found of any more 'Loaisel de Tréogate' after Alexandre Prosper, who died in 1849.[51]

Just, what role, if any, Loaisel played in the Revolution is not known. According to an anecdote of highly questionable authenticity, and for which the original source has not been discovered, Loaisel was 'président d'un club révolutionnaire' and as such had the audacity to threaten the audience before the opening performance of the *Forêt périlleuse* with these words: 'Citoyens, je vous préviens que le premier scélérat qui sifflerait mon drame serait arrêté par mes ordres et que sa tête serait en grand danger de ne pas rester sur ses épaules'.[52] Not only did the *Forêt périlleuse* open in the middle of the Directoire (7 May 1797),

[48] *Soirées de mélancolie*, 'Au lecteur', p.158; 'Avertissement', p.xii.

[49] 'promesse de mariage' and 'contrat de mariage' cited in note 12 above.

[50] A. D. Seine: Etat civil, baptême, 5 juillet 1789, Alexandre Prosper Loaisel Tréogate; Etat civil, baptême, 29 mai 1790, Angélique Eulalie Loaisel Tréogate.

[51] 'Décès' cited in note 8. The *fichier* of the A. D. Seine contains no marriages, births, or deaths of persons with surnames 'Loaisel de Tréogate' other than those cited here.

[52] Ginisty, *Le Mélodrame*, p.28, n.1; repeated in Henri Quentin [pseudonym: Paul d'Estrée], *Le Théâtre sous la Terreur (théâtre de la peur), 1793-1794* (Paris 1913), pp.397-98.

Biography and literary career

when such language would not have been totally appropriate, but in fact none of Loaisel's plays opened during the *Terreur*, at which time such an occurrence might have been more logical. The information that Loaisel was 'président d'un club révolutionnaire' is probably just as unreliable as the rest of the anecdote.

The Convention thermidorienne awarded Loaisel an 'encouragement' of 2000 livres on 4 September 1795, a clear indication of his acceptance by that régime.[53] He had by that time established quite a reputation as a dramatist, and it was under that designation that he was listed in the official decree. Around this time and for the next several years, he may have attempted to support himself and his family by the proceeds of his writing, for in 1800, he officially listed his profession as 'homme de lettres'.[54] His most successfully dramatic productions fall within this period, from 1793 to 1801.

Right at the height of his literary career, Loaisel lost his first wife, who died of tuberculosis on 16 February 1800. She left him nothing, having sold all her possessions to pay for trips – presumably cures for the disease – and for operations. Strangely, at the time of her death, she was not living with Loaisel but with her brother-in-law, Achille Dey, an employee of the 'subsistances militaires'.[55] Whatever the reasons for this situation might have been, no ill will survived between the two men. Quite to the contrary, Dey was present at Loaisel's deathbed in 1812, which seems to indicate a close, enduring friendship.[56]

Loaisel's profitable literary career was short-lived. If indeed he had ever been able to support himself by his writing, the time came – somewhere between February 1800 and September 1804 – when he could no longer do so and had to take a job in the postal administration, where he remained until his death.[57] on 10 October, 1804, he married Jeanne Sophie Delaville, sister of another postal employee. Jeanne Sophie, daughter of an employee of the Trésorerie nationale, brought with her a

[53] Noël Gabriel Luce de Villar, *Rapport et projet de décret présenté à la Convention nationale, dans la scéance du 18 fructidor (an III, 4 septembre 1795), au nom du comité d'instruction publique, sur les encouragemens destinés aux savans, gens de lettres et artistes* (Paris An III), p.8.

[54] A. D. Seine, Etat civil, acte de décès, 16 février 1800, Marie Opportune Prout.

[55] 'Acte de décès' cited in preceding note; A. N., Minutier des notaires, Etude XLIV (Hua), 737, 3e jour complémentaire an XII [20 septembre 1804], 'Procès verbal de Carence après le décès de Made Loaisel'.

[56] A. D. Seine, Etat civil, acte de décès, 11 octobre 1812, Joseph Marie Loaisel.

[57] 'Acte de décès' cited in preceding note; 'Procès verbal de Carence après le décès de Made Loaisel', cited above in note 55.

48

modest dowry, which permitted them to live in limited comfort with the luxury of a maid.[58] This second marriage produced no children.

The evidence does not seem to support the claim by Loaisel de Saulnays that in the midst of misery, Loaisel was 'accueilli ou plutôt recueilli par un parent (Jean David Loaisel de Saulnays, chef d'escadron au 1er Hussards de la Garde [23 mai 1783-1858]), en son château de Thierville, par Brionne, dans l'Eure', and then returned to die in Paris.[59] Loaisel's continued presence in Paris between the time of his second marriage in 1804 and his death in 1812 is supported by a document drawn up in 1809 listing the couple as residing in Paris[60] and also by the repeated references to his continued employment in the postal service in 1804, 1809, and 1812.[61] Again, Saulnays's information is undocumented and may be based on the verbally transmitted tradition of family history.

An anecdote reported by Alphonse Rabbe recounts Loaisel's death as a result of shock and hurt over a supposed plagiarism: 'Cubières Palmezeaux prétend que la comédie des Marionnettes de M. Picard n'est qu'une copie de cette dernière pièce de Tréogate [*La Bisarrerie de la fortune*], et que celui-ci, simple, modeste et timide, n'osant pas réclamer contre ce plagiat, en conçut tant de chagrin qu'il en mourut au mois d'octobre 1812.'[62] The two plays have little in common other than a roughly similar plot based on contrived coincidences, and both owe a debt of inspiration – acknowledged by Picard – to the comedy of Dufresny *La Coquette du village, ou le lot supposé*. But more important

---

[58] A. D. Seine, Etat civil, Mariage, 10 octobre 1804, Joseph Marie Loaisel – Jeanne Sophie Delaville; A. N., Minutier des Notaires, Etude XLIV (Hua), 738, 18 vendémiaire an XIII [10 octobre 1804], Contrat de mariage.

[59] Saulnays, p.10. The château of David-Jean Loaisel de Saulnays is identified as the Château de Freneuse (Eure) in Henry J.-G. de Milleville, *Armorial historique de la noblesse de France* (Paris 1845), p.146. Although the château is not indicated on modern maps under either name, towns of Thierville and Freneuse-sur-Risle are located about 4 kilometres apart on either side of the Risle and approximately 8-10 kilometres north of Brionne (Eure).

[60] 'Etat des meubles appartenant à Madame Loaisel de Tréogate', 1er mai 1809, contained in 'Description après décès de Joseph Marie Loaisel, 12 octobre 1812 (A. D. Seine, D4 U1 51 no.535).

[61] 'Procès de Carence après le décès de Made Loaisel', cited above in note 55; 'Contrat de mariage' Loaisel–Delaville, cited above in note 58; 'Etat des meubles' and 'Description après décès de Joseph Marie Loaisel', cited in preceding note; 'Acte de décès' Joseph Marie Loaisel, cited above in note 56.

[62] *Biographie portative et universelle des contemporains* (Paris 1836), ii;318-19.

49

still, *Les Marionnettes* opened on 14 May 1806, making Loaisel's death of 'chagrin' an extremely slow one![63]

Loaisel died 'à la suite de longue maladie' on 11 October 1812. He had almost literally no personal possessions besides the clothes on his back and a 'paquet de fouillis ne méritant pas de description'.[64] Perhaps the expenses of his medical care had driven him to sell everything that could have brought him any money as had been the case at the time of his first wife's illness. It is remarkable that the 'homme de lettres' left no library or personal papers of any value and evidently not even a collection of his own works. The disillusionment that Loaisel met in the Gendarmerie set the tone for his entire life. His literary career, in spite of the temporary popularity of some works, ended without glory eight years before his death. He seems just to have faded away in his final years – ill, poor, completely forgotten by the public, and probably still disappointed over the lack of fulfilment of the ambitions that had governed most of his life.

[63] Louis B. Picard, *Théâtre* (Paris 1812), v.219, 221.
[64] 'Description après décès', cited above in note 60.

2

Literary career

⚜

THREE distinct periods in the evolution of Loaisel's literary career are revealed by analysing the novel prefaces, the literary production, and contemporary reactions.[1] They are best described in his own terms. In his earliest works, at which time he refers to himself as 'le triste Eleve d'Apollon', he chooses to seek literary glory by emulating the writers of *le genre sombre*. This period, which runs from 1776 to 1782, includes the following works: the three short novels *Valmore*, *Florello*, and *La Comtesse d'Alibre*; the *Soirées de mélancolie*, a collection of short stories and prose poems; and the two works in verse, *Aux âmes sensibles* and *A m. le chevalier de Parny*. Then in 1783 with the appearance of *Dolbreuse*, Loaisel shifts to the full-fledged novel and evinces a strong interest in philosophical matters. This is the period of his highest ambitions. He aspires to become a true 'savant', to make an impression on the intellectual world, and to contribute to 'le bien public'. In *Ainsi finissent*, he announces his intention to abandon the novel for more socially useful pursuits, most probably in the domain of philosophical expository writing. However, these ambitions never materialise. Instead, in 1788, Loaisel turns to writing for the theatre and creates some of the first examples of the melodrama. He calls himself at this time an 'homme de lettres' and probably earns his living from writing, but he has no higher ambitions than producing good entertainment.

[1] the general conception and methodology of this portion of the study have been discussed in the introduction. Much material has been drawn from the annotated listing in Part II and is presented here without cross-reference notation, which would have been a considerable encumbrance. The reader would do well to be generally familiar with the type of information contained in the listing as well as the format of presentation so that he can refer to it easily when desiring further elucidation on points that can be only touched upon here. Appendix B and table 1 (p.87) summarise the data on publication and performance histories.

i. Triste élève d'Apollon: le genre sombre

The 'Lettre à m. Coll', so important for the biographical information on Loaisel's military career, provides an excellent starting point from which to examine the early years of his literary career. In the three opening paragraphs, Loaisel states with rhetorical modesty his limited intentions, concluding 'Puissiez-vous être attendri sans rien admirer!' (*Florello*, p.4*). He then proceeds to unveil his future literary ambitions and recounts how he first became involved in literature (pp.5*-7*):

Si la sensibilité, comme on l'a dit, influe sur les productions en tous genres, si elle donne à l'ame un ressort prodigieux, si elle est la mere du génie & le germe des plus grands talens, je dois m'engager sans crainte dans la plus épineuse de toutes les carrieres. Je dis plus; quoique je ne fasse qu'entrevoir dans le plus obscur lointain la palme destinée aux Grands-Hommes, il m'est permis de me repaître de l'espoir de l'obtenir un jour. Car j'ose assurer que jamais la Nature ne forma un cœur plus sensible que le mien. Cependant je n'attache aucune prétention à ces œuvres éphémeres. Enfoncé dans la solitude, désabusé de l'erreur de l'Optimisme, à laquelle je croyois autrefois, dévoré d'ennui, livré à moi-même, je cherchois un baume salutaire aux blessures qu'a reçu [*sic*] mon ame dans le commerce du monde. Je voulois, par quelque distraction agréable, faire treve à mes chagrins. La culture des Beaux-Arts, que j'ai toujours aimés, m'a paru une occupation consolante; j'ai pris la plume, & j'ai écrit. J'ai lu mes passe-temps à une bonne Dame, qui n'est pas bel-Esprit, mais qui aime à faire le bien. Elle en a été enchantée, & il y a tout lieu de croire qu'elle l'eût été à moins: elle a même versé des pleurs. Il m'a paru touchant de faire pleurer le beau sexe. Je suis revenu sur mes pas; j'ai développé des caracteres qui n'étoient que nuancés; je me suis appliqué à mieux soigner mon style, à répandre plus d'intérêt sur les détails, & je me suis fait imprimer. Voilà la cause bien simple de mon entrée dans la carriere des Lettres.

There seems little doubt that the 'blessures' to which Loaisel refers resulted from his failure to fulfil his ambitions for a glorious military career. Just two pages further on, he launches into the long comparison between his past as 'Disciple joyeux de Mars' and his present condition as 'triste Eleve d'Apollon'.[2] He closes that passage with an explicit description of the transfer of goals from one career to another: 'Je finirai par m'y égarer sans doute; mais le monde étant un labyrinthe,

---

[2] pp.9*-10*; the entire passage is quoted above, p.40.

il vaut encore mieux s'égarer au chemin de la renommée, que dans toute autre route. Autrefois je n'avois d'ennemis que ceux de la Patrie; aujourd'hui j'ai à combattre des chagrins, des préjugés, & tous les Aristarques de la Littérature' (pp.10*-11*). Through the maze of rhetoric stands out the very real and absolutely identical goal of both careers – 'la renommée', or as stated in the passage quoted earlier, 'la palme destinée aux Grands-Hommes'.

This interpretation is most important to keep in mind when trying to evaluate Loaisel's claims that he came to literature searching for a 'baume salutaire', a 'distraction agréable', or an 'occupation consolante'. No doubt these aims could have played a part in his early interest in 'la culture des Beaux-Arts', but they certainly were not the final goal of his career. The role, real or imaginary, played by the 'bonne dame' in these early days is of little significance. Whether or not, 'désabusé de l'erreur de l'Optimisme', Loaisel originally took recourse to literature as therapy for either his general disillusionment with life or for his specific disappointment over failure to fulfil worldly ambitions of glory in the military, the essential fact remains that he quickly turned to pursuing literature still in hopes of attaining worldly glory but by different means.

Another most important fact disclosed in the 'Lettre à m. Coll' is that Loaisel was unaided in his early literary career. Again the counsels of the 'bonne Dame' notwithstanding, Loaisel seems not to have been involved in a literary society or even to have had a literary guardian: 'Encore étranger dans le Monde littéraire, inconnu à tous ceux qui le composent, je n'ai pu soumettre mon début à la censure de quelque Homme instruit, qui auroit pu guider ma marche' (p.3*). In fact, there is little evidence of any significant contacts between Loaisel and other intellectuals or writers throughout his entire lifetime. He is not mentioned in the literary memoirs or correspondences of Bachaumont, Grimm, or La Harpe. Periodicals took note of his works, but never said anything about the man himself in their reviews. There are only three documented contacts with other writers. The first is a letter Loaisel sent from Nancy to Baculard d'Arnaud in 1774, saying that he had used Baculard's address in arranging for some money to be forwarded to Paris.[3] Although he calls Baculard 'mon cher bienfaiteur',

---

[3] Bibliothèque nationale, Département des manuscrits, Nouvelles acquisitions françaises, no.14893, François-Thomas de Baculard d'Arnaud, *Œuvres diverses et correspondance*, ff.50-51. This letter was discovered by Robert Dawson and published in

there is practically no information at all in the letter as to the relationship that existed between the two. Loaisel's claim in the 'Lettre à m. Coll' that he lacked the advice of 'quelque Homme instruit' in the early days of his literary career suggests strongly that Baculard served no active role as mentor, although Loaisel certainly admired him and sought to emulate his example.[4] The second documented contact between Loaisel and a literary figure is the exchange of poems with Parny: Loaisel's *A m. le chevalier de Parny, après avoir lu ses Poésies érotiques*, composed in 1782 and Parny's *Réponse aux vers précédens*. Finally, there is the melodrama *Le Grand chasseur*, written in collaboration with Pixerécourt. Unfortunately there is no information available on this collaboration other than the finished product. The insertion of the short story *La Folle de Saint-Joseph* into *Ainsi finissent* would seem to indicate some access to Parisian literary circles in 1785 provided that there is some autobiographical truth – as there appears to be – in the claim that the story was copied from a manuscrit circulating in Paris at the time.[5]

The reference to 'la culture des Beaux-Arts, que j'ai toujours aimés' brings up the question as to just what Loaisel's literary culture might have been. Although he never addresses the matter directly, it is possible to ascertain the authors and works with which he was familiar just by drawing up a list of the identifiable quotations and explicit mentions of the names and works. Most of these mentions and quotations come from the novel prefaces, epigraphs, and the passage in *Dolbreuse* (i.13-20) discussing the reading programme of Dolbreuse and Ermance. Although no information has been found to give any idea of Loaisel's formal education, he shows a grasp of Latin sufficient to have produced familiarity with Horace's *Odes*, *Epistles*, and *Satires*, Ovid's *Tristia* and *Metamorphoses*, Pliny's *Letters* and *Panegyricus*, Tibullus's *Elegies*, and Virgil's *Aeneid*, *Georgics*, and *Eclogues*. All of these works

his *Baculard d'Arnaud: life and prose fiction*, Studies on Voltaire 161-62 (1976), ii.596-97. There is one minor correction to be made to Dawson's transcription. The first sentence should read, 'Mon cher bienfaiteur, je suis en Route pour aller chez moi en Semestre', and not 'je suis en honte'. The latter reading would certainly have added to what is known concerning Loaisel's reasons for leaving the army, but the correct reading contributes little of interest.

[4] Dawson's brief comment on Loaisel's letter to Baculard provides no further information on their relationship (i.254).

[5] the publication history of *La Folle de Saint-Joseph* is discussed in detail in the listing under entry no.35.

are quoted in Latin, the quotations serving mostly as epigraphs in the earliest works. A wide background in the letters and history of antiquity is evident also in the many references to mythology, critics, statesmen, and philosophers of the ancient world. As might be expected, Loaisel is particularly attracted to the baroque and romantic aspects of the writings of the ancients. He also demonstrates some familiarity with epic and legend of the French middle ages – Roland, Ferragus, Renaud de Montauban – and of the Italian renaissance – *Orlando furioso* and *Gerusalemme liberata*. A number of seventeenth-century writers are mentioned including Pascal, Boileau, Ménage, Balzac, Sorbière, Chaulieu, Bourdaloue, and Chapelain. Spanish novels are represented by *Amadis de Gaule* and by *Don Quixote*. Racine is given particular attention in *Valmore* and in *Dolbreuse*. Dolbreuse and Ermance are described as being especially attracted to his tragedies for the 'code sublime de tendresse et de grands sentiments' (*Dolbreuse*, i.15). As to his own century, Loaisel detests the 'sales poésies de Grecourt' and the 'plates farces de Vadé' (*Comtesse d'Alibre*, p.ix). Voltaire is criticised for his 'fureur presque risible' when attacking literary enemies in his works (*Dolbreuse*, ii.113). Loaisel praises the *Télémaque* and also the various newer literary tendencies of the period: the elegiac and lyrical mode of Parny's *Poésies érotiques*; descriptive poetry, represented by *Les Saisons* of Saint-Lambert and *Les Jardins* of Delille; the moral and sentimental novel, represented by Richardson, Rousseau, and Marmontel; and finally the 'sombre', led by the English mode setters Hervey and Young, backed up by Crébillon père and Baculard d'Arnaud in France. Among all of these writers, the strongest allegiance is expressed for Young, Rousseau, and Baculard d'Arnaud.

Returning once more to the passage recounting Loaisel's literary ambitions, one must examine his claim that 'jamais la Nature ne forma un cœur plus sensible que le mien'. Rather than reading this as pure unadulterated autobiography, how very much more logical to interpret this and similar passages which invoke popular labels of the then current literary fashions as attempts by Loaisel to incite enthusiasm and anticipation over the novel to follow. In the passage under consideration, the process works in the following manner. Loaisel first announces that 'la sensibilité, comme on l'a dit [...], est la mere du génie et le germe des plus grands talens'. He then sets out to build himself up as possessing such genius and great talents, but he does so indirectly by asserting instead his 'sensibilité', from which the other qualities inevitably flow. At the same time he has invoked the magic word 'sensibilité'. A similar rationale is also undoubtedly behind many of the passages which describe his disposition as 'sombre' and 'mélancolique', two other very popular literary labels of the time. The degree of autobiographical truth contained in such passages can never be determined accurately, nor is it really important to attempt such a determination. They can be studied more profitably for the role they play in contributing to the 'autobiographical myth' that Loaisel seems quite consciously to be trying to establish in the early novel prefaces. This myth is indeed worthy of consideration on its own right as a work of imagination.

The 'Lettre à m. Coll' contains the first phases of the 'autobiographical myth'. The following passage provides one of the most striking illustrations and also helps to explain the reasons for establishing the myth (pp.7*-9*; emphasis in original):

J'ai à répondre à un de vos reproches. Vous vous plaignez de cette teinte lugubre répandue sur tous mes Ecrits, de cette misanthropie éternelle que je porte, dites-vous, dans les Cercles, dans les Spectacles, & même au sein de l'amitié. Il est vrai, mon ami; je sacrifie sans relâche à la noire mélancolie, & le soleil dans son cours me retrouve sans cesse aux pieds de son idole. Je voudrois bien abjurer un culte contre lequel mon cœur réclame encore quelquefois. J'aimerois, dans des vers légers, à chanter Glycere, à rire des Héraclites du jour, à vanter mon *insouciance*; mais cela n'est plus en mon pouvoir. Les saillies de mon imagination sont éteintes; mon esprit, devenu maussade et nébuleux, ne trouve plus rien de plaisant. Je vous offrirois plutôt la triste image d'un Lappon, enseveli dans ses frimats, que le tableau frais & colorié d'un Petit-Maître sémillant, ou d'une Nymphe de Coulisse. Je peindrois plutôt les fonctions funebres des Ministres d'Atropos, que les scenes délicieuses d'une nuit passée au Bal de l'Opéra, ou d'un voyage d'été, fait par la Galiote à Saint-Cloud. Je suis d'un pathétique, d'un sombre qui effaroucheroit le Docteur Young lui-même.

Si vous veniez à me voir au moment où je vous écris, vous me prendriez sans peine pour un Légat des Trépassés, tant ma mine est funéraire! Le Philosophe d'Abdere, avec tous ses ris, ne viendroit pas à bout de me faire rire; tous les efforts de l'ironie, tous les sels de l'épigramme ne dérideroient pas mon front; je crois même que mon sérieux seroit à l'épreuve des agaceries d'un minois séduisant. C'est m'avouer atteint d'un mal incurable, c'est me confesser mort, & me mettre dans le cas de m'entendre dire de tous les côtés: *fuis au fond des bois avec les ours tes pareils.* Mais qu'y faire? A cela je répondrai par le vieux proverbe: *les jours se suivent, & ne se ressemblent pas.*

At the same time that he sets the tone for his literary productions – no

laughter, no irony, only the most serious of styles and the most lugubrious of subjects – Loaisel indirectly claims 'le Docteur Young' as his
patron saint. What may appear at first to be an apology to the reader
for the author's morose and tragic personality, or perhaps an expression
of deep personal sorrow, is much more probably designed as an incite-
ment to further reading. By placing, himself under the sign of Young,
Loaisel has joined a highly popular literary vogue. It just so happened
that an 'autobiographical myth' of personal tragedy was an integral
part of Young's success, at least on the continent.[6] If Loaisel was to
achieve similar success, he had also to create the aura of personal tragedy
in addition to imitating the spirit of the works.

Loaisel undoubtedly knew Young's *Night thoughts* through Le
Tourneur's 1769 translation, *Les Nuits d'Young*. In the 'Discours
préliminaire' to this translation, Le Tourneur records the popular
legend surrounding the author and points out the effect of this tragic
life on his composition. After first recounting the untimely deaths of
Young's wife and two stepchildren, he then goes on to describe the man
himself and his book:

Donnez du génie à cet homme infortuné, une imagination vive & brûlante,
une ame profondément sensible [. . .] & vous pourrez aisément deviner le ton,
le genre, les beautés & les défauts de l'ouvrage.

Que le début doit en être sombre! Comme l'état de son cœur aura tout à
coup changé l'aspect de l'univers! Qu'il doit voir l'espéce humaine misérable
dans le sentiment de sa propre misère! Comme toutes ses idées, toutes ses
réflexions doivent aboutir à la mort & au tombeau! Qu'il doit chérir les
ténèbres & la solitude de la nuit! Qu'il doit aimer à n'entendre que sa voix
gémissante au milieu du silence & de l'obscurité! Il cherchera tous les objets
qui peuvent flater & nourrir sa douleur. Qu'il sentira de violens desirs d'être
toute autre chose que ce qu'il est, de mourir pour changer d'état, de rejoindre
ses amis dans les lieux où il les croit heureux, en se voyant si malheureux dans
le monde où ils ne sont plus! Qu'il tourvera bien plus de douceur à s'entretenir
avec leurs fantômes chéris, que dans le commerce des hommes! Il ne pourra
plus souffrir de visage joyeux dans un monde qu'il ne voit qu'au travers d'un
crêpe funèbre.[7]

---

[6] Young's legend in France and its effect on the reception of *Les Nuits* is discussed in
detail in Paul Van Tieghem's 'La poésie de la nuit et des tombeaux', in his *Le Préromantisme: études d'histoire littéraire européenne* (Paris 1930), ii.21-25.

[7] Pierre Le Tourneur, 'Discours préliminaire', *Les Nuits d'Young* (Amsterdam, Paris
1769), i.LV-LVII.

It is certainly more than just coincidence that Loaisel's self-portrait in the 'Lettre à m. Coll' should so closely resemble Le Tourneur's description of Young. The whole story of thwarted ambitions of military glory and of regrets over the loss of a former mistress – including a 'héroïde' of over sixty verses – help to establish for Loaisel his own 'autobiographical myth' of misfortunes with which he can seek to rival the reputation of Young (*Florello*, pp.11*-14*). For just as Young's tragic life assured the reader of 'le ton, le genre, les beautés & les défauts de l'ouvrage', so will Loaisel's.

Speaking of his imagination, which he accurately describes as comprising a penchant for melodramatic action and the bucolic idyll, Loaisel stresses above all else his natural inclination toward the *genre sombre* (pp.3*-4*). Both he and his critics see this 'sombre' and 'lugubre' aspect of the early works as their most remarkable quality. However, the critics are not favourably impressed either with the *genre sombre* or with Loaisel's exploitation of it. The ensuing series of exchanges between reviews and prefaces finally erupts into an actual *querelle* over *La Comtesse d'Alibre*.

Throughout the 'Lettre à m. Coll', Loaisel frequently proclaims the insufficiency of his talents, the limited scope of his goals, and his doubts over achieving even those goals. The purely rhetorical nature of such modesty seems evident fom the clash between these statements and the accompanying discussions of his ambitious dreams of attaining the highest literary glory. However, Loaisel's anticipation of criticism and his concern with preparing defences in advance of attack reveal a somewhat less rhetorical attitude, which may in fact reflect a very real apprehension over the acceptance of his works by the critics. The preoccupation with potential criticism is already visible in *Valmore*. Although this first novel lacks a preface, two footnotes to the text are addressed directly to potential criticism to fend off possible attacks on the work's morality and verisimilitude (*Valmore*, pp.66, 75). But it is in a short note at the end of the text that Loaisel's apprehension is most apparent: 'Des raisons m'ont empêché de mettre à cet Ouvrage toute la correction dont je suis capable. Persuadé d'ailleurs de l'insuffisance de mes talens, je me soumets d'avance & sans murmure à tous les arrêts des plus séveres Aristarques de la Littérature. Mais je suis jeune, je suis Militaire, je débute: voilà des droits sur lesquels je compte: voilà mes titres à l'indulgence du Public' (*Valmore*, p.96). Fear of a lack of stylistic proficiency is also evident in the opening lines of the 'Lettre à m. Coll': 'Voilà, mon Ami, une seconde Anecdote que je donne au Public; elle n'est probablement pas mieux achevée que la premiere (*Florello*, p.3*). Also, to a certain degree, a defence of the *sombre* is inherent in the discussion of Loaisel's literary proclivities and in the 'autobiographical myth'. Loaisel claims Young as his patron saint probably with no small thought going to the protection offered by this association. If the date of the 'Lettre à m. Coll', 'Le 2 Mars 1776', accurately reflects the date of its composition, Loaisel had not yet had any indication of the critical reaction to *Valmore*, since the first published review did not appear until 1 May 1776. But by the time he wrote the 'Avertissement' and the section 'Au lecteur' of the *Soirées de mélancolie*, he had evidently read most of the reviews of both the earlier works. In the 'Avertissement' appears a long defence of his 'goût pour les sujets lugubres' and in 'Au lecteur', a justification of his style. Both times Loaisel mentions that he had been criticised on the point he is addressing. A brief examination of the contemporary criticism of *Valmore* and *Florello* will help to interpret the motivation behind the remarks in these two sections of the *Soirées de mélancolie*.

Several periodicals took note of Loaisel's first two works only in passing with very little if any commentary. The *Année littéraire*, which in 1776 was undergoing the double crisis of official condemnation and a change in direction as the result of the death of Fréron père,[8] published only one combined announcement of *Valmore* and *Florello* along with the *Soirées de mélancolie* without commenting on any of the works (1777, i.288). The *Journal des sçavans*, whose principal interest was in scientific works,[9] announced the publication of *Valmore* and *Florello*, but it neither reviewed these works nor made any mention at all of Loaisel's future works (août 1777, p.575). The *Almanach littéraire ou étrennes d'Apollon*, while praising *Valmore* as a work which 'rempli d'intérêt et de sentiment, fait verser des larmes', passed right over *Florello* (1777, p.210). The *Journal encyclopédique* had almost as little to say but did compliment Loaisel for the 'manière forte et vigoureuse' in which he treated in *Valmore* and *Florello* the oft told tale of the misfortunes of love. It criticised in both works the occasional lack of verisimilitude and of 'correction' in the style (1er juillet 1776, p.158).

Two other periodicals devoted more space to Loaisel and continued to follow his future works with interest and some praise, even defending

[8] *Histoire générale de la presse française*, ed. Claude Bellanger *et al* (Paris 1969), i.267.
[9] *Histoire générale de la presse française*, i.205-206.

him to a limited degree during the controversy over *La Comtesse d'Alibre*. One of these was the prestigious *Mercure de France*. The review of *Valmore* lacked comments and was little more than a summary of the moral elements, consisting mostly of a paraphrase of Loaisel's two notes defending the work's morality (janvier 1777, premier volume, pp.97-99). However, *Florello* received a more balanced summary and was praised for its 'chaleur' and 'intérêt'. The only other comment pointed out Loaisel's 'imagination vive et sensible, mais mélancolique et sombre' (juillet 1776, pp.103-106). Loaisel also found support in the continuations of the *Journal de Trévoux*. His first three works were all reviewed while the journal was under the direction of the frères Castilhon and published under the title *Journal des sciences et des beaux-arts*. Unfortunately for Loaisel, the influence of this journal was on the decline as judged by the number of readers, which dropped to 200 by November 1778.[10] It committed itself right from the start in Loaisel's favour by stating in the review of *Valmore*, 'L'Auteur annonce un vrai talent'. A few faults were noted: a style 'parfois négligé', excessive wordiness, too many 'réflexions', and 'une imagination trop féconde' (1er mai 1776, pp.277-79). This same imagination was again noted as responsible for the lack of versimilitude in the plot of *Florello* but then was highly praised for inspiring the forceful and vigorous depiction of passions in this second work. In spite of the continued imperfections of style, the journal found that on the whole, *Florello* justified the earlier positive judgement of *Valmore* (15 juin 1776, pp.539-42).

Loaisel was less fortunate at the hands of the *Affiches de province*, as he would continue to be through 1779, during which period Querlon was director.[11] While *Valmore* went unnoted, *Florello* was attacked head-on with not a single word of praise or encouragement. In addition to receiving severe criticism for the style and overabundant moral reflections, Loaisel was brought to task for his literary taste: 'L'Auteur de cet Ouvrage prévient dans une lettre qui sert de Préface [...] qu'il aime les sujets lugubres: il a certainement rempli son objet. On peut même dire qu'à force de vouloir approfondir ce genre, quelques-unes de ses peintures sont dégoutantes d'horreur' (5 juin 1776, p.90).

Turning to the 'Avertissement' of the *Soirées de mélancolie*, one can see from Loaisel's opening words just exactly which review he is reply-

---

[10] a fact signalled in the *Correspondance secrète*, 8 novembre 1777 (quoted in Eugène Hatin, *Histoire politique et littéraire de la presse en France* (Paris 1859-1861), ii.272).

[11] *Histoire générale de la presse française*, i.323-26.

ing to: 'J'avois prévu le reproche qu'on m'a fait de mon goût pour les sujets lugubres' (*Soirées de mélancolie*, p.ii). The only review to offer any real criticism on the taste for 'sujets lugubres' was the article on *Florello* in the *Affiches de province*. The characterisation of certain passages as 'dégoutantes d'horreur' seems to have been too much for Loaisel to let go by without a reply. But perhaps more important still is that this review gives Loaisel another opportunity to vaunt himself as champion of the *genre sombre*. Indeed, how much more appropriate is an unfavourable review, since it enhances the image of the misunderstood, unappreciated, isolated, and now even more *sombre* and *mélancolique* disciple of Young.

Naturally, the defence will be a very personal one. First comes a long Lockean explanation of how each individual develops a distinct and different personality determined solely by the uncontrollable 'évenements', 'sensations', and 'circonstances' of his own separate existence. Supposedly at the moment one realises how powerless man is over this external conditioning, he develops a spirit of indulgence and tolerance for the varied personalities of others. It is only just that such tolerance be extended to writers regarding their preference for 'tel genre à tel autre', for a writer is just as powerless in the selection of his genre as in the determination of his personality (pp.ii-vi). He can write well only about things he has experienced: 'Il n'est pas facile de se donner des passions, des idées & des sentimens étrangers à l'état actuel de son ame' (p.vi). His genre is therefore determined by his personality, and from his powerlessness to determine his personality follows his powerlessness in the selection of a genre. 'Voilà du moins ce que je pense, & ce que je crois', concludes Loaisel. 'Je ne sçais écrire que ce que je sens; je ne puis exprimer que mes affections à mesure qu'elles naissent & se succedent en moi; je plains celui qui n'écrit pas d'après son cœur' (pp.vii-viii). In spite of the confident tone of these last words, Loaisel rounds off his defence with a reminder that this is indeed a defence: 'Ce que je viens de dire est plus que suffisant pour justifier mon penchant à la mélancolie' (p.viii). He cannot resist the temptation to exploit this opportunity to mention again the 'autobiographical myth': 'Si je suis triste & sombre, il est indubitable que ce n'est pas sans un motif puissant, sans une cause invincible, qui m'éloigne des jeux & des ris: peut-être qu'à force de répandre mes regrets, il s'adouciront, & feront place à des idées plus calmes & moins nébuleuses' (p.viii). But such references to personal tragedy are rare in the 'Avertissement' to the *Soirées de mélancolie*. The emphasis is much less on the 'autobiographical myth', which Loaisel may be reluctant to push any further in its own right, than on literary theory. In *Florello*, he felt comfortable enough justifying his genre solely by setting up a parallel between himself and Young; however, in a response directed clearly at his literary critics, he feels obliged to base his defence on more theoretical and philosophical grounds.

This analysis of the 'Avertissement' is of importance to the question of autobiographical interpretation of the novels, for at the very heart of Mornet's reading of 'confidences personnelles' into the texts is the statement quoted above 'Je ne sçais écrire que ce que je sens'. Taken out of context, this sentence can be quite easily interpreted as a literary principle in its own right so as to justify an autobiographical reading of the works. This is precisely what Mornet does when he quotes it as proof of 'le goût de l'auteur pour la confession'.[12] But a close literal reading of Loaisel's statement, even out of context, reveals that he claims as auto-biographical only the *feelings* he describes in his novels. He says nothing at all to indicate that the *adventures* he recounts have any basis in reality, autobiographical or not. Reading this statement in context, as demonstrated above, reveals that Loaisel is less concerned with declaring a penchant for autobiography than with providing himself an excuse for writing in the *genre sombre*. His excuse is that the nature of his personality leaves him no other choice, whence the necessity of discussing that personality.

In the section 'Au lecteur', Loaisel admits that past criticism of his style was actually warranted. He offers a rather apologetical sounding expression of the insufficiency of his literary talents along with the assertion that he is trying to improve: 'Voilà bien des rêveries que je donne au public; malgré l'indulgence qu'il a bien voulu avoir pour mes foibles essais, je crains fort qu'il ne m'engage à ne plus rêver; néanmoins j'ai mieux soigné mon style que je n'avois fait dans Valmore & Florello, j'ai tâché d'éviter les fautes qu'on m'a justement reprochées' (p.158). The past criticism of his style seems to have instilled some grave doubts about his future literary success. He therefore proceeds to justify the style of the *Soirées de mélancolie* in hopes of deterring further criticism. He anticipates charges of 'des longueurs, des tableaux chargés, & quelquefois des redites', otherwise stated, 'une monotonie abondante,

---

[12] Daniel Mornet, 'Un "préromantique"', p.497. This article is discussed above, p.16.

fastidieuse pour bien des gens; mais qui a ses charmes pour l'ame sensible, qui sçait en saisir les touchantes beautés' (pp.158-59). His primary defence is to quote from the 'Deuxième préface' of *La Nouvelle Héloïse* the passage on the style of passion: 'La passion pleine d'elle-même s'exprime avec plus d'abondance que de force' etc.[13] Loaisel must have hoped that this association of his own theories with those of Jean-Jacques would lend him a protective shield against the critics. But it is a long way from theory to practice, and the shield was to be badly pierced.

A more significant revelation contained in 'Au lecteur' is Loaisel's announcement of plans for his future writing: 'Un assez long voyage, qu'il ma [*sic*] fallu faire, m'a empêché de publier les Anecdotes que j'avois promis de donner successivement de deux mois en deux mois, après celles que j'ai déjà mises au jour; mais aujourd'hui que débarrassé de toute contrainte gênante, je puis m'abandonner sans réserve à mon goût pour la littérature, je vais tâcher de remplir incessamment ma promesse' (p.158). That 'promesse' appeared in the 'Avertissement': 'Je me propose d'ajouter encore quelques Anecdotes à celles qui ont déja paru (Je parle ici de Valmore & de Florello); je leur donnerai un but moral, & les réunirai sous un titre universel' (p.xii). This project is highly significant since it is a direct imitation of the *Epreuves du sentiment* of Baculard d'Arnaud. It was only in 1775 that Baculard had finally perfected this formula, which he and his publishers had been playing with ever since around 1764. Aside from the *Décaméron français* of Louis d'Ussieux, published from 1772-1775, no one else had yet taken up this idea of writing a series of short stories for separate publication but belonging to a single, unified collection.[14] The similar presentation of *Valmore* and *Florello*, both 'anecdotes', leads one to wonder if this project may not perhaps have been in Loaisel's mind even before he wrote those two works. They were, in fact, published only three months apart, thus meeting the criterion of rapid composition and publication that was part of this new project. Whatever the case with *Valmore* and *Florello*, the project announced in the *Soirées de mélancolie* never

[13] the passage quoted from Rousseau is found on page 741 of the Pléiade edition (*Œuvres complètes* (Paris 1959), i).

[14] a very illuminating discussion of the idea of 'séries de nouvelles' is found in Angus Martin, 'Baculard d'Arnaud et la vogue des séries de nouvelles en France au XVIIIe siècle', *Revue d'histoire littéraire de la France* 73 (1973), pp.982-92. See especially pp.983-84 concerning Baculard and pp.987-89 for Louis d'Ussieux. Baculard's development of the concept is also discussed by Dawson (i.267-74).

materialised. It is none the less an important indication of Loaisel's plans at that stage of his literary career.

Closely connected with the plans for a series of *anecdotes* is Loaisel's search for a suitable and respectable literary form. He draws a clear distinction between the 'anecdote', represented by *Valmore* and *Florello*, and the form of the various pieces comprising the *Soirées de mélancolie*, which he calls 'petits Contes Moraux' (*Soirées de mélancolie*, p.i). It is evident that he sees the *anecdote* as a higher form of literature than the *conte moral*, for he precedes the promise of more *anecdotes* with a renouncement of any further attempts in the vein of the *Soirées de mélancolie*: 'Mon intention n'est point de donner d'autres productions dans ce genre; je sçais le peu de mérite qu'on attache à ces sortes d'ouvrages, & la foible considération qui en resulte' (p.xi). But Loaisel never gives any clear explanation of the characteristics that distinguish the *anecdote* from the *conte moral*. The fact that he fails to do so most probably reflects an uncertainty that he shares with his contemporaries regarding the proper use of these terms. In his *Histoire de la nouvelle française aux XVIIe et XVIIIe siècles* (Genève 1970) René Godenne points out that a change in terminology accompanied changing conceptions of content and form of the *nouvelle* after 1759 when Marmontel published his first *Contes moraux* (pp.173-86). If at the outset the term *conte moral* had seemed to serve well to distinguish the new, shorter form of fiction imitating Marmontel from the declining mode of a more *romanesque* 'nouvelle-petit roman', writers soon sought to dispel the ambiguity surrounding the term *conte*, which 'depuis 1700 avait surtout désigné des histoires faisant appel à des données imaginaires (conte de fées, conte oriental, conte mythologique, conte allégorique)' (Godenne, p.181). Some settled upon the term *anecdote*, which definitely carried no such allusions. Among them was Baculard d'Arnaud, who by 1777, when the *Soirées de mélancolie* were published, had written nine *anecdotes* (Godenne, p.181, n.62). Loaisel may well have been concerned with indicating the difference between the content of the *Soirées de mélancolie*, in which 'données imaginaires' abound, and the content of the other works, which recount only realistic adventures. Furthermore, it is highly likely that he followed the lead of Baculard d'Arnaud in adopting the term *anecdote* for these other works and particularly for those in the series, which is a direct imitation of Baculard.

Loaisel's search for a respectable literary form is an indication of a deeper dissatisfaction visible already in *Florello*. In the 'Lettre à m. Coll' he says of his first two works, 'Je n'attache aucune prétention à ces œuvres éphémeres' (*Florello*, p.6*). This is not empty rhetoric to Loaisel. Indeed, after renouncing the form of the *conte moral*, he goes on in the 'Avertissement' to the *Soirées de mélancolie* to degrade even the projected series of *anecdotes*: 'Voilà quels seront mes Passe-temps, en attendant que mon foible génie tâche de prendre un essor plus élevé & cherche la véritable gloire dans des fonctions plus grandes & plus nobles' (*Soirées de mélancolie*, p.xii). This statement seems to suggest that the quest for 'fonctions plus grandes et plus nobles' may go beyond the struggle with specific forms of fiction and extend outside the domain of literature altogether. It may reflect a desire to enter a more worldly and more respected profession, perhaps even a return to the military, as the listing of his profession in 1788 as 'officier de cavalerie' would seem to suggest (see above, p.45). The problem appears again to be very much on Loaisel's mind in the prefaces to *Dolbreuse* and to *Ainsi finissent* as will be discussed below.

Although the 'Avertissement' contains a defence against anticipated criticism of the *Soirées de mélancolie* for multiplying 'les scenes et les descriptions champêtres', no such criticism appeared (pp.ix-xi). The *Journal encyclopédique* referred the reader back to the reviews of *Valmore* and *Florello* for comments on the faults as well as strengths of the *Soirées*, indicating thus that they saw no improvement in the style worthy of noting (15 avril 1777, pp.350-51). The *Almanach littéraire ou étrennes d'Apollon* passed over them briefly, noting simply that they were 'le fruit d'une imagination forte et sombre' (1788, p.129). The *Journal des sciences et des beaux-arts* was less enthusiastic about the *Soirées* than the earlier works. In spite of 'quelques figures trop hardies', the overall judgement was that 'les cœurs sensibles liront ce recueil avec délices' (1er mars 1777, pp.452-53). In the *Mercure*, the *Soirées* received a much fuller and more enthusiastic treatment than did the first two works. While praising Loaisel's imagination, described in approximately the same terms as in the review of *Florello*, it criticised his composition for disorder, uniformity, repetition, and particularly 'une trop grande abondance d'images tristes'. But the most interesting of all the *Mercure*'s remarks is the praise for Loaisel's prose style, in which it noted particularly 'de la grâce', 'de l'harmonie', and 'les images [...] poétiques' (août 1777, pp.96-100). The prose style that is being praised here is obviously what the modern critic calls *prose poétique*. The *Mercure*, in a later review of the *An* III re-edition of the *Soirées*, reprinted *Le Port,*

65

one of the most accomplished pieces of *prose poétique* in the collection (30 décembre 1794, pp.226-28). Perhaps in reply to the remarks in the *Mercure*, the *Affiches de province* found that Loaisel had, to the contrary, failed in his effort to lend the tone of poetry to his prose: 'Elle n'en a ni le feu, ne l'harmonie, ni l'élévation'. They again attacked the 'sujets lugubres' and furthermore accused the *contes* of being 'rien moins que moraux' (15 octobre 1777, p.166). The *Journal de Paris*, which started publishing too late to pick up Loaisel's two earlier works, gave an unenthusiastic and mildly sarcastic review of the *Soirées de mélancolie*. It summed up various pieces in the collection as common and unoriginal, dismissed the *prose poétique* as 'déclamations', and criticised the inappropriate mixture of a 'funèbre histoire' with a 'style fleuri' in the *conte L'Empire de la beauté*, which it condescendingly summarised nevertheless, because it was 'l'histoire qui frappera le plus l'imagination du Lecteur' (8 juin 1777, p.1). As Loaisel had feared, the critics did little to encourage him to write more. The *Mercure's* praise for his *prose poétique* was counterbalanced not only by the attacks of the *Affiches de province* and the *Journal de Paris* but also by the *Mercure* itself in other observations of an unfavourable nature. The *genre sombre* was widely attacked again in spite of the long defence in the 'Avertissement'.

It is not surprising then to read in the preface to *La Comtesse d'Alibre* that Loaisel had become too discouraged to pursue the plans he had announced in the *Soirées de mélancolie* (*Comtesse d'Alibre*, pp.v-vi):

Malgré l'indulgence du public pour mes foibles essais, j'avois abandonné une carriere si difficile à parcourir, où j'avois à peine fait quelques pas, & dont le but glorieux me paroissoit si éloigné [. . .] J'avois refermé les livres de nos maîtres, où je puisai l'amour des beaux-arts, que je dévorois autrefois; mais qui depuis quelque tems faisoient naître dans mon ame, à côté d'une continuelle admiration, la méfiance de mes forces, & le désespoir de ne pouvoir jamais égaler ces fameux modeles.

Most surely, the unfavourable reception of the previous works was primarily responsible for this temporary abandonment of literature. Loaisel's sensitivity to criticism has been amply demonstrated already and will be so again even more clearly in the *querelle* over *La Comtesse d'Alibre*. He further explains that he abandoned literature at the same time he departed from Paris and retreated into the calm of country life next to nature. Following the logic of the widespread contemporary philosophy which proclaimed the good influence of country living as

opposed to the evil influence of the city, he explains his return to literature as a result of his return to Paris: 'Un incident me ramene à Paris, &
la maudite influence du sol me remet la plume à la main. Des idées
tristes ont fermenté dans ma tête, & dans l'essor impétueux d'une
imagination presque toujours abandonnée à elle-même, j'ai écrit l'anecdote qu'on va lire' (p.vi). This explanation fits in a bit too perfectly with
one of the pervasive philosophies of the novel to be taken at face value.
The true reason for the return to literature, and the influence of country
and city living thereupon, will have to be left to conjecture. The abandonment of the plans announced in the *Soirées de mélancolie* is, however,
a fact. And that abandonment was almost surely caused by adverse
criticism.

Anticipating that his critics will again cry out 'à l'homme noir, à
l'esprit vaporeux', Loaisel launches into another justification of the
genre sombre in the preface to *La Comtesse d'Alibre* (p.vi). He first calls
again for tolerance of others' literary opinions (pp.vii-ix) and then
presents a very brief theoretical justification of the genre (pp.ix-x):

Si je voulois justifier mon genre, je pourrois entrer dans des discussions
raisonnées; dire qu'un écrivain qui se pique d'être original, ne doit avoir qu'une
sorte de pinceaux. Je pourrois prouver par des exemples que les ames humaines
ont besoin de secousses, que la douleur & la pitié les dispose, les amene par
degré, à cette philosophie de l'homme réfléchissant, qui l'éclaire & le guide
dans le chaos des événemens de la vie; que l'Héloïse de Jean-Jacques a guéri
plus d'un cœur, de passions terrestres, pour l'élever aux transports sacrés du
véritable amour, qu'enfin le Télémaque, les chef-d'œuvres de Richardson, les
Tombeaux d'Hervey & les Nuits d'Young, ont corrigé plus d'un libertin.

Loaisel refuses to develop the theoretical discussion any further, having
already indulged in lengthy preterition. Instead he refers the reader to
the 'préfaces très bien faites de M. d'Arnaud' (p.xi), undoubtedly having
in mind above all the prefaces to *Les Amans malheureux, Euphémie,*
and *Fayel,* which discuss at length the *genre sombre* – or *genre terrible*
in the case of *Fayel* – and justify the 'secousses' referred to here. Loaisel
seems actually to be less intent on expounding theory than on associating
his novel with similar works which had already achieved full acceptance
by the public and were in fact among the best sellers of that period, a
tactic he had already employed with *Florello* and the *Soirées de mélancolie.* But if he expected thus to ward off the anticipated hostile attacks
of the press, he was quite mistaken. *La Comtesse d'Alibre* provoked a

minor *querelle*, which was most probably the major cause for Loaisel's temporary abandonment of the *genre sombre* until he could come back to it through melodrama.

The *Affiches de Paris*, which published the first review of *La Comtesse d'Alibre*, precipitated the affair by the viciousness with which it attacked the work. The review opened by critising the character of Lucile: 'L'Auteur a voulu donner un pendant à Gabrielle de Vergy; mais sa *Lucile* est encore plus coupable que la femme de Fayel. Epouse adultere, il nait un fruit de ses criminelles amours' (9 novembre 1779, p.2500). It went on to attack the *sombre* scene near the end in which the cruel Comte d'Alibre throws his adulterous wife into a dungeon to starve to death along with the infant born of her affair with Milcourt, a childhood sweetheart. Loaisel paints the scene in the following manner (*Comtesse d'Alibre*, pp.124-25):

[Le Comte d'Alibre] avoit fait jetter la comtesse dans un caveau ténébreux, creusé sous les fondemens de son château; résolu de la laisser mourir dans les angoisses de la faim; & pour donner un raffinement plus cruel à sa barbarie, il avoit envoyé des satellites prendre & enlever l'enfant de cette femme infortunée, pour le mettre entre les mains de sa mère, & la contraindre ou de manger le fruit de ses entrailles, & de périr ensuite dans les horreurs de l'épouvante, ou d'expirer avec lui dans les agonies de la rage. Et il avoit fait suspendre une lampe au milieu du cachot pour qu'elle pût observer toutes les progressions de la douleur & du trépas sur le visage de cette créature souffrante.

Two days later, they are both dead but not until after the Comtesse had cut open a vein in a futile attempt to keep her child alive by nourishing him with her blood. The *Affiches de Paris* left no doubt as to how they judged the literary taste of the author of this passage (pp.2500-2501):

Qu'une imagination échauffée par la lecture de nos tristes Romans & de nos Drames lugubres, invente & rapproche de pareilles horreurs, il n'y a rien là d'étonnant; mais qu'un homme se plaise à les écrire, à les publier, qu'il les donne comme des Anecdotes prises dans l'Histoire de la nation, de cette nation si douce, si généreuse, si peu portée à la vengeance, c'est ce qui a lieu d'exciter notre surprise, nous avons presque dit, notre indignation.

The attack was thus quite personal and certainly spared no effort to display the scorn and contempt felt for the author.

Shortly after the review was published in the *Affiches de Paris*, Loaisel's reply appeared in the preface to his *Aux âmes sensibles*. Although he opens by stating, 'Je ne prétends point commencer une querelle', he must surely have realised that such a *querelle* would add to the notoriety and popularity of *La Comtesse d'Alibre*. (p.7) First, he observes that the dungeon scene, so severely attacked, is but a very small part of the entire work and is more than counterbalanced by the remainder: 'L'Aristarque ne laisse entrevoir qu'un coin du tableau [. . .]; il ne donne point à juger par le coup-d'œil de l'ensemble si le tout est bien distribué, & si les couleurs sont heureusement contrastées' (p.9). After describing at length the virtuous actions of father and daughter at the beginning of the novel, Loaisel concludes that in so far as the review in the *Affiches de Paris* is concerned, 'toutes ces situations, tous ces tableaux si touchants n'ont point été mis en opposition avec le morceau du cachot' (p.12). He likens this review to a review of Cré-billon's *Atrée et Thieste* based solely on the horror-filled fifth scene of the fifth act (pp.12-13). This of course permits Loaisel to point out in passing the similarities between their literary theories and practice and thus to place himself under Crébillon's protection, as he had done with other writers on repeated occasions before. He goes on to defend the verisimilitude of Lucile's fall into the sin of adultery by pointing out that the reviewer should have recognised 'que les exemples de perfection sont rares, que les plus grandes fautes sont presque toujours à côté des plus grandes vertus, & que conséquemment il seroit contre les regles de peindre toujours des Héroïnes. Il auroit vu que ma *Lucile* est douée d'une grande sensibilité; que cette sensibilité fit son héroïsme, & que par une raison contraire elle peut la conduire aux plus grandes foiblesses' (p.14). Furthermore, far from his defending the actions of Lucile, as the review seems to intimate in the opening words, Loaisel has con-demned them by the severity of the punishment meted out to the young lovers: 'Loin de justifier mon Héroïne, je mets le remords & le grand châtiment près du forfait; [. . .] elle est punie de trop de foiblesse, comme son époux de trop de barbarie' (p.16).

But the severity of the punishment was not only determined by the severity of the crime. Another consideration was the nature of the reading public and the effect the author hoped to produce: 'Si je rends la punition si terrible, c'est qu'il m'a semblé que les plus grands exemples étoient sans pouvoir; que la plupart des hommes n'étoient aujourd'hui que des especes de Zoophytes qui veulent des commotions puissantes & extraordinaires pour être avertis de leur existence, & que d'ailleurs l'effroi causé par les grands crimes & le châtiment qui les suit, faisoit mieux sentir l'attrait & le besoin de la vertu' (p.16). In other words, the contemporary reader needs severe jolts – or 'secousses' in the words of the preface to the novel itself – in order that literature take its moralising effect. The time-honoured argument that a story of vice punished inspires virtuous behaviour lends an air of sophistication and legitimacy to the official defence but can hardly be seen as the primary motivation for writing the dungeon scene. However, a significant insight into that motivation is revealed here in Loaisel's judgement that he was writing in a society that reacted most favourably to 'commotions puissantes & extraordinaires'. That is to say, he saw a public demand for works written in the *genre sombre*. Thus, still aiming for popularity and literary glory, he resorted to the means necessary to attract as wide an audience as possible. In his final point in reply to the *Affiches de Paris*, Loaisel manages to catch the reviewer in error. To reproach the Comte d'Alibre's desire for revenge as an affront to the character of the French nation is to overlook the fact that the comte is indeed 'un étranger venu du fond de l'Italie demeurer en France' (p.17). Loaisel concludes with an imaginative declaration of his will to continue writing despite, and indeed because of, continued criticism. But the closing lines are perhaps nearer to his actual state of mind at the time: 'Si chacun a sa folie, celle d'écrire est la moins dangereuse, & assurément la plus excusable. On a donc bien tort de ne pas laisser en paix les pauvres Auteurs' (p.20).

The *Mercure's* review of *La Comtesse d'Alibre* was in part also a reply to Loaisel's defence in the preface to *Aux âmes sensibles*. In its opening statement, it recommended an open-minded attitude toward this work in particular and the *genre sombre* in general: 'Si la sensibilité est le principe le plus fécond en vertus [. . .], pourquoi s'élever contre des ouvrages dont la teinte sombre & touchante porte à la sensibilité? Pourquoi proscrire un genre intéressant pour beaucoup de personnes, dont l'âme tendre et réfléchie aime à se nourrir d'Ouvrages analogues à leur sentiment? Malheureux qui raisonne toujours, & ne sent jamais que les défauts!' (26 février 1780, pp.175-76). It went on to point out the very limited audience to which such works appeal: not to the 'gens de lettres' or 'gens d'un goût sévère' but rather those 'qui adoptent sans examen un genre quelconque dès qu'il leur fait plaisir, et les instruit en les intéressant'. Rather than attempt an analysis of the entire novel, the review stated that it would give only an 'examen du principal caractère, qui est celui de Lucile, ou de la Comtesse d'Alibre: ce caractère est dans la nature' (p.176). On this point, the *Mercure* thus supported Loaisel's argument in the preface to *Aux âmes sensibles,* parts of which

it paraphrased and quoted directly, adding on its own that, 'Tous les
incidens préparent sa faiblesse et la justifient en quelque sorte' (p.177).
But if the *Mercure* sided with Loaisel as to the verisimilitude of Lucile's
character, it failed to support his use of the *genre sombre* in the dungeon
scene. The commentary is an important pronouncement on the *genre
sombre* (pp.178-79):

L'Auteur a cru, sans doute, que les lecteurs d'aujourd'hui, accoutumés aux
secousses du style emporté de nos Modernes Youngs, & à leurs sombres
imaginations, avoient besoin d'être électrisés fortement. Des émotions, même
extraordinaires, ne lui ont pas paru suffisantes; il lui falloit des convulsions.
Nous esperons qu'il nous pardonnera à ce sujet quelques réflexions générales,
dont il n'est tout au plus que l'occasion, & qui nous sont dictées par l'intérêt
du bon goût, & par celui que doit inspirer un Littérateur sensible et honnête,
'qui, selon ses propres expressions, ne demande que des lumières, & qui les
reçoit avec reconnoissance quand elles sont dictées par le décence & par la
bonne foi.' Il est des excès, même dans le genre terrible, qu'une certaine
convenance doit proscrire. Ce sont ces atrocités révoltantes, ces scènes
d'horreurs qui répandent sur notre âme une melancolie sombre & farouche:
ce n'est plus du pathétique, c'est de l'horrible. L'Auteur, en ces occasions, a
beau dire que sa plume se détrempe dans ses larmes, qu'elle lui échappe des
mains: le Lecteur n'éprouve qu'une horreur sèche. Le cœur est serré, mais non
pas attendri; on frémit et on ne pleure pas; l'émotion que l'on ressent alors
n'est plus un plaisir, c'est une angoisse; & malheureusement il n'y en a déjà
que trop dans la vie, sans qu'il soit besoin de s'exalter la tête pour en inventer
d'imaginaires.

These are strong words of criticism indeed, and they must surely have
had an effect on Loaisel. Unlike the hostile attack of the *Affiches de Paris*,
this partially favourable review is moderate in the tone of its criticism
and less likely to provoke immediately a defensive attitude. It even
quotes Loaisel's pretentions of openness to well-intentioned suggestions
for improvement, thus leaving little room for counter-attack.

The *Journal encyclopédique*, in its first substantial review of one of
Loaisel's works, found that 'la vengeance atroce du comte fait frissonner
et n'attendrit pas' (1er mars 1780, p.289). It devoted most of its commentary to an attack on the *genre sombre* and the imitators of Baculard
d'Arnaud. First, most practitioners of the genre had no sense of control
or proportion (pp.289-90):

On remarque en général que les auteurs des productions de ce genre, qui se
sont si fort multipliées depuis quelque tems, manquent toujours leur but, en

s'élançant au-delà. S'ils se proposent de toucher le cœur, ils le déchirent, & plus souvent encore ils le révoltent; ils ne sçavent employer que les couleurs les plus sombres; & leurs tableaux qu'ils veulent simplement rendre terribles, ne sont qu'horribles & dégoûtans; c'est dans des tombeaux, c'est dans des charniers qu'ils vont monter leur imagination.

Furthermore, the genre lacked verisimilitude: 'Le *genre sombre*, comme ils l'appellent, depuis qu'il se sont imaginé d'en créer un, n'est jamais vrai ni naturel'. Finally, although these imitators of Baculard d'Arnaud constantly quoted his writings to justify their own, they could not emulate his success by simply copying the *sombre* aspect of his works (p.290):

Ils ne sentent pas que l'écrivain qu'ils s'empressent de citer, & qui a donné en effet le plus de productions de cette espece, ne doit pas la sorte de succès qu'elles ont eu, à ces tableaux noirs, qui, nous le répétons, ne sont pas dans la nature, & que la raison, le goût & la vérité proscrivent également. Il la doit à cette sensibilité qui caractérise plusieurs de ses écrits; ce qui quelquefois rachete ou fait oublier ces détails prétendus sombres qu'on lui reproche avec raison, & que s'empresent de copier tous ceux qui ont entrepris de l'imiter.

In addition to highlighting the controversial nature of the *genre sombre*, this review is a highly significant indication of the extent of this literary vogue at the time Loaisel wrote *La Comtesse d'Alibre*.

The *Journal de Paris*, in a short review, refused to talk of 'l'horrible tableau' or of the 'violentes secousses', thereby condemning them by preterition. It also criticised the style as 'précieux et à prétention' but noted that there were some details 'touchans dans le fond' (31 mars 1780, pp.373-74). The *Almanach littéraire ou étrennes d'Apollon* repeated, perhaps copied, these last two observations, but offered only a slightly sarcastic remark in reference to the controversial element, calling the work an 'Anecdote dans ce qu'on appelle le genre sombre' (1781, p.165). The *Année littéraire*, the *Journal de littérature, des sciences et des arts*, and the *Affiches de province* failed to mention the work at all. The omission in the *Année littéraire* could well signal an unfavourable judgement, as could also the omission in the similarly oriented *Journal de littérature, des sciences et des arts*, a continuation of the *Journal de Trévoux*. Since 1779, this second periodical had been under the direction of a former editor of the *Année littéraire*, the abbé Grosier, who had fallen out with Fréron *fils*.[15] The *Affiches de province* had just undergone

[15] information reported in the *Mémoires secrets*, mai 1779 (quoted in Hatin, ii.273-74).

a change in direction in mid-1779 and could have missed *La Comtesse d'Alibre* owing to administrative problems.[16] However, under the new director, the abbé Fonteney, this journal refused to comment on any of Loaisel's future works, giving at most a one-sentence paraphrase lifted from the prefaces. At least, with Querlon gone, Loaisel lost one of his severest critics. The abbé Fonteney did, in fact, make one comment. In the review of *Aux âmes sensibles*, he complimented Loaisel for the moderation of his reply to the attack on *La Comtesse d'Alibre* by the *Affiches de Paris* – the reply that filled the preface to *Aux âmes sensibles* – and remarked that 'M. de Tréogate a de la sensibilité et surtout beaucoup d'honnêteté dans le caractère' (31 mai 1780, p.86).

La Comtesse d'Alibre certainly received publicity from the *querelle*, but this did not arouse the public's interest enough to send it into a second edition during this period, although a publisher's decision to quash such a highly criticised work could also have been responsible for the lack of immediate re-editions. It is significant, however, that a first edition of this work made its way into the library of Marie-Antoinette (see listing entry no. 6). There was also an English translation in 1781. The translator may have thought that the tone of gothic horror as well as the sentimental character of the work would have appealed to an English audience at the time, but the English literary journals failed to take note of the translation. In 1781, the gothic novel was barely starting to achieve recognition in England and was not yet a popular mode. Only two of the gothic masterpieces had appeared by then – Walpole's *Castle of Otranto*, in its third edition (1769), and Clara Reeve's *The Old English baron*, in its second edition (1778).[17] *La Comtesse d'Alibre* does possess some of the most important qualities of the gothic novel, or 'roman noir'. In addition to the horror of the dungeon scene, the principal characters fit very well into the mould of the common typological trio of hero, villain, and damsel-in-distress, and the struggle between good and evil is depicted with the required simplicity and obviousness. It is no surprise, then, that *La Comtesse d'Alibre*, after being re-edited twice in *An* II, under the title *Lucile et Milcourt*, went through another re-edition in *An* X, when the 'roman noir' was at the height of its popularity in France (Killen, pp.94 ff.).

16 *Histoire générale de la presse française*, i.326.

17 Alice M. Killen, *Le Roman terrifiant ou roman noir de Walpole à Anne Radcliffe et son influence sur la littérature française jusqu'en 1840* (Paris 1923), pp.220-21; Maurice Lévy, *Le Roman 'gothique' anglais, 1764-1824* (Toulouse 1968), pp.685-86.

Valmore and *Florello,* on the other hand, were both translated into German, the first in 1777 and the second in 1780. Undoubtedly, *Valmore* appealed because of the Wertherian themes of melancholy, resignation, and suicide. Goethe's *Die Leiden des jungen Werthers* had been published in Germany in 1774. *Florello* may have exercised a somewhat similar attraction but also the bucolic and idyllic theme fit right in with the vogue of Gessner, at its height at that time.[18] *Valmore* and *Florello* were re-edited and issued as a single volume in *An* III. They were both extensively revised for this re-edition, indicating that Loaisel may have been truly in agreement with the early criticism of his style in these two works. In 1802, they were translated into Russian. The *Soirées de mélancolie* were re-edited in *An* III but seem never to have been translated.

Loaisel's short-lived excursion into poetry produced no significant works. *Aux âmes sensibles* may have been published actually as an excuse for printing the polemical preface. The poem itself takes up only ten of the volume's thirty pages. This 'élégie' is actually a revised and much enlarged version of the thirty-verse 'heroïde' that appeared in the 'Lettre à m. Coll' in *Florello.* The original version has been stripped of the amatory and idyllic themes, while the *sombre* and elegiac mode of the remainder has been further developed. The only periodical to take note of the poem was the *Affiches de province,* and it devoted its limited commentary to the preface, as discussed above.

The only other poem known to have been written by Loaisel is *A m. le chevalier de Parny, après avoir lu ses Poésies érotiques.* Although published in the *Nouvel almanach des muses* in 1802, the work was written in 1782. The admiration Loaisel expresses for Parny's *Poésies érotiques* confirms the poetic tendencies demonstrated in *Aux âmes sensibles.* The fourth book of *Poésies érotiques,* containing the *élégies,* was published in 1781, joining the first three published in 1778.[19] The tone of these *élégies* is certainly similar to that of Loaisel's *élégie,* published in 1780. Parny's *Réponse,* published following Loaisel's poem, praises Loaisel's talents in turn, but there is no way of knowing which works Parny had in mind. It is not clear exactly when Parny actually wrote his reply. Since Loaisel's poem is dated and Parny's not, it may be that the reply was written in the same year as the *Almanach*'s publication, 1802.

[18] Paul Van Tieghem, 'Les idylles de Gessner et le rêve pastoral' (in his *Préromantisme,* ii.249).

[19] Raphael Barquissau, *Les Poètes créoles du XVIIIe siècle* (Paris 1949), pp.35-36.

74

If so, Parny's compliment would be addressed most probably to Loaisel's talents as a dramatist and not as a poet.[20]

ii. Savant: le bien public

The experiments with poetry constitute a transitional phase during which Loaisel abandons short narrative fiction in the *genre sombre*, probably because of the *querelle* over *La Comtesse d'Alibre*, and finally turns to long narrative fiction with a predominantly philosophical orientation. This period before 1783 is also the time he would have written the articles on Louis le Débonnaire and Philip II of Spain for Delisle de Sales's *Histoire des hommes*, if that collaboration ever took place at all (see 'Miscellaneous works' in the listing). An interest in expository writing would fit quite logically into Loaisel's intellectual development at this time as a signal of other such works he announces in *Dolbreuse* and *Ainsi finissent*. A considerable amount of philosophical argumentation was already apparent in the earlier novels. In *Florello*, almost, the entire *première partie* was devoted to examining the philosophy of the solitary life. But the second and longer part was a fast-moving adventure with a most *sombre* ending. In both *Valmore* and *La Comtese d'Alibre*, in spite of the ever present moralising, the action and sentimental plot dominated the works. With *Dolbreuse*, philosophical argumentation assumes equal importance with the story line, often overwhelming it.

The switch to long narrative fiction and the expanded concern with philosophical matters are accompanied by the adoption of a new patron saint, Rousseau. In the past, Loaisel had called upon Rousseau chiefly in defence of literary practices. A Rousseauistic philosophy is apparent in several passages of *Florello*. But with *Dolbreuse*, Rousseau is the main inspirational force behind the philosophical and moralistic discussion that runs throughout the novel. This is evident already in the 'Préface' but is particularly noticeable in the body of the work, where Rousseau and *La Nouvelle Héloïse* play an explicit role. To some extent Loaisel's preoccupation with philosophical considerations in *Dolbreuse* may have been merely a necessary part of his obvious imitation of *La Nouvelle Héloïse*. But evidence does exist that, for a certain period of

---

[20] Loaisel's poem and Parny's reply are reproduced below in appendix C.

time, he was indeed very strongly interested in 'l'esprit philosophique' for its own sake.

The 'Préface' of *Dolbreuse* strongly emphasises the philosophical purposes of the novel. One familiar with eighteenth-century novel prefaces may be tempted to see in this preface nothing more than the normal insincere mask of pure-sounding intentions designed to protect the author against attacks on the immorality of the novel's contents. But the content of *Dolbreuse* is so overwhelmingly and unmistakably philosophical and the tone of the philosophy is so straightforward and transparently serious that a literal reading of the preface in terms of the philosophical intentions is quite justified. The very subtitle of the novel – 'l'homme du siècle, ramené à la vérité par le sentiment et par la raison' – reveals Loaisel's desire to synthesise a modern, universal view of mankind based on two of the most vital philosophical concepts of the century – *sentiment* and *raison*. Furthermore, one should note, as did most of the contemporary reviewers, that the work is labelled 'histoire philosophique'. There is no doubt that this is an entirely different world from that of the 'anecdote française', to which category the first three novels belonged.

From the very first words of the 'Préface', Loaisel proclaims that he intends *Dolbreuse* to serve a useful purpose for the good of mankind: 'Dans quelque genre que l'on écrive, on doit se proposer d'être utile. On doit avoir pour objet de contribuer, au moins en quelque chose, au bien public' (*Dolbreuse*, i.v). These pretensions toward social utility are more than mere rhetorical posturing, as will be seen in the final words of the 'Préface'. The reason that so many well-intentioned writers have failed to achieve such goals is that they have lacked the necessary qualifications (i.vi-vii):

Avant d'écrire, même des ouvrages d'imagination qui doivent offrir un but d'utilité comme les autres productions de l'esprit, il faudroit que l'on eût toujours un fond d'expérience & d'observations, d'où dérive & procede, pour ainsi dire, cette sagacité philosophique qui distingue les nuances les plus fugitives, les effets les plus imperceptibles des passions, & en tire ces combinaisons & ces résultats qui, rassemblés un jour par des mains habiles, formeront une somme de matériaux suffisante enfin pour achever le grand édifice de la morale.

Quite obviously, the reader is being led to understand that Loaisel possesses these qualifications. Perhaps the reader is also to believe that

Dolbreuse is that long-awaited 'grand édifice de la morale'. In a later paragraph discussing 'le but de l'Ouvrage', the goals start out sounding specific and limited but end up in the realm of the universal and ultimate (i.ix-x):

Le but de l'Ouvrage que nous mettons au jour, est de remettre en honneur parmi nous l'amour conjugal, dont le nom seul est presque devenu un ridicule; de ramener les meres aux sentimens de la nature, de faire sentir le prix de plaisirs faciles & trop négligés de la vie libre & innocente des campagnes, & d'arracher au luxe & à la corruption des villes, des hommes nés loin des villes, des hommes nés pour ressentir & inspirer le goût de cette simplicité antique qui nous rapproche de notre état primitif, & peut-être de notre destination.

But for the public to be persuaded, it must first be interested; and for the public to be interested, a work must be written in a genre that appeals to current tastes: 'Pour nous amener & nous intéresser à la pratique du bien [...] il faut (aujourd'hui particulièrement, qu'on veut une forme dramatique à presque tous les ouvrages de l'esprit) posséder l'art plus difficile qu'on ne pense, de montrer l'homme en action; il faut savoir [...] mêler habilement le langage d'une philosophie séduisante, à l'intérêt des situations' (i.vii). In *La Comtesse d'Alibre* and the other earlier works, Loaisel had created interesting situations by resorting to the *genre sombre* and horror. But with *Dolbreuse*, he adopts a new approach: 'Dans un tems où l'imagination fait les frais de tous les plaisirs, peut-être faut-il parler davantage à l'imagination, & revêtir les idées de la raison des images de la volupté' (i.ix). This shift from the *genre sombre* to concentrate on 'la volupté' is one of the more important aspects of Loaisel's later novels. Brief scenes of somewhat suggestive love-making were already present in both *Florello* and *La Comtesse l'Alibre*. But the first extended treatment of *libertinage* comes in *Dolbreuse*. This theme is further exploited in *Ainsi finissent*, and when that novel is rewritten and published as *Valrose*, scenes have been added that are indeed highly erotic.

There are indications both in the 'Préface' to *Dolbreuse* and in a note in the body of the work that Loaisel's interests are no longer confined solely to writing fiction. At the beginning of the final paragraph of the 'Préface', a rhetorical denial of the sufficiency of his talents and of the scope of his ambitions reveals a change of interests confirmed later in *Ainsi finissent* (i.x-xi):

Nous sommes bien loin de nous supposer les talens qu'on a droit d'attendre de celui qui donne des tableaux d'histoire dans la vue de réformer les mœurs.

Nous sommes encore plus éloignés de nous flatter d'avoir fait quelques pas
sur les traces de ces génies privilégiés, qui attirent sur eux les regards de leur
siecle, & impriment un mouvement au monde intellectuel. Le genre dans
lequel cet Ouvrage est écrit, nous sauve du ridicule d'une pareille prétention.

The last sentence reveals that, although he has presented a full justification for his selection of fiction as the form best suited to communicat-
ing his philosophical concerns, Loaisel is probably still plagued with
doubts about its value and acceptability, doubts he had expressed earlier
regarding the specific forms of the *conte moral* and the *anecdote*, as
discussed above. His doubts about the value of fiction could easily lead
him to experiment with other types of writing as he seeks to fulfil his
new and different ambitions in the realm of intellectual and philosophical
matters. But what is most important here is the profound change in
Loaisel's personal ambitions. The all too obvious preterition in the
first two sentences quoted above indicates that Loaisel would like indeed
to attract the attention of his century and make a lasting impression on
the intellectual world. To use the terms of *Valrose*, he is now aspiring
to be a 'savant' (*Valrose*, i.xvi). His proclaimed hope that *Dolbreuse*
serve a useful purpose by helping to reform the customs of society is
more than either protective moralising to ward off attacks against
scenes of *volupté* or an attempt to align his intentions with those of the
author of *La Nouvelle Héloïse*. Loaisel is beginning to develop a sincere
desire to play a socially useful role in society.

Dolbreuse, currently regarded as one of Loaisel's most important
works, merits a moment's pause to consider an important point recently
raised by Michel Delon in his internal analysis of the novel. Delon
demonstrates that Dolbreuse, the central character, was unsuccessful in
his effort to return to 'la vérité' by way of a synthesis based on 'le
sentiment' and 'la raison'. Delon concludes as follows (p.836):

Dolbreuse n'est donc pas seulement un roman à verser au compte du courant
anti-philosophique et du renouveau chrétien. Si la religion y représente une
composante importante, elle ne résume pas cette œuvre hétérogêne où se
retrouvent toutes les tentations du siècle. La crise des Lumières marque sans
doute le moment où les synthèses harmonieuses ne sont plus possibles, où il
faut abandonner tel ou tel terme du dilemme, à moins d'adopter la position
tragique. La vérité à laquelle l'évolution de la société ramène le héros contre
son cœur et sa raison, n'est qu'hypothétique et mal assurée. La seule vérité est
finalement l'écriture.

To the extent that Dolbreuse speaks for Loaisel the writer, Delon's conclusion might be construed as applying equally well to Loaisel's own situation in 1783 – his doubts about his own intellectual capabilities and his reluctantly continued pursuit of literature as the only means he currently has for obtaining the high goals of his announced intentions. But Loaisel the writer has not given up yet as has Dolbreuse the character. The discussion below of *Ainsi finissent* will clearly demonstrate that despite doubts about his personal abilities and the best means to achieve his goals, Loaisel still seeks to become a 'savant' and to serve 'le bien public'.

Clear evidence of Loaisel's expansion into new fields of interest and new forms or writing appears in a long footnote in *Dolbreuse* announcing a 'projet de discipline militaire' (i.52-54, note). The note outlines some ideas on the training of an army in peacetime and stresses particularly the importance of rural garrisons and rigorous physical training. It then announces, 'Nous avons rassemblé sur cette matiere, quelques idées neuves & faites peut-être pour être accueillies. Elles seront développées dans un projet de discipline militaire que nous devons publier bientôt' (i.54, note). The first person of this note is the voice of Loaisel as author, not that of the fictional narrator or of a fictional editor of the memoirs. Loaisel certainly had the background for writing such a treatise and, as pointed out in the biography, he still considered himself to be of the military profession at this time. This indication of new interests in writing works outside the domain of fiction prepares the way for the dramatic shift of ambitions explicitly proclaimed in *Ainsi finissent*.

Dolbreuse was reviewed at some length by most of the important periodicals, the only exception being as pointed out earlier, the *Affiches de province*, which devoted only a few words to the work, paraphrasing a sentence in the preface regarding the moral intentions (30 juillet 1783, pp.122-23). With two exceptions, to be discussed later, the reviews were mostly favourable. The *Bibliothèque universelle des romans* honoured the novel by publishing an extract. It placed the work in the class of 'Romans d'amour' and chose to concentrate on the episode recounting the seduction of the Comtesse d ... by Dolbreuse (août 1783, pp.181-216). This may indeed be the most interesting and best written section of the work considered from the point of view of character portrayal and plot development, but it is hardly typical of the work as a whole, since philosophical discussions are here held to a minimum. The *Journal de littérature, des sciences et des arts* praised *Dolbreuse*, saying it revealed 'l'empreinte d'une vraie sensibilité' and contained 'des situations intéressantes, des peintures touchantes, déchirantes même, et par-tout l'enthousiasme d'une âme fortement passionée pour la vertu', although this last quality at times led to a 'ton de déclamation un peu trop uniforme' (1783, iv.244-59). The *Journal de Paris* praised the high moral intentions and found the descriptions of the 'égarements' quite realistic and capable of producing 'de fortes impressions'. But it too criticised the writing and composition, pointing out such faults as an overabundance of reflections and 'termes précieux' and a style that was 'emphatique et exagéré' (11 octobre 1783, pp.1171-72). The *Journal encyclopédique* repeated the general enthusiasm of the other reviews and concluded, 'L'Auteur connoît le cœur humain et la société, qu'il peint de couleurs un peu dures, mais naturellement trop vraies'. This was a significant tribute to Loaisel's sense of realism, coming as it did from a journal very much concerned with verisimilitude, the very grounds upon which it had previously attacked the *sombre* element in *La Comtesse d'Alibre*. Loaisel's style was criticised, in somewhat the same terms as it had been in the case of the previous novel, for the 'prétentions', 'des tournures forcées et des images gigantesques' (1783, vii, seconde partie, pp.279-86). The review in the *Mercure* differed little from the previous ones either in its praise or criticism. It did, however, open with a lengthy discussion of the utility of novels for teaching morality and emphasised this aspect of *Dolbreuse* most of all (1er novembre 1783, pp.13-24). The brief review in the *Almanach littéraire ou étrennes d'Apollon* followed the same patterns as the others thus far mentioned (1785, p.136).

Both the *Année littéraire* and the *Journal de monsieur* attacked *Dolbreuse* quite severely but did not limit the criticism to the style as had the more favourable reviews. The major portion of each review was devoted to a lengthy and detailed critique of the philosophical questions, particularly those relating to morality. They also both agreed that the scenes of 'volupté' were among the most reprehensible. The *Année littéraire* singled out for particular reproof the very episode that the *Bibliothèque des romans* had chosen to reprint.[21] The similarity of content and of the sarcastic tone of these two reviews were to be expected, since the *Journal de monsieur* was at the time under the direction of

---

[21] *Année littéraire* (1783), vii.270-80; *Journal de monsieur* (1782), vi.25-56.

Geoffroy and Royou. They had been formerly associated with the *Année littéraire* but had left when Fréron fils took over the direction, which they had hoped to obtain. They decided to set up a rival journal. The influence of the *Journal de monsieur* was limited, however, since it had but 200 subscribers at about the time of the review (Hatin, iii.209-11).

While the influence of Rousseau was noted by the *Mercure, Année littéraire*, and *Almanach littéraire ou étrennes d'Apollon,* no particular emphasis was placed on this aspect of the work. The reading public, however, may well have been excited by another work in the tradition of *La Nouvelle Héloïse*, since re-editions of *Dolbreuse* appeared in 1785 and 1786 and a German translation in 1790. Another re-edition appeared in 1792 and a final one in *An* II. But unlike *La Comtesse d'Alibre, Dolbreuse* did not excite enough interest for any further reeditions after *An* II. The vogue of the 'roman noir' had replaced that of the sentimental, Rousseauistic 'roman somme'. Like *La Comtesse d'Alibre*, which appears to have been owned by Marie Antoinette, *Dolbreuse* achieved the honour of making its way into the personal library of one of the century's notables. The marquis de Sade came into possession of a copy of the first edition during his imprisonment at the Bastille.[22]

Dolbreuse contained many hints and suggestions of changing interests and goals. In the last paragraph of the 'Préface de l'éditeur' in *Ainsi finissent*, stepping out of the fictional role of 'éditeur' to speak in his own voice, Loaisel flatly announces his intention to abandon the genre of *roman* and perhaps the whole domain of fiction (i.12-14)

Ce Roman est le dernier que je mets au jour, soit comme Auteur, soit comme Editeur, si toutefois on peut appeller Roman un Livre où il n'y a point d'aventures, où l'action est bien moins dans les incidens que dans les images, où les sentimens abondent, où tout est en réflexions & en développemens. Quoique ce genre d'Ouvrage soit loin de me paroître frivole & sans utilité, comme je viens de le dire, mon esprit cependant s'est tourné vers des objets plus importans. J'ai réparé, autant qu'il étoit en moi, les années perdues de ma première jeunesse; j'ai tâché de n'être pas toujours un anneau stérile dans la chaîne des individus qui composent la société dont je suis membre; & si ma santé affoiblie & presque détruite par des travaux forcés ne trompe pas mon vœu le plus ardent, je laisserai avant de mourir un monument de mon zèle pour le bien public, & des efforts que j'ai fait pour y contribuer. Heureux si

[22] Gilbert Lély, *Vie du marquis de Sade,* in *Œuvres complètes* of Sade (Paris 1972), ii.166-67. See Delon, p.837, n.16.

l'épuisement de mes forces & le sacrifice de ma vie ne sont pas sans fruit pour le bonheur de quelques-uns de mes semblables!

Loaisel's continued struggle with literary form is evident here in the opening lines of the passage. At the time he wrote *Dolbreuse*, he was clearly attempting to combine philosophy with fiction. The results were not well received. Indeed the overabundance and interrupting influence of the 'réflexions' had been attacked by most of the reviewers. This criticism probably explains why Loaisel states here in the preface to *Ainsi finissent* that he hesitates to call this new work, 'où tout est en réflexions et en développements', a *roman*. He thus admits that incorporating philosophy into the *roman* can, if the practice is exaggerated, stretch the genre beyond its limits. But by refusing to eliminate the 'réflexions' from *Ainsi finissent*, he indicates that he is really more interested in developing the philosophical matters that they contain than in producing a work that will earn critical acclaim as a well-written *roman*. *Ainsi finissent* is thus an intermediate stage on the way toward abandoning the *roman* altogether as an inappropriate form for expressing his proccupations with 'des objets plus importans'. Although Loaisel denies that he is abandoning the *roman* because it is 'frivole & sans utilité', this consideration probably did enter into his decision, for he has yet to express any whole-hearted belief in the value of the genre.

In addition to the struggle with literary form, this last paragraph of the 'Préface de l'éditeur' reveals a much deeper preoccupation. Loaisel clearly expresses a very real social consciousness as well as a desire to play an active role in society when he states, 'J'ai tâche de n'être pas toujours un anneau stérile dans la chaîne des individus qui composent la société dont je suis membre.' He arouses no small amount of curiosity by promising a 'monument de mon zèle pour le bien public' before he dies. The 'Préface de l'éditeur' gives no further hint of the nature of this 'monument' other than that it surely will not be another *roman*. The solution to this enigma is to be found in letter 57.

This letter recounts a philosophical discussion between the Chevalier de . . . , who is author of the letters, and M. de B. . . concerning the effectiveness of efforts by a single individual to influence morality and politics for the betterment of society. Le Chevalier de . . . , at first sceptical, is inspired by M. de B. . . to make an attempt: 'Je me suis promis à moi-même [d'essayer mes forces et mes moyens], et de les employer quelque jour'. A note to this statement reads, 'Le Chevalier de . . . a tenu sa promesse; il a composé un grand Ouvrage sur un sujet neuf & important. Cet Ouvrage est entre les mains de l'Editeur de ces Lettres' (ii.126). From the continuation of the discussions, it appears that the 'sujet' is nothing less than a call to revolution (ii.126-28):

Rien de plus vrai que cette dernière réflexion de M. de B.... Le bien ne se fait pas sur la terre, parce que ceux qui ont le courage de l'entreprendre, manquent de force pour l'exécuter. Les hommes ne sont vicieux & malheureux, que parce qu'ils sont foibles, que parce que les ames humaines n'ont en elles-mêmes rien qu'elles puissent opposer victorieusement à toutes les affections nuisibles qui s'y introduisent & s'y établissent avec une sorte de tyrannie. Mais la foiblesse qui fait nos malheurs, nous vient-elle de nous ou de la nature? Nous voyons que la destinée des foibles est entre les mains des forts, que ceux-ci sont rares, que ceux-là composent presque toute la société; mais & les forts & les foibles, sont-ils nés tels ou le sont-ils devenus? Cette question n'est pas si aisée à décider qu'on se l'imagine. On sait ce que sont les hommes façonnés & défigurés par d'autres hommes dans nos sociétés corrompues; mais a-t-on vu la nature humaine abandonnée à ses facultés primitives & usant de ses propres forces? A-t-on observé, a-t-on pu observer si elle est aussi susceptible d'amélioration & de perfectionnement qu'elle nous paroît l'être de dégradation: à quel point de grandeur & de force, à quel dégré de bonheur elle pourroit atteindre; jusqu'où iroit l'esprit humain éclairé d'une lumière nouvelle qui viendroit tout-à-coup reculer les limites de son savoir; excité par l'exemple inoui des bonnes mœurs répandues & pratiquées universellement, & dirigé par un autre gouvernement, d'autres loix, d'autres institutions, meilleures & plus sages que les institutions, les loix & les gouvernemens connus?

Such is the 'sujet neuf et important' of the 'grand Ouvrage' promised in the note. Ostensibly this note can be interpreted as merely an attempt to lend more credibility to the illusion that Loaisel is only 'éditeur' of supposedly real letters. A note concerning the existence of additional works by the Chevalier de... could reinforce this illusion in the same manner as do the notes which mention lost letters. But there is good reason to believe that this note is actually a further explanation of the 'monument' Loaisel spoke of in the preface. For just as he is author of the letters of Le Chevalier de..., he would obviously be author of the 'grand Ouvrage'. Such a work calling for revolution and a better society would certainly be the ultimate fulfilment of Loaisel's dream of becoming a 'savant', making a lasting impression on the intellectual world, and contributing to 'le bien public'. Given the subversive character of this work, it is obvious why Loaisel would not want to specify its exact nature in the preface speaking in his own voice. The note in letter 57, written in the fictional voice of 'l'éditeur', provides the perfect camouflage to avoid difficulties with censorship. Such procedures of using cross references and footnotes to hide politically sensitive matters were of course often employed in the *Encyclopédie* and various dictionaries of the eighteenth century, so Loaisel was not acting without precedent.

The 'Préface de l'éditeur' mentions other aspects of *Ainsi finissent*, besides the emphasis on 'réflexions et developpemens', that reveal Loaisel's evolving conception and exploitation of the *roman*. One noteworthy feature is that 'il n'y a point d'aventures' (i.12-13). Already in *Dolbreuse* the frenetic, unreal action and melodramatic adventures that filled the *anecdotes* and the *Soirées de mélancolie* had yielded to more believable motivation and events. In *Ainsi finissent* there is increased concentration on an even more realistic internal psychological and intellectual conflict, while action is reduced to a minimum. Since this work is essentially a *roman libertin*, the preface presents another justification of 'peintures voluptueuses' in approximately the same terms as the preface to *Dolbreuse* (*Ainsi finissent*, i.7-8, 11-12). The hindsight permitted by knowledge of the blatant eroticism in some passages of *Valrose* leads one to suspect that even in the earlier works, Loaisel's interest in 'la volupté' was a good deal less pedagogical than it appears from the arguments he offers in the prefaces. These arguments do afford, however, a perfect excuse for calling attention to the 'peintures voluptueuses' and thus arousing the interest of many a prospective reader. This particular aspect of popular taste was clearly demonstrated to Loaisel when the *Bibliothèque universelle des romans* chose to publish the libertine episode of *Dolbreuse* as the most appealing portion of the novel. Another interesting characteristic of *Ainsi finissent* explained in the preface is the inclusion of 'quelques citations de morceaux connus, & assez étrangers aux amours du Chevalier de ...' (i.12). This is one of the stranger aspects of the work and rather puzzling for what it signifies about Loaisel's conception of the *roman*. The 'morceaux connus' include newspaper articles and short literary works not by Loaisel, and most of them do indeed have nothing at all to do with the plot.[23]

Reactions to *Ainsi finissent* in the periodical press were restrained and limited. The *Affiches de province* noted the appearance of the book

[23] for further discussions of the 'morceaus connus', see listing nos 1, 2, and 35.

and quoted the passage 'si toutefois on peut appeller Roman' etc. as the only commentary (12 avril 1788, p.178). The *Journal de Paris* listed a publication announcement but never gave a review (10 mai 1788, p.574). The *Année littéraire* was the only periodical to review the novel. The tone of the review and the comments were much less deprecatory that those in the review of *Dolbreuse*. It found the plot common, the melancholy tone monotonous, and the style at times too exalted and obscure. Loaisel was criticised for failing to exploit the epistolary form by offering letters from the heroine as well as those from the hero. He was also chided for presenting 'des peintures un peu trop galantes et trop voluptueuses'. But in spite of all these faults, the review stated that there were letters 'parsemées de détails fort agréables et d'une bonne morale'. It quoted several examples including the 'promenade du matin'.[24] The *Almanach littéraire ou étrennes d'Apollon* offered no commentary but again quoted the 'promenade du matin' (1789, pp.200-201).

Loaisel's development on the stylistic front had never evoked much praise. The style of *La Comtesse d'Alibre* had been referred to as 'précieux' and 'à prétention'. Commenting on *Dolbreuse*, the reviewers again employed the same terms and added such epithets as 'emphatique' and 'exagéré'. With the exception of the simple, direct, smooth *prose poétique* employed in a few pieces in the *Soirées de mélancolie*, the early novels are written in a highly formal, ornamental style, which abounds with periphrasis, apostrophe, exclamations, and rhetorical questions. Loaisel adopts the long complex sentence form in *Dolbreuse*, probably thinking this would help create the serious, intellectual tone required by the philosophical emphasis of the work. But with *Ainsi finissent*, an overall change in style is quite noticeable. The sceptical philosophical tone of the work is reflected in a less emphatic and less pretentious prose. The 'promenade du matin', praised by both the *Année littéraire* and the *Almanach littéraire ou étrennes d'Apollon* is written in a *prose poétique* reminiscent of the *Soirées de mélancolie*. These two periodicals thought highly enough of this passage to reprint portions of it with their reviews. The evolution toward a simpler, more natural prose continues as Loisiel turns to drama.

The publication history of *Ainsi finissent* is one of the strangest to be encountered among all of Loaisel's works. This appears to have been the

---

[24] 1788, ii.217-28. The 'promenade du matin' is found in letter 26.

only work which provoked censorship problems, or at least it is the only one for which evidence of unauthorised publication has been found (see listing entries nos. 2 and 3). After the 1787 edition with 1788 re-issue, there appeared a 1789 re-edition in a greatly reduced form. The 12° format was unchanged, but there were some 200 fewer pages. Since no copies of this edition have yet been located, it is impossible to know what if any revisions appear. It could have been that the printer used a much smaller type. But another possibility is that extraneous passages, including those 'morceaux connus', were eliminated reducing the work to the bare sentimental plot. When this same plot is again taken up for use in *Valrose*, all the extraneous matter of the 1787 edition has disappeared and much new material has been added. Thus, the 1789 re-edition could well represent the interim stage before the new material had been written.

iii. Homme de lettres: le mélodrame

Neither the 'projet de discipline militaire' announced in *Dolbreuse* nor the 'grand Ouvrage' mentioned in *Ainsi finissent* ever appeared. Loaisel did indeed adhere to his resolution to abandon the novel, at least temporarily. Instead he turned to another genre – drama. His first three plays were 'comédies': *L'Amour arrange tout*, *Lucile et Dercourt*, and *Virginie*, all very similar in nature according to the reviews.[25] Only the first was published, which seems regrettable since the reviewer of *Virginie* believed this third work to be 'ce qu'il a fait de mieux au théâtre'. The subject of *L'Amour arrange tout*, according to a note published on page 2 of the printed edition, was taken from a short story 'L'Amant ennobli par l'amour' contained in the collection *Lettres de tendresse et d'amour*.[26] This is indeed the case. Moreover, a few passages

[25] only the last two were reviewed, *Lucile et Dercourt* in the *Almanach générale de tous les spectacles de Paris et des provinces* (1795, p.95), and *Virginie* in the same volume (p.118).

[26] in volume ii, pp.213-31. This is a very rare work. The copy examined came from the United States Library of Congress. It is an undated, two-volume edition carrying the following imprint: 'A Amathonte, et à Paris Chez Cailleau, Imprimeur-Libraire, rue Saint-Severin'. The *Almanach littéraire ou étrennes d'Apollon* (1781, pp.151-52) describes an edition of 'petit in-8' format. The copy examined was definitely not of this format and probably coincides with the edition Gay dates as 1781 ([Jules Gay], *Bibliographie des ouvrages relatifs à l'amour, aux femmes, au mariage*, 4th ed., rev. J. Lemonnyer (Paris 1894-1900), ii.830).

	1788	1789	1790	1791	1792	1793	1794	1795	1796	1797	1798	1799	1800	1801	1802	1803	1804	1805	1806–1813
L'Amour arrange tout	24	20	15																
Lucile et Dercourt			18																
Virginie			23	3															
Château du Diable					14	63			49	12	9		39		16	13		1	
Bisarrerie de la Fortune						23	9		7				13	4	6				
Combat des Thermopyles							4				3								
Vol par amour								16	15										
Forêt périlleuse										22		19	1	54	12	19	25	29	77
Amans siciliens												1							
Roland de Monglave												29				13		1	
Fontaine merveilleuse												20							
Adélaïde de Bavière														19					
Grand chasseur																	16		

Table 1. *Chronological chart of play performances*

are transcribed word for word. *L'Amour arrange tout,* the first play to be produced, opened on 22 July 1788, the day after Loaisel's first marriage. It remained for over two years in the repertory of the Théâtre des Beaujolais. The other two plays were much shorter-lived.

While these first three plays were rather refined *comédies de mœurs,* the fourth play, *Le Château du Diable,* labelled a 'comédie héroique', was of a completely different nature. It provides a clear signal of Loaisel's evolution toward melodrama and is one of the very earliest examples of this genre in its embryonic form. A review of the work's first performance, on 5 December 1792, was not enthusiastic and saw the play only as a vehicle for the miracles of the *machiniste,* who was applauded for his efforts after the opening performance.[27] Although the play's success undoubtedly depended upon careful execution of the illusions, as the short duration of the poorly staged and poorly executed run at the Théâtre de l'Emulation clearly shows, this play was the first to bring real renown to Loaisel himself. [28] The *Mercure* mentioned it in a review of one of his later plays as 'un ouvrage qui a joui d'un grand succès au Théâtre de Molière et qui est pleine d'imagination'.[29] The *Courrier des spectacles,* in reviewing a successful *reprise,* described it as a play which 'dans sa nouveauté fit courir tout Paris'.[30] The 77 performances in its first year make *Le Château du Diable* Loaisel's most popular play during a first run.[31] It is second only to *La Forêt périlleuse* for overall length of the period of performances, closing out its final run in late 1805. This play has two more very considerable distinctions to its credit. In 1801, Kotzebue adapted it as a 'Zauber-Oper', with music composed by Frederick Reichart, for the opening of the 'Théâtre de la Patrie' in Berlin. Victor Hugo's first melodrama, also called *Le Château du Diable,* is actually a loosely adapted version of Loaisel's play.[32]

Shortly after *Le Château du diable,* Loaisel produced another successful play, *La Bisarrerie de la fortune,* a *comédie de caractère et d'intrigue* of a traditional nature, which opened on 16 April 1793. The reviews were unanimous in proclaiming the success of the play during its run at the Théâtre du Marais, although the number of performances is only

[27] *Chronique de Paris,* 8 décembre 1792, p.1370.
[28] *Courrier des spectacles,* 9 février 1798 (21 pluviôse an VI), no.353, p.2
[29] *Mercure français,* 25 mai 1793, pp.154-55 (a review of *La Bisarrerie de la fortune*).
[30] 12 octobre 1800 (20 vendémiaire an IX), no.1317, p.2.
[31] the criteria for defining a 'run' are discussed below, p.113.
[32] see Fargher. Only a fragment of Hugo's play has survived (*Théâtre complet,* Bibliothèque de la Pléiade (Paris 1964), ii.1283-301).

one-third that of *Le Château du Diable*. Reviews and lengths of performances during succeeding runs do not indicate great approval or popularity, but most reviewers refer none the less to a successful run at the Théâtre de la République beginning on 22 July 1794. At this time the Théâtre de la République, the branch that survived after the scission of the Comédie-Française, was the most pre-eminent theatre in Paris.[33] The prestige of having his play performed at all by this theatre was enough to establish a considerable reputation for Loaisel. After the performances at the Théâtre de la République, *La Bisarrerie de la fortune* was immediately translated into German in two separate editions. It received another German edition in 1808 and before then, in 1803, a Dutch translation. It was revived several times, the last in late 1803, but each run consisted of only a very few performances.

Loaisel's next play was most probably conceived as a patriotic gesture to the *Terreur*. This work, *Le Combat des Thermopyles ou l'école des guerriers*, opened on 2 August 1794 and survived for only four performances. Perhaps its failure was due to an accident of timing, for it opened five days after the fall of Robespierre, at which time a strong reaction against revolutionary plays was taking place (Carlson, p.207). There was an equally unsuccessful attempt at a reopening in 1798. That time the play survived for only three performances.

The reputation Loaisel acquired through *Le Château du Diable* and *La Bisarrerie de la fortune* probably had much to do with prompting the re-editions of his novels. Just two days after the last performance of *La Bisarrerie* at the Théâtre de la République, the *Journal de Paris* announced the re-editions of *Dolbreuse* and of *La Comtesse d'Alibre*, the latter under the new title *Lucile et Milcourt*.[34] The *Soirées de mélancolie* and the combined re-edition of *Valmore* and *Florello* followed soon thereafter. It was at this stage in his career that Loaisel received the 'encouragement' from the Convention.

The 'encouragement', dated 4 September 1795, awarded Loaisel 2000 *livres*. He was designated in the official document as 'auteur dramatique' (see above, p.48). Thus, in spite of the recent re-edition of his novels, he was singled out for his accomplishments and promise as a dramatist. This designation may say as much for the official scorn of the novel as it does for Loaisel's reputation in the theatre. It is most important to note that this 'encouragement' was offered by the

---

[33] Marvin Carlson, *The Theater of the French Revolution* (Ithaca, New York 1966), p.175.
[34] 18 août 1794 (1er fructidor an II), p.2402.

'Convention thermidorienne' and almost fourteen months after the fall of Robespierre. It is not likely, therefore, that Loaisel was being honoured specifically for his patriotic *Combat des Thermopyles*, which had in fact excited no enthusiasm at all during the first days of the new regime, as was pointed out above. The recognition then was most probably for *Le Château du Diable* and *La Bisarrerie*. The importance of these two works to Loaisel's reputation in 1795 is strongly emphasised by the title page of *Roland de Monglave* in the *An* VII edition, which identifies the author as 'Loaisel-Tréogate, auteur de la Bizarrerie de la Fortune, du Château du Diable, etc.'

Le Vol par amour, the first new play by Loaisel since *Le Combat des Thermopyles*, opened on 2 November, 1795, less than a month after the award of the 'encouragement'. No reviews of the performances have been located, but the number of performances and length of the run suggest that it was a fair success even though it was never revived after the initial run. The play was performed at the Théâtre de l'Ambigu-Comique and marks the beginning of Loaisel's long association with that theatre. The work is labelled 'comédie' and has many of the trappings of a traditional *comédie de caractère et d'intrigue*.

With *La Forêt périlleuse ou les brigands de la Calabre*, not only did Loaisel again exploit the 'brigand' motif, this time as the central element of the plot, but also he created a play that is in every way a full-fledged melodrama. This was his most successful play both in terms of immediate success and future popularity. It opened on 7 May 1797 at the Théâtre de la Cité and was praised by Lepan in the *Courrier des spectacles* for such outstanding qualities as 'exposition sage et naturelle, marche assez vite, intrigue fortement conçue, intérêt toujours soutenu, dénouement bien preparé'. The first performance was 'très applaudie', and one scene even provoked an incident in the audience. In this scene, the body of the supposedly dead hero, who has a blood-soaked bandage wrapped about his head, is presented to his unsuspecting beloved at the orders of a sadistic, jealous villain. Several ladies in the audience were shocked at this sight and ran screaming from the theatre. The performance came to a halt, and a few indignant spectators called for the curtain to be lowered, but the play went on. This scene, which LePan found too violent, probably contributed to the play's success.[35] *La Forêt périlleuse* moved to the Théâtre de l'Ambigu-Comique, where it opened on 23 January 1801 and remained in the repertory until 1813

[35] *Courrier des spectacles*, 8 mai 1797 (19 floréal an v), no.122, pp.2-3.

and probably beyond.[36] In the meantime it had been translated into Dutch and also English. It went through eight French editions, the last published in the collection 'Théâtre contemporain illustré' in 1862. The English translations, of which there were at least three separate versions, the latest edition being re-issued in 1879, testify to the play's appeal to audiences in both England and America as a classic of the melodramatic repertory.

The year 1799 saw Loaisel's most feverish literary production since the period of the earliest novels and the years 1793-1795, when he wrote *Le Château du Diable* and *La Bisarrerie de la fortune* and revised the novels for their re-editions. This is the period when he legally designated his profession as 'homme de lettres' (see above, p.48). On 19 January, another 'comédie' entitled *Les Amans siciliens ou les apparences trompeuses* was premiered and suffered a 'chute complete' according to the *Mercure*.[37] It was never performed again or published and thus attained the dubious honour of being Loaisel's most complete failure in the threatre. He had much better luck with another melodrama, *Roland de Monglave*, produced at the Ambigu-Comique. This was his second work to be performed at this theatre, the first having been *Le Vol par amour*. The first performance, on 28 January, was a 'succès brillant et mérité'. But Loaisel, perhaps stung by the failure of *Les Amans siciliens* just nine days earlier, was not present to receive what would have been a great boost to his morale. For the *Journal des théâtres, de littérature et des arts*, after praising the play in the words just quoted, went on to report that when an actor came on stage to name the author who had been 'vivement demandé', 'le public a montré beaucoup de regret de ne pouvoir témoigner à l'auteur lui-même la vive satisfaction qu'il avoit éprouvée à la représentation de cet ouvrage'.[38] The play had a short, successful run at the Ambigu-Comique and a not so successful revival in 1803 at the Théâtre de la Porte Saint-Martin. Frederic Reichardt, the German composer of the musical accompaniment to Kotzebue's adaptation of *Le Château du Diable*, saw *Roland de Monglave* during the run at the Porte Saint-Martin and had nothing at all complimentary to say about either the play or its author.[39] There was a Dutch

---

[36] research on performance histories covered only the period up to 1813.

[37] 29 janvier 1799 (10 pluviôse an VII), p.60.

[38] 30 janvier 1799 (11 pluviôse an VII), no.62, pp.246-47.

[39] letter dated 20 janvier 1803 (A. Laquiante, *Un hiver à Paris sous le Consulat – 1802-1803 – d'après les lettres de J.-F. Reichardt* (Paris 1896), pp.286-88).

translation of *Roland de Monglave* in 1800, the same year that saw the translation of *La Forêt périlleuse* by the same translator. The Ambigu-Comique premiered another play by Loaisel, *La Fontaine merveilleuse*, on 13 September in this same busy year of 1799. It seems to have been fairly well received initially but played off and on for less than six weeks and was not revived. Loaisel's part in this work was minimal, however, for the spectacle – ballets, music, scenery, costumes – greatly over-shadows the words. Furthermore, the subject and some of the lines were taken from the tale *Sadak et Kalasrade* in the *Contes des génies*, so that Loaisel's literary efforts were more of adaptation than creation.[40] The *Mercure* notes this source, and while it does not directly accuse Loaisel of having copied the lines, it does remark sarcastically that the style 'semble appartenir à deux plumes: il y a des morceaux de dialogue très bien écrits; d'autres qu'on ne pardonnerait pas à un écolier'.[41] *La Fontaine merveilleuse* was Loaisel's last dramatic effort for almost two years. But towards the end of 1799 or early in 1800, he must have been working on *Valrose*, for it was announced in the *Journal de Paris* of 21 March 1800.

Loaisel is identified on the title page of *Valrose* as 'auteur de Dol-breuse, de Lucile et Milcourt, etc.' Thus, at least in the estimation of his publisher Leprieur, these two earlier works had established for Loaisel a reputation that could be exploited in order to attract readers to the new work. The *An* x, 'Quatrième Edition' of *Lucile et Milcourt* confirms the popularity of that work during this period. For some reason, *Valrose* seems not to have been reviewed. This may have been due to the highly erotic nature of some episodes or to the fact that the novel is actually a rewritten version of *Ainsi finissent* and like most re-editions would not normally have been reviewed at all. Even though the basic sentimental plot of the earlier novel is preserved and many passages only retouched, *Valrose* has to be classified as a new work because of the importance and number of the additions, omissions, and revisions. The narrative form has changed. *Ainsi finissent* was an epistolary novel, whereas *Valrose* is a memoir novel divided into chapters with descrip-tive titles. Place and character names have been changed, and two of the four principal character roles have been considerably altered and ex-panded. Five new chapters have been added at the end, and two new chapters towards the middle, all relating directly to the action. Most of

[40] in *Le Cabinet des fées* (Genève, Paris 1786), xxx. Other editions of the *Contes* appeared earlier.
[41] 16 septembre 1799 (30 fructidor an VII), pp.272-76.

the abundant material extraneous to the plot has been omitted. The most significant aspects of *Valrose* as compared to *Ainsi finissent* are the new melodramatic and erotic episodes. The melodrama comes as no surprise and is a clear reflection of Loaisel's experience in the theatre during the years since he wrote *Ainsi finissent*. But the emphasis on eroticism is a bit of a surprise. The 'peintures voluptueuses' of *Ainsi finissent* are starkly puritanical compared to such episodes as the graphically described assault by sex-starved outlaws upon the virginity of the naked heroine of *Valrose*. This episode was chosen as the subject of the frontispiece for the second volume. The caption, a quotation from the text, reads as follows: 'Pour mieux s'en assurer la possession, à la quelle ils prétendent tous, ils la depouillent toute nue'. The operation is conducted in full view of our hero, suspended in chains from a nearby boulder. Obviously, by choosing this episode for the subject of a frontispiece, someone – author, illustrator, or publisher – had decided to draw particular attention to the erotic aspects of the work. The fontispieces for both volumes of *Valrose* were designed by Binet, who also illustrated many of the novels of Restif de La Bretonne. The publisher Leprieur paid quite a tribute to Loaisel and *Valrose* by engaging the services of such an eminent illustrator.

The preface to *Valrose* provides an extremely valuable final insight into Loaisel's inner conflicts and also presents his last evaluation of the role of literature and the novel in particular. The 'Préface de l'auteur' is enclosed within the fictional convention of the mysteriously discovered manuscript. It combines certain elements of the 'Préface de l'éditeur' of *Ainsi finissent,* which was written in the voice of Loaisel as author, along with elements of letter 1 and letter 25 of *Ainsi finissent* and several pages of entirely new material. In the 'Préface de l'auteur' of *Valrose*, the only concern is to define the purpose and function of the *roman*. It therefore speaks most probably in the voice of Loaisel as author, as the inclusion of material from the 'Préface de l'éditeur' of *Ainsi finissent* would also indicate. If indeed this is the case, then the elements of letters 1 and 25 of *Ainsi finissent* transposed therein were probably written in Loaisel's voice when they appeared in *Ainsi finissent*.[42] Some highly significant indications of Loaisel's intellectual

---

[42] in the section of letter 1 of *Ainsi finissent* later transposed into the 'Préface de l'auteur' of *Valrose,* the Chevalier de . . . is actually describing the thoughts of the friend to whom he is writing, the Comte de P. . . . But the Chevalier goes on to explain that his own state of mind is even more discouraged than that of the Comte.

evolution can be deduced from this rather complicated textual transposition.

First, it will be recalled that in the preface to *Ainsi finissent*, Loaisel renounced the *roman* for 'des objets plus importans'. In a note to letter 57, he seemed to promise a 'grand Ouvrage' that would practically be a call to revolution. As was further pointed out, within the fiction of letter 57, the Chevalier de . . . was undergoing an intellectual crisis, specifically regarding the effectiveness of efforts by a single individual to bring about social change. In fact, this intellectual crisis is a leitmotif that runs throughout all of *Ainsi finissent*. In the sections of letters 1 and 25 later to be transposed into the 'Préface de l'auteur' of *Valrose*, Le Chevalier de . . . seriously questioned the value and accomplishments of 'l'esprit philosophique'. However, letter 57 indicated a resolution of the crisis establishing a belief in the benefits of 'l'esprit philosophique' and in the possibility that individual action can indeed lead to improvement of society. To the degree that these passages also spoke for Loaisel himself, at the time he wrote *Ainsi finissent*, they announced a similar resolution of his own inner conflicts and together with the preface, indicated his proposed abandonment of fiction for writings of a philosophical, perhaps even revolutionary, nature.

But Loaisel did not produce any such writings, nor did he abandon fiction. And when *Valrose* is published, the 'Préface de l'auteur' restates the same intellectual crisis evoked in *Ainsi finissent* but with a very different conclusion. The note to letter 57 in *Ainsi finissent* is gone in *Valrose*, thus removing any mention of the 'grand Ouvrage'. At the outset, the 'Préface se l'auteur' definitively renounces the potential benefits of 'l'esprit philosophique'. The following passage recounts the past hopes and this present disillusionment of 'l'auteur', ending with the words of letter 1 of *Ainsi finissent*, indicated here with brackets (*Valrose*, i.xvi-xvii; *Ainsi finissent*, i.16):

J'eus, comme bien d'autres, la prétention d'être un savant. Pendant un tems je m'enfonçai dans l'étude des sciences abstraites; mais à la place des lumières que j'y cherchois, je ne trouvai que ténèbres; et bientôt j'appréciai à sa juste valeur [cet esprit philosophique qui voit toujours dans les objets, des propriétés, des analogies, un nouvel ordre de choses; quand il ne fait que tâtonner dans la nuit des conjectures.

Je vis, et c'est peut-être tout ce qu'il nous est permis de voir bien clairement, qu'il est une foule de vérités placées à une distance infinie de la sphère de notre savoir, que Dieu tient cachées dans les abîmes de sa sagesse; que l'étude des sciences n'est pour nous qu'une suite d'humiliations; et que nous ne sommes rien en comparaison de l'immensité de la nature, qui se joue perpétuellement de notre curiosité.]

Repeating the words of letter 25 of *Ainsi finissent*, the 'Préface de l'auteur' of *Valrose* goes on to state that 'les prétendus progrès de l'esprit ne sont que les raffinemens bizarres de l'esprit' (*Valrose*, i.xvii; *Ainsi finissent*, i.125). However, the conclusion to this state of affairs, wholly new with *Valrose*, is that there is *no* definite resolution to the crisis. The solution proposed is merely a method of coping with this hopeless situation (*Valrose*, i.xviii-xix):

La science, il est vrai, nous retient dans les limites du monde réel; elle réduit l'homme à ses vraies dimensions; elle le soumet au joug de l'impérieuse nécessité: mais est-ce pour lui un avantage dont il ait à se féliciter? Si le sentiment de notre foiblesse s'accroît avec nos lumières, n'avons-nous pas besoin d'illusions pour nous détourner de la triste vérité? Et où les chercher ces illusions si nécessaires à notre bonheur, si ce n'est dans les bons romans dans les fictions intéressantes? C'est là que notre ame épuisée, par le long et pénible exercice de ses facultés, retrouve ses douces chimères, et des êtres créés à la mesure de ses desirs.

No doubt by this time Loaisel had read the *Confessions* of his earlier idol Jean-Jacques, for the last words of this passage certainly bring to mind Rousseau's description of his consolation in 'le pays des chimères', the 'monde idéal que mon imagination créatrice eut bientot peuplé d'êtres selon mon cœur'.[43] Thus, in his last pronouncement on literary theory, Loaisel vindicates the *roman*, which he had earlier intended to abandon. But no longer does he see it as fulfilling a role of moral utility. Although there is a small concession to moral utility, it is buried within a long list of purely esthetic qualities which distinguish the superior *roman* and place it in 'la classe de bons livres'. Loaisel's disillusionment with 'l'esprit philosophique' has brought him back to the *roman* primarily for its function as fiction, a work of imagination destined for the entertainment of the imagination.

This vindication of the *roman* for its function as entertainment is highly significant as a key to Loaisel's intellectual evolution in this last period of his literary career. Loaisel's plays are certainly most remarkable for their value as light entertainment and as such are far removed from the world of high literature he attempted to enter as 'triste Eleve

---

[43] *Œuvres complètes*, Bibliothèque de la Pléiade (Paris 1959), i.427.

d'Apollon'. With the exception of *Le Combat des Thermopyles* and a few isolated speeches in the melodramatic plays, there is no hint of the 'savant' desirous of serving 'le bien public'. Writing has become for Loaisel 'homme de lettres' a way to make a living, and money is to be made by entertaining the public. The additions of the melodramatic and erotic episodes to refashion *Ainsi finissent* into *Valrose* seem best interpreted as just such catering to public taste for entertainment.

The last two melodramas that Loaisel wrote did little to enhance his reputation. *Adélaïde de Bavière* opened on 2 July 1801 at the Ambigu-Comique but was not a tremendous success. 'L'auteur a souvent fait mieux', wrote LePan in the *Courrier des spectacles*.[44] Although the play was not revived in France after the initial run, it was translated into Dutch the same year it opened. Loaisel's next melodrama, *Le Grand chasseur ou l'isle des palmiers*, was probably written in collaboration with Guilbert de Pixerécourt. Pixerécourt's actual contribution may have been minimal, but the very fact of a collaboration shows that Loaisel's talent was acknowledged by the foremost melodramatist of the period.[45] The play, which opened on 6 November 1804, had only a short run and was not performed again. In LePan's opinion, whatever success the play enjoyed had little to do with the author's talents. Loaisel alone was announced as author of the play.[46]

In March of 1803 appeared the first announcement of Loaisel's last novel, *Héloïse et Abeilard ou les victimes de l'amour*. It is certainly regrettable that this work has completely disappeared. Moreover, no review of it has been located, so that its contents remain a mystery. The significance of this novel as Loaisel's last attempt in the genre coupled with the fact that it appears to be his longest novel underline the necessity of locating a copy to complete the history of his literary career.

Le Grand chasseur was the last literary work of confirmed authenticity to be written by Loaisel. When it opened, he was already an employee of the postal service. This was his sole known occupation for the last eight years of his life. There are no definite indications as to why he completely stopped writing. The long illness of which he died may have been partly responsible, but he must also have been

[44] 3 juillet 1801 (14 messidor an IX), no.1586, p.2.

[45] Willie G. Hartog believes the play to be 'de l'invention de [Loaisel], car la pièce n'est pas du tout dans le genre de Pixerécourt' (*Guilbert de Pixerécourt: sa vie, son mélodrame, sa technique et son influence* (Paris 1913), p.121).

[46] *Courrier des spectacles*, 7 novembre 1804 (16 brumaire an XIII), no.2810, p.4.

discouraged at not having produced a really successful play since *Roland de Monglave* in 1799. The fact that his last two novels were completely ignored by the periodical reviewers may have added to his disillusionment.

The story of Loaisel's hopes and ambitions and of his reactions to public reception of his works, as told in the novel prefaces, announces and explains in large part the evolution of his literary production. It is a story just as interesting as any of those told within the novels or the plays. Loaisel suffered in real life from a 'mal du siècle' not unlike that inflicted on his characters. The initial failure he suffered in the military created a continued yearning for personal fulfilment that he never actually realised.

First he set out to achieve glory in 'pure' literature by writing short prose fiction and poetry in the *genre sombre*. Except for a few translations, these early works went through no immediate rereditions. Perhaps because of discouragement over this apparent lack of enthusiasm by the general public, perhaps because of the cool to downright hostile reaction of the periodical press, particularly in regard to *La Comtesse d'Alibre*, Loaisel began espousing more socially useful ideals hoping sincerely to contribute to the improvement of society. Turning to the longer novel in the tradition of the moralistic *roman somme*, he attempted to enter the domain of the century's great thinkers seeking to solve life's problems through philosophy and the sciences while at the same time receiving the recognition he still sought to give meaning to his life. He seems indeed to have shared in the true revolutionary spirit of the late 1780s, but there are few facts to confirm these suspicions other than isolated remarks in *Ainsi finissent*. The two novels he published during this period enjoyed some immediate success, especially *Dolbreuse*, which was even included in the *Bibliothèque universelle des romans*. Significantly, the selection chosen by the *Bibliothèque* was a libertine adventure. Along with his high-minded philosophical intentions, Loaisel yielded to public taste by shifting to more emphasis on the sensual elements culminating in the highly explicit eroticism of *Valrose*. For reasons not immediately apparent, Loaisel turned to writing for the theatre and a less cultured audience. His marriage, which coincided with the appearance of the first play, may have placed financial burdens on him that required his changing to a less lofty and more lucrative field of literature. He evidently earned his living from writing during the

97

1790s until the first years of the Empire, and achieved his greatest popularity at this time. His success in the theatre was accompanied by re-editions of all the novels. Ironically, *La Comtesse d'Alibre*, which may have been responsible for his turning away from the *genre sombre*, was the most popular of the re-edited novels. While an early *comédie d'intrigue*, *La Bisarrerie de la fortune*, brought Loaisel some recognition through translations and a run at the Théâtre de la Nation, his creation in 1797 of *La Forêt périlleuse*, one of the first true melodramas, assured his survival into the late nineteenth century. It was his most popular play during his lifetime and the only one of his works to survive after his death.

The success of Loaisel's plays evidently did not satisfy his deeper yearnings for solving the essential problems of life. But while the preface to *Valrose*, Loaisel's last communication on a personal level, reveals a continued desire for the unattainable, it also concludes his search for the true function of literature. He finally descends from the heights of Parnassus to proclaim that the goal of literature – specifically, the novel – is to entertain and, in so doing, to provide an escape from the malaise of the meaninglessness of a confusing world. Beneath the deceptively mundane surface of this pronouncement lies a profound and strikingly modern attitude toward life as well as an equally modern vindication of imagination – both the author's and the reader's – as the ultimate concern of literature.

II
Annotated listing of
the works of
Loaisel de Tréogate

I

Scope, sources, and procedures

∼∼∼∿∘⎇∘∿∼∼

i. Scope and concept

THIS listing is intended to be as complete as possible and thus includes all known or suspected editions of all works ever attributed to Loaisel, whether published under his name, anonymously, or pseudonymously. Unpublished plays, a legitimate part of Loaisel's overall literary endeavours, are included. So also are translations of his works, which provide important indications concerning their survival and diffusion. The general nature and extent of textual revisions in re-editions are noted. In addition to the publication histories of the texts, the listing also presents performance histories of the plays, since a play lives on the stage as well as on the printed page. All library locations discovered for extant copies are noted as are all secondary source references pertaining to Loaisel's works. All bibliographical problems encountered are discussed and, to the extent possible, resolved. The aim has been to provide a firm basis for future research and to eliminate duplication of effort while providing the possibility for rechecking and verifying results.

ii. Sources consulted

Compiling the data contained in this listing necessitated extensive and thorough research not only in existing library collections but also in a wide variety of secondary sources ranging from contemporary periodicals to the most recent bibliographies. It became apparent during the preliminary efforts to locate extant copies of Loaisel's works that systematic searching in existing library collections would most probably yield meagre results with the obvious exceptions of the British Library,[1] the Bibliothèque nationale, the Bibliothèque de l'Arsenal, and the

[1] formerly the Library of the British Museum.

American libraries covered in the *National union catalogue, pre-1956 imprints*.[2] Efforts toward reasonable thoroughness were, however, directed toward research in secondary sources. A brief discussion follows of the bibliographies and guides used to select these secondary sources.

Besides the well known general research bibliographies and guides of Besterman, Cabeen, Cioranescu, and Maclès,[3] a very informative general orientation, including a list and discussion of sources, appears in Robert Barroux's 'Indications bibliographiques' in the *Dictionnaire des lettres françaises: le XVIIIe siècle* (i.19-32). Robert Estival's *La Statistique bibliographique de la France sous la monarchie au XVIIIe siècle* (Paris, La Haye 1965) contains many helpful comments on both manuscript and printed sources appearing up to the time of Quérard, but only those sources that treat books printed before the Revolution. Cioranescu's article 'Notes sur la *Bibliographie littéraire du XVIIIe siècle*' suggests a variety of types of sources and assesses their value.[4] Jean Sgard's 'Tableau chronologique des périodiques de langue française publiés avant la Révolution'[5] combined with the critical comments in Gabriel Bonno's Cabeen article, 'Periodical literature' (Cabeen, iv.308-21), provide a first basis for selecting periodicals published in the pre-Revolutionary period.[6] For the period after 1789 the proliferation of periodicals renders even semi-comprehensive listings, such as that of Martin and Walter, extremely difficult to handle.[7] An absolutely indispensable guide to those periodicals which first appeared *during* the Revolution is contained in Maurice Tourneux's *Bibliographie de l'histoire de Paris pendant la révolution française*; it contains no information, however, on periodicals that started into circulation before the begin-

United States Library of Congress (London 1968-   ).

[3] Theodore Besterman, *A world bibliography of bibliographies*, 4th ed. (Lausanne 1965-1966); David C. Cabeen, ed., *A critical bibliography of French literature* (Syracuse, New York 1947-1968): vol.iv, *The Eighteenth century*, ed. Georges R. Havens and Donald F. Bond (1951), and vol.iv supplement, *The Eighteenth century*, ed. Richard A. Brooks (1968); Alexandre Cioranescu, *Bibliographie de la littérature française du dix-huitième siècle* (Paris 1969); Louise Noelle Maclès, *Les Sources du travail bibliographique* (Geneva 1950-1958).

[4] *Dix-huitième siècle* 3 (1971), pp.361-70.

[5] in *L'Etude des périodiques anciens: colloque d'Utrecht*, 9-10 janvier 1970 (Paris 1972).

[6] Sgard's 'Tableau' supersedes Bonno's 'List chronologique des périodiques de langue française du XVIIIe siècle', *Modern language quarterly* 5 (1944), pp.3-25.

[7] Bibliothèque nationale, Département des imprimés, *Catalogue de l'histoire de la révolution française*, ed. André Martin and Gérard Walter: vol.v, *Ecrits de la période révolutionnaire: journaux et almanachs* (Paris 1943).

ning of the Revolution.[8] The *Catalogue collectif des périodiques* provides the surest and least confusing aid in differentiating among similar sounding periodicals and in following name changes and evolutions of a single periodical.[9] The most detailed and complete guide to almanachs is John Grand-Carteret's *Les Almanachs français (1600-1895)* (Paris 1932).

The most comprehensive and knowledgeable discussion of eighteenth-century novel bibliography for works appearing between 1750 and 1788 is found in the introductory remarks to Angus Martin's 'Towards a checklist of French prose fiction 1751-1788'.[10] The list of sources in the *Bibliographie du genre romanesque français, 1751-1800* expands coverage to include also sources treating the last years of the century. For the theatre, the 'guide' section of Auguste Rondel's *Catalogue analytique sommaire de la collection théâtrale Rondel, suivi d'un guide pratique à travers la bibliographie théâtrale et d'une chronologie des ouvrages d'information et de critique théâtrales* (Paris 1932) lives up to all one might expect from the title and author. It and the bibliography of Seymour Travers's *Catalogue of nineteenth-century French theatrical parodies (1789-1914)* (New York 1941) are unsurpassed for thoroughness in their listing of both periodical and non-periodical sources for the period here under consideration: 1788-1812. Additional information in Rondel's 'Conférence sur la bibliographie dramatique et sur les collections théâtrales' is also helpful.[11]

In a much more limited sense, some useful selections of sources were found in monographs on two contemporaries of Loaisel with similar literary proclivities: Baculard d'Arnaud and Pixerécourt.[12] Robert Barroux's article on Loaisel in the *Dictionnaire des lettres françaises* and the short monograph on Loaisel by Henry Loaisel de Saulnays list some of their sources. Much of the criticism studied yielded leads to source material of interest, and prefaces to some of the bibliographies consulted contained useful discussions of their own sources.

---

8 (Paris 1900), iii, chapters 6-7.

9 Bibliothèque nationale, Département des périodiques, *Catalogue collectif des périodiques du début du XVIIIe siècle à 1939 conservés dans les bibliothèques de Paris et dans les bibliothèques universitaires des départements* (Paris 1967-1977).

10 *Australian journal of French studies* 3 (1966), pp.345-69.

11 *Bulletin de la Société d'histoire du théâtre*, janvier-mars 1913 (reprint: Lille 1913).

12 Dawson; Hartog; and Guilbert Van de Louw, *Baculard d'Arnaud, romancier ou vulgarisateur: essai de sociologie littéraire* (Paris 1972).

a. Periodicals and literary correspondences

(See below, pp. 231-33, for a list of the sources consulted in this category.)

Research in periodicals concentrated on locating reviews and announcements of texts and play performances. Many of the bibliographies and reference works consulted are based on just such data, whence the advisability of returning to original sources for verification of accuracy. There was also a hope of locating heretofore unreported works by Loaisel published only in the periodical press.

The research performed in periodicals was far from exhaustive. During the course of this study, references were discovered to several specific periodicals which were known or believed to mention Loaisel's works. All these periodicals were selected for examination. But beyond these, a selection had to be made based on relevance, an estimate of promise, facility of examination, and availability of copies. With a few exceptions, it was decided to concentrate primarily on the Parisian literary press. Additional problems related to specific areas of research imposed further limitations.

Aside from their interest to critical considerations, reviews also have a bearing on textual history. First, they confirm that a book was published and distributed by a certain date or that plays were performed on the days announced. Second, inasmuch as reviews of a text often consist largely, if not wholly, of extracts of the work reviewed, they are in a limited sense also part of the text's history, since they serve as supplemental distribution for a selected portion of that text. Third, reviews sometimes identify authors of anonymously or pseudonymously published works. Finally, they provide information on the authenticity and content of unpublished or unlocated works. The most consistent sources for novel reviews were the following: *Almanach littéraire ou étrennes d'Apollon, Année littéraire, Affiches de Province, Journal encyclopédique, Journal de Trévoux* (continuations), *Journal de Paris,* and *Mercure de France.* The *Courrier des spectacles* and the *Courrier de l'Europe et des spectacles* regularly reviewed opening play performances in the issue of the following day. Play reviews in other periodicals were sporadic, especially for the smaller theatres, where Loaisel's plays were performed.

Publication announcements, while not confirmations of publication and distribution, are none the less important data. They suggest what may have been the earliest dates a text was available on the market. Sometimes they are the only data available on a text. Five periodicals existed that were devoted solely to such current bibliography: *Catalogue hebdomadaire* (1763-1781), *Journal de la librairie* (1782-1789), *Journal typographique et bibliographique* (1797-1810), *Journal général de la littérature de France* (1798-1848), and *Bibliothèque française* (1800-1808). For the period 1790-1796, other sources not specialised in bibliography had to be relied upon, such as the *Journal de Paris* or the *Décade philosophique*.

The systematic *dépouillement* for reviews and publications announcements covered only those works of Loaisel previously identified from other sources. Aside from a few theatre almanachs that contain articles on individual authors, research in periodicals is severely hampered by an almost total lack of indexing by author. In those cases when *tables* do exist, they generally list works by title only. Since a page by page examination of periodicals was quite beyond the scope of this project, it was necessary to rely upon the *tables* or in their absence to conduct a limited page by page search restricted to a reasonable time period around the publication or performance date, whence the limitation to previously identified works.

Dates of play performances can be found in the theatre announcements published in the daily press, but very few periodicals carried complete listings on a regular basis. Of those few that did so, the following were used for this study: *Affiches de Paris* for the period prior to 1797; *Courrier des spectacles* for 1797-1805; *Courrier de l'Europe et des spectacles* for 1805-1811; and *Journal de l'Empire* after 1811. The only method possible to gather the desired data on play performances – dates of first performances and of reopenings, numbers of performances, and names of theatres where performed – was to examine the theatre announcements day by day. This was done for the period running from January 1788 to December 1812, thus covering all performances to the year of Loaisel's death.

Efforts were made to locate works published by Loaisel in the periodical press during the period from 1776 to his death in 1812. The lack of author identifications in the *tables* was again a hindrance. The only periodicals found to identify authors consistently in the *tables* were the *Almanach des muses* and the *Nouvel almanach des muses*. These were thus the only ones in which the *dépouillement* may be said to be definitive. Since some bibliographies had indicated that Loaisel published 'poésies fugitives' and prose in the *Mercure de France* and the *Journal encyclopédique*, the *tables* of these two periodicals were systematically checked, but no works ascribed to Loaisel were found to be listed other than the novels being reviewed.

Of the vast number of literary correspondences, only the principal ones were consulted, the selection being based on Cioranescu's remarks in his 'Notes sur la *Bibliographie littéraire du XVIIIe siècle*' (*Dixhuitième siècle* 3 (1971), p.370). The *Correspondance littéraire secrète* of Métra and Imbert had to be excluded because of a lack of any sort of index. Of the remaining works in Cioranescu's selection, only Bachaumont, Grimm, and La Harpe treated the period under consideration. None of them produced any information whatsoever on Loaisel or his works.

b. Bibliographies, répertoires, reference works, and sale catalogues

(*See below, pp.233-39, for a list of the sources consulted in this category.*)

A vast amount of data can be gathered from the sources contained in this category. Much is incomplete, of questionable reliability, and sometimes obviously in error, thus calling for judicious comparison with other data as well as attempts to discover and verify original sources. However, these sources provide information available nowhere else and sometimes shed light on otherwise unresolvable problems. With the exception of booksellers' catalogues, library sale catelogues, and works specifically dealing with illustrators and illustrated books, a concerted effort was made toward thoroughness in this category of sources.

Desessarts's *Siècles littéraires*, Ersch, and Laporte are the most valuable of the bibliographies, since similarity of wording and repetition of errors show that they were probably the original sources of many later bibliographies. Also, like the periodicals, they appeared at the time Loaisel's works were being published and thus could be based on firsthand knowledge and examination of editions that may have disappeared since. Quérard's *France littéraire* and Michaud contain original entries. Michaud is both incomplete and inaccurate in a number of respects but is important to keep in mind as the chief source of Arnault for all entries and Rabbe for the novels. Rabbe produced the first thoroughly researched listing of Loaisel's plays, both published and unpublished, having drawn his data from theatre almanachs. Hoefer provides no new data nor does Levot, who is based principally on Quérard's *France littéraire* and Rabbe.

The monumental manuscript play bibliographies of Douay, Duval, Goizet, and Lecomte ('les Fiches Lecomte') as well as the modern published works of Brenner and of Wicks and Schweitzer are all based on considerable original research. Sometimes they provide general indications of sources, but rarely do they list sources of individual entries. Thus, they were of little help in solving the difficult problems of locating the original evidence for ascribing to Loaisel unpublished or pseudonymously or anonymously published plays. The period from 1790-1799, not covered by either Brenner or Wicks and Schweitzer, has yet to inspire a modern bibliography other than Tourneux's rather incomplete product. This is the most confusing period of all as regards Loaisel's plays.

The MMF is a model research guide in every respect. Prior to its publication, the authors generously shared the results of their research regarding Loaisel's works, including the recently discovered location of the one and only copy of *Valrose* known to exist. Their bibliography and that of Delcro are the only ones which consistently list sources for each entry.

Gay is unique and of particular value in having sifted through a large number of nineteenth-century catalogues of booksellers, thus providing the first listings of some titles that had escaped all previous bibliographies. His listing of the bookseller's catalogue as reference for an entry is also a confirmation of the existence of that work at a certain moment in history. Cohen and Lewine also provide evidence of a work's existence in cases where the data they give on illustrations could only have come from a visual inspection. In several of the problems encountered, these three sources provided the only suggestions toward solutions.

Direct consultation of booksellers' catalogues would have been beyond the scope of this project, given the vast quantity available and the complete lack of indexing even in individual catalogues. The collection in the Bibliothèque nationale (the Q 10 collection) was consulted to track down a few leads to specific booksellers, such as Lefilleul. The catalogues of Leprieur and Louis published in the back of Loaisel's *Valmore et Florello* (*An* III) and *Soirées de mélancolie* (*An* III), respectively, offered some helpful information. Catalogues of library sales, like booksellers' catalogues, are valuable research aids for confirming existence of works. Here again the collection in the Bibliothèque nationale (the 'delta' collection) is so vast that systematic consultation was entirely out of the question. Only the most important, or those to which there were leads, were consulted: La Vallière, Pixerécourt Soleinne, and Taylor.

Of the many works consulted which concern illustrated books, engravers, artists, etc., only Cohen and Lewine qualify strictly as bibliographical sources. It was hoped that the others might yield a clue to the origin of a reference to the missing *Héloïse et Abeilard*. They are all listed under 'Works consulted' to prevent future duplication of the unrewarded efforts of that research.

There are only five modern attempts at complete listings of Loaisel's works. The bibliography in Loaisel de Saulnays's monograph, while unprofessional in many respects, none the less has the advantage of being based at least partially on the highly important *fonds Rondel* at the Bibliothèque de l'Arsenal. It suffers from a confusing and ambiguous compiling of data. Saulnays includes a useful list of many of the sources used but rarely links sources to individual title or edition entries. Of the more recent listings, Cioranescu and Barroux are clear and fairly accurate as far as they go, although both contain errors and are incomplete, especially as regards re-editions. Unpublished plays and works of doubtful authenticity are not mentioned at all by either one, nor is there any discussion of the significant bibliographical problems concerning some of the works that are listed. Bousquet's listing, which seems primarily based on Barroux, provides no new information and fails to correct some errors. Morabito's bibliography is based mainly on the holdings of the Bibliothèque nationale with Cioranescu (although not an acknowledged source) apparently having provided the remaining entries.

c. Library collections and catalogues

(*See below, p.240, for a list of the library catalogues consulted.*)

Works from the following libraries were examined either on the spot, through interlibrary loan, or in microfilm copy:

Belgium:
Bibliothèque générale de l'Université de Liège

England:
  The British Library
France:
  Bibliothèque de l'Arsenal
  Bibliothèque nationale
  Bibliothèque de l'Opéra, Paris
  Bibliothèque universitaire de Rennes
  Bibliothèque Sainte-Geneviève, Paris
Union of Soviet Socialist Republics:
  Saltykov-Shchedrin State Public Library, Leningrad
United States of America:
  American Antiquarian Society, Worchester, Massachusetts
  Boston Public Library
  Library of Brown University
  Library of University of California at Los Angeles
  Library of Case Western Reserve University
  Library of University of Chicago
  Library of Columbia University
  Library of Congress
  Library of Cornell University
  Library of University of Florida
  Library of Harvard University
  Library of Indiana University, Bloomington
  Library of University of Iowa
  Library of University of Michigan, Ann Arbor
  Newberry Library, Chicago
  New York Public Library
  Library of Northwestern University
  Library of Oberlin College
  Library of University of Pennsylvania, Philadelphia
  Library of Tulane University
  Library of Vassar College
  Library of Yale University

With the exception of translations, all copies of Loaisel's works located in the BN, Ars, BUR, Rennes, Opéra, NN, and NNC were examined firsthand. Many of the copies listed in the *NUC* were examined firsthand through inter-library loan, but in some cases only photocopies could be furnished. In all but three cases (two translations and one re-edition of doubtful attribution), it has been possible to examine either firsthand or by photocopy at least one copy of all those editions for which extant copies could be located. A query was sent to verify significant BL listings. A query for the German translations listed in Fromm was sent to the Deutsche Staatsbibliothek in East Berlin, which instituted a search throughout both the German Democratic Republic and the Federal Republic of Germany.

As it turned out, library copies are in several instances the only record of re-editions. This was especially true of plays, but also pertained to two novels. The Ars collection of Loaisel's plays, as might be expected, turned out to be the most complete known, lacking only one re-edition of one play. No collection, however, was complete in the novel holdings. Except for the first edition of *Dolbreuse*, all editions of the novels must be considered extremely rare. No manuscripts were found for any of the works.

iii. Bibliographical procedures and format[13]

a. Organisation

The listing is divided into four sections: novels, plays, poems, and miscellaneous works. Articles on works are listed alphabetically within each section. Articles on plays present the performance history separately before the publication history of the texts. All editions and translations of a given work are listed together chronologically within the article on that work. There is a separate entry for every edition that can be either confirmed through an existing copy or inferred through source references or other evidence.

Many discrepancies were found among secondary source format descriptions of an edition of a given date.[14] These could have indicated

---

[13] ideas concerning bibliographical procedures were drawn mainly from the following sources: MMF and Martin's 'First listings'; R. L. Frautschi and J. Moreland, 'Toward a list of French prose fiction', *Romance notes* 9 (1968), pp.341-43; Fredson Bowers, *Principles of bibliographical description* (Princeton 1949; re-issue, New York 1962). Also helpful were Ronald B. McKerrow, *An introduction to bibliography for literary students* (Oxford 1927) and Philip Gaskell, *A new introduction to bibliography* (Oxford, New York 1972).

[14] an extremely valuable treatment of the complicated problem of format – the only satisfactory work on the subject regarding French printing – is found in Charles Mortet, 'Le format des livres: notions historiques et pratiques', *Revue des bibliothèques* 3 (1893),

simultaneous printings in different formats, but all appeared to be in error. Instead of complicating the listing with separate entries for each erroneous format description, explanations of the errors are included in the comments to the edition to which the reference in question most probably refers. Library catalogue errors in description of format are not discussed when the copies have been examined, since the examination provides indisputable proof of the error. Isolated cases of apparent source errors in edition dates also are discussed under the edition to which they most probably refer. However, when several sources contain identical apparent errors in dates or when the nonexistent edition seems to have established a reputation, a separate entry is given. Edition entries are designated by the Gregorian or Revolutionary calendar year according to the dates actually printed on the title page, or suspected as printed on the title page in instances when no extant copies have been located. Source references frequently cite Gregorian calendar dates for editions now known to bear the imprint dates designated only in the Revolutionary calendar. (There are, of course, two possible Gregorian calendar equivalents for each Revolutionary year.) The fact that these dates could actually have indicated other editions was always taken into account, but there was never any evidence that this was the case. All such source references citing imprints converted to Gregorian dates are included under the entries of the editions to which they actually refer.

b. Definitions

The following terms are used throughout the listing. Although their general meanings are widely understood, their precise definitions are far from standardised. Their use in the listing adheres strictly to the definitions given below.

Edition: 'The whole number of copies of a book printed at any time from substantially the same setting of type-pages' (Bowers, p.39).

Original edition: the first edition of a work to be printed.

Re-edition: an edition printed after the original edition from a different type setting. It may contain changes in both title-page and text.

Rewritten version: no hard and fast rule has been devised for drawing the line between a re-edition with extensive revisions and a rewritten

pp.305-25 (reprint: Paris 1894). The most common discrepancies in secondary sources and even library catalogues were the format descriptions, making this one of the most important bibliographical problems to be resolved.

version. The problem presented itself in only one case where an arbitrary decision was made.[15]

Issue: all copies of an edition put on sale at the same time.[16]

Re-issue: all copies of an edition put on sale at one time after the first issue and containing a cancellans title page or changes to the title page other than those designed to correct errors or to perfect copy.[17]

Variant state: term applied to any part of an edition exhibiting variations in type-setting, where no changes are made to the original title page other than those designed to correct errors or perfect copy.[18]

Cancellans: 'Any part of a book substituted for what was originally printed. It may be of any size from a tiny scrap of paper bearing one or two letters, pasted on over those first printed, to several sheets replacing the original ones. The most common form [. . .] is perhaps a single leaf inserted in place of the original leaf' (McKerrow, p.222).

Translation: employed here in a wide sense to include adaptations as well as renditions completely faithful to the original French versions.

c. *Problems of attribution and unlocated editions*

Each separate edition entry heading (including translations), and in a few cases the heading for the entire article on a given work, will contain a brief parenthetical note of the status of any outstanding problems concerning either authenticity of attribution or the actual existence of the work or edition. A detailed discussion of the problems will appear in the 'comments' section of the entries. References in secondary sources are of extreme importance in solving such problems. Although they contain some examples of verifiable error, they often provide the only existing evidence concerning a specific problem. One of the basic considerations in each case is whether secondary source data are confirmed, that is, whether there is more than one reference containing independently obtained evidence. The reliability of the sources is of course another major concern (see discussion above under 'Sources consulted').

---

[15] the case involved *Ainsi finissent* and *Valrose*. *Valrose* is listed as a separate work with a cross-reference under *Ainsi finissent*. The problem is fully discussed in the 'comments' section to *Valrose*.

[16] an adaptation of Bowers's definition (p.40).

[17] an adaptation of Bowers's definition (p.40).

[18] an adaptation of Bowers's definition (pp.41-42).

Three categories have been selected to designate the degree of authenticity of attribution of works published anonymously or pseudonymously or, in the case of some plays, not published at all. Assignment to these categories does not follow any standard set of criteria since each case is unique. A work of 'confirmed attribution' is judged to be as authentic a part of Loaisel's *œuvre* as a work published under his name. A work of 'unconfirmed attribution' seems authentic according to the known evidence but needs additional confirming evidence before it can legitimately be considered part of the *œuvre*. Those works labelled 'doubtful attribution' are considered spurious.

Only those editions of which a copy has been examined firsthand by this writer are listed with no parenthetical note concerning their actual existence. In a few cases when firsthand examination of a copy was not possible, there was sufficient proof of an edition's existence for it to be considered an edition of 'confirmed existence'. Such proof consisted of at least a sale or library catalogue reference, *reported* firsthand examination of a copy, or *two* reliable independent source references based on sources which had apparently examined actual copies. Editions labelled 'unconfirmed existence' are supported in all cases by only one independent reference but in a highly reliable source. Because of the extreme rarity of surviving copies of Loaisel's works, only one copy having survived in ten cases, it was not felt that the failure to locate an extant copy should outweigh a *reliable* source reference; thus, editions of 'unconfirmed existence' are considered part of the *œuvre*. Editions of 'doubtful existence' are not considered part of the *œuvre*, because they are supported only by a single independent reference of *questionable* accuracy. 'Nonexistent' editions are those for which the references flatly contradict known evidence or can be shown convincingly to be in error. Plays for which no editions have been located, nor references to editions found, are designated 'unpublished?'.

d. Format of play performance histories

The performance history of each play will contain a separate entry for each 'run' of that play. A new 'run' is determined by the announcement of a 'reprise', a change of theatre, or a lapse of at least six months' time since the last previous performance. For each run, the following data will be given: the opening and closing dates, the theatre where performed, and the number of performances during that run. Sources referring to a particular run will be listed immediately following the presentation of the preceding data. Comments will be provided when problems exist, such as discrepancies in sources, attribution of authorship, or the possibility that the play was not published.

e. *Format of publication histories*

There will be a separate entry for each individual edition (or re-issue) of a published text. Each individual entry will consist of the following sections, when applicable:

1. *Bibliographical description.*

(a) Title pages will be transcribed in simplified facsimile and will include complete title, complete imprint, and, when applicable, ornament descriptions and epigraphs. Original spelling and punctuation are preserved as well as the distinction between upper and lower case. No attempt is made, however, to duplicate or describe original type or to distinguish between small and large capitals. Line endings are indicated by a virgule (/). The presence of ornaments and vignettes is noted, but they are described by dimensions only, height first. Dates printed in roman numerals are transcribed as such; dates in arabic numerals are transcribed in arabic numerals. Since dates are transcribed exactly as they appear, Gregorian calendar equivalents for Revolutionary calendar dates are not given unless they are actually printed on the title page. All errors will be transcribed as they appear and will be followed by a '[*sic*]' notation. In the absence of an existing copy, the description will be based on what appears to be the most reliable compilation of data from source references.

(b) The presence of frontispieces will be noted, but they will not be described. If they are signed, the names of the artist(s) will be listed as printed.

(c) The physical description of the book will include the number of volumes when more than one, format, and pagination in all series. In describing pagination, a distinction is preserved among arabic, upper case roman, and lower case roman numerals. The pagination of the plays is so simple, never involving more than one series, that only the total of numbered pages will be indicated. The pagination of novels, however, is more complex requiring that all series either partially or fully printed be described. In fully printed series, only the first and last pages will be listed. In partially printed series, the beginning and end of each printed portion and of each inferred portion will be indicated, with inferred pagination being placed in brackets; however, pagination will not be inferred for unnumbered end pages following the last numbered page of final partially printed series nor for unnumbered pages preceding the first partially printed series. When duplicate series appear within the same volume they will be differentiated in the following manner: a single asterisk (*) will indicate a duplicate series preceding the series numbering the main body of the text (e.g., 1*-16*[1]2-92); a double asterisk (**) will indicate a duplicate series following the series numbering the main body of the text (e.g., [1]2-92[1**]2**-6**). A semicolon will mark the end of pagination for a given volume in a multi-volume work.

(d) A content note will be given for the novels only.

2. *Textual revisions.* A brief note will summarise the nature and extent of revisions in all re-editions.

3. *Library locations.* A single dagger (†) following a library location will indicate a firsthand examination by this writer of the copy (copies) in that library. A double dagger (‡) will indicate the location of the copy used for the bibliographical description. Examinations and descriptions based only on photocopy or microfilm will be noted as such. Firsthand examinations by others when known will be noted in cases of copies not examined by this writer. In all other cases when copies could not be examined, the source which provided the location – usually the library's printed catalogue – will be cited except for those locations furnished by the *NUC*.

4. *Sources.* All sources mentioning the edition are cited. Periodicals will be listed first with an indication as to whether the reference is to a simple announcement (an) or to a review (rv). Periodicals consulted for performance announcements (perf an) will also be noted. Bibliographies will be listed second. Sources will be listed chronologically by publication date within each of the two categories.

5. *Comments.* The comments section will contain discussions of the following: discrepancies and possible errors in source references; attribution of authorship for anonymous and pseudonymous works and unpublished plays; distinction between re-edition and re-issue; spurious material contained in the text; and specific problems concerning isolated cases.

Annotated listing

f. Note on library and source citations

Periodicals are referred to by either their full titles or their popular designations. An author's surname and, when necessary, a short title are used to refer to most manuscript and printed book sources. Libraries and a few sources are referred to by abbreviations. All such references – abbreviations, surnames, and short titles – are identified in the list of abbreviations and sigla at the head of the volume. In the case of frequently cited sources in which all bibliographical references to Loaisel's works are grouped together, precise locations of those references within a source are given below and are not specified when that source is cited under individual entries in the listing.

Arnault, xii (1823).63
BL, *Cat*, cxl.437
BN, *Cat*, xcix.48-50
Bousquet, pp.412-13
Cioranescu, *Bibl*, ii.1134-35
Cohen, 6th ed, cols 647-48
Cohen, 5th ed, col.335
Cohen, 4th ed, col.281
Cohen, 3rd ed, col.267
Desessarts, *Dict*, p.260
Desessarts, *Siècles litts*, iv(An IX).169-70
Didier, p.326
Ersch, *Fr lit*, ii.281-82
Ersch, suppl, p.292
Ersch, sec suppl, pp.330-31

Fantin des Odoards, ii.168
Fromm, iv.185
Godenne, *Nouvelle*, p.288
Grieder, *Trans*, p.103
Hoefer, xxxi(1860).414-15
Levot, ii(1857).349-50
Lewine, p.320
Michaud, xxiv(1819).594-95
Morabito, pp.XI-XV
NUC, cccxxxvii.326-27
Quérard, *Fr litt*, v(1833).328-29
Rabbe, iii.318-19
Sabin, xxvi(1935).25
Saulnays, pp.17-20
Worp, ii(1908).444

2

Novels

~~~~~~~

Ainsi finissent les grandes passions; ou les dernières amours du Chevalier de . . .

1. *Ainsi finissent*: 1781 edition (nonexistent)
'Ainsi finissent les grandes passions, ou les Dernières amours du chev. de . . . . , par Loaisel de Tréogate. Paris, 1781 [. . .] 2 vols in-12' (Gay, i.39).
Source: Gay, i.39.
Comments: Gay's description applies to all editions he lists. Martin ('First listing, 1784-1788', p.128) suspects that this date might be a mistaken reference to the 1787 edition. This is almost surely the case, since Gay does not list the 1787 edition at all. In addition, the text of the 1787 edition of *Ainsi finissent* contains several reprints of publications or manuscript works, three of which can be dated as having appeared after 1781: the funeral oration of the duc d'Orleans by abbé Fauchet, dating from 1785 (i.110-13); the story 'La Folle de Saint-Joseph', which appeared in manuscript and published form in mid-1786 and perhaps as early as 1785 (ii.55-65; see comments to no. 35 below); and a description of the Tour de Vincennes taken from a 'nouvelle description des environs de Paris', which mentions the opening of the prison by the baron de Breteuil in 1784 (ii, note on pp.224-30). This internal evidence plus the lack of any other reference to a 1781 edition make it practically certain that no such edition ever existed.

2. *Ainsi finissent*: 1787 original edition
AINSI FINISSENT / LES GRANDES PASSIONS; / OU / LES DERNIÈRES AMOURS / DU CHEVALIER DE . . . . / Publiées par M. LOAISEL DE TRÉOGATE. / [*double full rule*] / PREMIÈRE PARTIE. / [*double full rule*] / [*ornament* (8×30 mm)] / A PARIS, / Chez POINÇOT, Libraire, rue de la Harpe, / près Saint-Côme, No. 135. / [*double half rule*] / 1787.

2 vols. 12°. pp.[1-4]5-14[15]16-240; [1-5]6-247.

Contents: Vol. i. [advertisement:] 'On trouve chez le même Libraire [...]', 2; 'Préface de l'éditeur', 5-14; 'Ainsi finissent [...]', 15-240. Vol. ii. 'Ainsi finissent '[...]', 5-247.

Library location: Liège‡ (photocopy of title page and microfilm of entire text examined).

Source: MMF, no.87.54 bis.

Comments: The BN 1788 copy actually represents a re-issue of this 1787 original edition (see no.3). As stated in the comments to no.1, *Ainsi finissent* contains several reprints of publications and manuscript works. The following remark in the 'Préface de l'éditeur' serves as a blanket acknowledgement for this borrowed material appearing in the text: 'On trouvera dans ces Lettres quelques citations de morceaux connus, et assez étrangers aux amours du Chevalier de . . . . ; ils étoient dans le recueil: je les y ai laissés, parce qu'il m'ont paru intéressans' (i.12). Specific sources are never cited, however. See no.35 for a discussion of the publication history of one of these 'morceaux connus', the story 'La Folle de Saint-Joseph' reprinted in letter 45 of *Ainsi finissent*.

3. *Ainsi finissent:* 1788-re-issue of original edition
AINSI FINISSENT / LES GRANDES PASSIONS; / OU / LES DERNIÈRES AMOURS / DU CHEVALIER DE . . . . / Publiées par M. LOAISEL DE TRÉOGATE. / [*double full rule*] / PREMIÈRE PARTIE. / [*double full rule*] / [*ornament* (17×28 mm)] / A PARIS, / Chez POINÇOT, Libraire, rue de la Harpe, / près Saint-Côme, No.135 / [*double half rule*] / 1788. / AVEC APPROBATION ET PERMIS SION.

2 vols. 12°. pp.[1-4]5-14[15]16-240; [1-5]6-247.

Contents: Vol.i. [advertisement:] 'On trouve chez le même Libraire [...]', 2; 'Préface de l'éditeur', 5-14; 'Ainsi finissent [...]', 15-240. Vol.ii. 'Ainsi finissent [...]', 5-247.

Library locations: BN‡; Bibliothèque du Château d'Oron, Oron-le-Châtel, Vaud, Suisse (listed as examined in MMF); NNC (copy lost); MH† (microfilm of BN copy).

Sources: *Journal général de France*, 12 avril 1788, p.178 (rv); *Journal de Paris*, 10 mai 1788, p.574 (an); *Année littéraire*, 1788, ii.217-28 (rv); *Almanach littéraire ou étrennes d'Apollon*, 1789, pp.200-201 (rv). Desessarts, *Siècles litts*; Fantin Des Odoards; Delcro, no.174; Quérard,

Fr. litt; Marc, p.183; Levot; Hoefer; Gay, i.39; Mornet ed., *Nouvelle Héloïse*, i.369; Saulnays; Barroux; Versini, p.663; Cioranescu, *Bibl*; Bousquet; Morabito; Y. Giraud, p.88; MMF, no. 87.54 bis.

Comments: The BN 1788 copy was printed from the same type-setting as the Liège 1787 copy except for some alterations to the title page. Examination of the BN copy revealed that the title page was not a cancellans. There is no way to determine positively just how much of the title page was reset, but this much is certain: the date was changed to 1788; the notation 'Avec Approbation et Permission' was added at the bottom of the page; the ornament was changed. Other minuscule differences in spacing or irregularities in type could have been just as much a result of wear as of resetting. The BN 1788 copy definitely shows more signs of type wear throughout than the Liège 1787 copy, so that the dates appear to reflect accurately the order of printing. The passage of time evident from the change in imprint date, maintenance of the same type-setting as the Liège copy, and the three changes to the title page which go beyond efforts to correct errors or to perfect copy constitute the necessary criteria to classify the BN copy as a re-issue of the original edition. Strictly speaking, there should also be evidence that the 1787 copies actually went on sale before the 1788 copies. Such evidence does not exist. In fact, the earliest mention of *Ainsi finissent* is a review that appeared on 12 April 1788. However, the absence of the mention 'Avec Approbation et Permission' on the title page of the Liège copy is most significant in this regard. Clandestine or unauthorised publication was fully in keeping with the practice of the editor Poinçot (see Darnton pp.227-28). He would certainly not be liable to advertise such publications in the French press. The absence of a publication announcement for the 1787 copies was in all probability intentional and should not be allowed to outweigh the change in imprint date and other evidence qualifying this copy as a genuine re-issue. The alternative designation as an original edition with variant title page simply would not adequately take into account this change in imprint date.

4. *Ainsi finissent*: 1789 re-edition (confirmed existence)
'Ainsi finissent les grandes passions, ou les Derniers [*sic*] amours du chevalier de... P., Poinçot, 1789. 2 parties in-12 de 124 et 127 pp. [...]' (Slatkine, no.2086).
Sources: Ersch, *Fr lit*; Michaud; Pigoreau, p.242; Rabbe; Gay, i.39; Slatkine, no.2086; Y. Giraud, p.88; MMF, no.87.54 bis.

Comments: The Slatkine reference, coming from a very recent book-seller's catalogue (1968) testifies to the edition's existence. It is the first source to give pagination. Slatkine is the source for the MMF entry (details concerning this reference were provided by professor Vivienne Mylne). Giraud cites no source but gives the same pagination as Slatkine. Ersch, Michaud, Pigoreau, and Rabbe list *only* a 1789 edition.

An VIII rewritten version as *Valrose*: see no.43.

La Comtesse d'Alibre, ou
le cri du sentiment

5. *La Comtesse d'Alibre*: 1778 edition (nonexistent)
'Comtesse d'Aligre [*sic*] ou le Cri du sentiment, 1778. in-8°' (Michaud).
Sources: Michaud; Delcro, no.2005; Rabbe; Saulnays.
Comments: The 1778 date is an error as the following note in the *An* II reedition (no.9) confirms: 'Cette anecdote a été imprimée et a paru, pour la première fois, en 1779' (p.13). Michaud, whom Delcro cites as a source, is evidently the originator of the error. Rabbe's use of Michaud has already been mentioned as has Saulnay's habit of compiling all references indiscriminately. Michaud is undoubtedly referring to the 1779 edition (no.6), which he fails to mention.

6. *La Comtesse d'Alibre*: 1779 original edition
LA COMTESSE / D'ALIBRE, / OU / LE CRI DU SENTIMENT, / ANECDOTE FRANÇOISE. / Par M. LOAISEL DE TREOGATE. / [*double ornamental full rule*] / La nature frémit, l'humanité pleure, & la raison se taît. / [*double ornamental full rule*] / [*ornament (39×43 mm)*] / A LA HAYE, / Et se trouve à PARIS, / Chez BELIN, Libraire, rue Saint-Jacques, / vis-à-vis celle du Plâtre. / [*double three-quarter rule*] / M. DCC. LXXIX.

8°. pp.[i-iv]v-xii[1]2-146.

Contents: [Preface], v-xii; 'La Comtesse d'Alibre [. . .],' 1-146.
Library locations: BN†; Ars†; ICU‡; MH† (microfilm of BN copy).
Sources: *Journal de Paris*, 11 septembre 1779, p.1034 (an); *Catalogue hebdomadaire*, 18 septembre 1779, article 14 (an); *Annonces, affiches et avis divers* (8°), 9 novembre 1779, pp.2500-501 (rv); *Mercure de France*,

26 février 1780, pp.175-79 (rv); *Journal encyclopédique*, 1er mars 1780, pp.285-90 (rv); *Journal de Paris*, 31 mars 1780, pp.373-74; *Almanach littéraire ou étrennes d'Apollon* (1781), p.165 (rv). Laporte, *Nouv suppl*, i.254 and ii.26; Nyon, *Cat La Vallière*, iii.108; Ersch, *Fr lit*; Desessarts, *Siècles litts*; Marc, p.183; Quérard, *Fr litt*; Levot; Hoefer; Gay, i.645; Mornet ed., *Nouvelle Héloïse*, i.369; Saulnays; Monglond, *Fr rév*, iii(1933). 160-61; Barroux; Cioranescu, *Bibl*; Bousquet; Morabito; Didier; Y. Giraud, p.74; MMF, no.79.22.

Comments: A mistaken subtitle 'ou les Loix des Sentiments' seems to have originated with Ersch and been picked up by Quérard. Quérard then adds another mistake, which he could have picked up from Michaud (see no.5), by misspelling 'Alibre' as 'Aligre'. These two errors are repeated successively by Levot, Hoefer, and Saulnays. Giraud gives 'histoire' for 'anecdote', but this term never appears in any edition nor in any other source. The bound copy in the BN reserve (Rés Y^2 1600) is engraved on both covers with the 'armes de Marie Anotinette' according to a handwritten note on the first leaf. No copy of the 1779 edition contained a frontispiece, nor were there any references to one. The frontispiece of the *An* II re-edition (no. 9) is evidently original with that re-edition.

7. *La Comtesse d'Alibre*: 1779 re-edition (doubtful existence)
'La Comtesse d'Alibre, La Haye-Paris, 1779 (1779)' (Mornet ed., *Nouvelle Héloïse*, i.369).
Sources: Mornet ed., *Nouvelle Héloïse*, i.369; MMF, no.79.22.
Comments: The MMF entry is based on Mornet. Mornet's description indicates by the date enclosed in parentheses a re-edition in 1779. According to his own criteria, he had to have located at least three similar descriptions of the entry before listing it (p.336, n.1). Of the sources he lists, Quérard, Barbier, and the catalogues of the BN and Ars provide no evidence of a second edition in 1779. However, the Ars catalogue (Ars, *BL*) lists one of its copies of *La Comtesse d'Alibre* as published in Paris only and the other as published in La Haye only. Each of these copies actually carries both places in the imprint, the title pages being identical to the one described above (no.6). Mornet could have taken these catalogue descriptions for two separate editions. His only other acknowledged sources – the catalogues of private libraries listed in his article 'Les enseignements des bibliothèques privées' (pp.492-96) – may possibly contain the answer, but this seems

doubtful. The only catalogue listed that was published late enough to carry the *Comtesse d'Alibre* is that of La Vallière, which was consulted for the present study and shows no indication of a second edition. The only remaining possibilities are the ten catalogues listed by Mornet as 'sans date' (p.496). The lack of any independent confirming evidence combined with the strong possibility that Mornet misinterpreted the Ars catalogue make the existence of this edition highly doubtful.

8. *La Comtesse d'Alibre*: 1781 English translation (unconfirmed existence)
'Trad. en angl. par Ed. Mante. London 1781' (Desessarts, *Siècles litts*).
Sources: Desessarts, *Siècles litts*; Ersch, suppl; Hoefer; Saulnays; Barroux.
Comments: Ersch's entry need not necessarily be based on Desessarts, since Ersch provides references to other translations not listed by Desessarts, indicating that he had additional sources. References in later sources are undoubtedly based on these two earlier ones. This translation is not mentioned by Block, Séguin, nor Grieder. No review or announcement could be found in either the *Monthly review* or *Gentleman's magazine*. Although definite confirmation is lacking, there is strong reason to suspect the actual existence of this translation, especially in view of the possibility that the two contemporary source references are independent of one another.

9. *La Comtesse d'Alibre*: *An* II, 214 pp. re-edition as *Lucile et Milcourt*
LUCILE / ET / MILCOURT, / OU / LE CRI DU SENTIMENT; / ANECDOTE. / Par LOAISEL DE TREOGATE. / [*full rule*] / La nature frémit, l'humanité pleure, / et la raison se taît. / [*full rule*] / [*ornament* (6×14 mm)] / A PARIS, / Chez LEPRIEUR, Libraire, rue de / Savoie, no. 12. / [*half rule*] / L'an second de la République.
frontispiece, unsigned.

18°. pp.[i-iv]v-xii[13]14-214.

Contents: [Preface], v-xii; 'Lucile et Milcourt [. . .]', 13-214.
Textual revisions: Some minor revisions, additions, and omissions.
Library locations: BN‡; NNC†; MH† (microfilm of BN copy).
Sources: *Journal de Paris*, 18 août 1794 (1er fructidor an II), p.2402 (an). Ersch, *Fr lit*; Desessarts, *Siècles litts*; Marc, p.183; Michaud; Pigoreau; p.242; Delcro, no. 5440; Quérard, *Fr litt*; Rabbe; Levot;

Hoefer; Saulnays; Monglond, *Fr rév*, iii(1933).160-61; Barroux; Cioranescu, *Bibl*; Bousquet; Morabito; MMF, no.79.22.

Comments: The frontispiece is new with this re-edition, there having been none in the 1779 original edition (no.6). Ersch's error in the title – 'Louise' for 'Lucile' – is repeated by Michaud, Quérard, Rabbe, Levot, and Saulnays, as is his description of format as 12°. Ersch could have based his format description on the *Journal de Paris*, which lists only 'petit format'. Since he makes no mention of the 18° edition, he is almost certainly referring to this edition and has made an error in the format. There is no other independent evidence for a 12° edition. The afore-mentioned sources which repeated his error in title obviously copied that much from him or each other and undoubtedly did the same for the 12° format description. Delcro, who also gives 12°, takes his information from Michaud, whom he cites. Monglond's 12° description is his own error, since it is based on a personal examination of the BN copy des-cribed above (see also nos 19 and 41).

10. *La Comtesse d'Alibre*: *An* II, 198 pp. re-edition as *Lucile et Milcourt* LUCILE / ET / MILCOURT, / OU / LE CRI DU SENTIMENT; / ANECDOTE. / Par LOAISEL DE TREOGATE. / [*full rule*] / La nature frémit, l'humanité pleure, / ET LA RAISON SE TAIT. / [*full rule*] / [*ornament* (2×6 mm)] / A PARIS, / Chez LEPRIEUR, Libraire, rue / de Savoie, n.o [*sic*] 12. / [*quarter rule*] / L'an second de la Ré publique.
frontispiece, unsigned, identical to frontispiece of *An* II, 214 pp. re-edition.

18°. pp.[i-iv]v-xii[13]14-198.

Contents: [Preface], v-xii; 'Lucile et Milcourt [. . .]', 13-198.
Textual revisions: Same text as *An* II, 214 pp. re-edition (no.9) except for modernisation of imperfect tense endings.
Library locations: None (personal collection of this writer‡).
Sources: Desessarts, *Siècles litts*; Hoefer; Saulnays.
Comments: Since the modernised spellings of the imperfect tense endings are used in the *An* x re-edition (no.11), this 198 page *An* II re-edition is certainly the later of the two *An* II re-editions. This copy was obtained from professor Vivienne Mylne, who had just purchased it herself but too late to enter it in MMF. The remark 'plusieurs éditions sous le titre de Lucile et Milcourt' appears in Desessarts, who is probably the source

for similar remarks in Hoefer and Saulnays. Since Desessarts's volume containing the reference to Loaisel appeared in *An* IX, thus before the *An* X re-edition, it suggests the possibility of additional re-editions after this second *An* II re-edition. See, however, comments to no.11.

11.   *La Comtesse d'Alibre*: *An* X re-edition as *Lucile et Milcourt*
LUCILE / ET / MILCOURT, / OU / LE CRI DU SENTIMENT; / PAR LOAISEL DE TRÉOGATE. / Quatrième Édition. / [*three-quarter rule*] / La nature frémit, l'humanité pleure, / ET LA RAISON SE TAIT. / [*three-quarter rule*] / [*ornament*; page is mutilated in area of ornament] / A PARIS, / Chez LE PRIEUR, Libraire, rue / S. Jacques, No.278. / [*half rule*] / AN X.
frontispiece, unsigned: mirror image of frontispiece in *An* II re-editions with some very slight modifications.
18°. pp.[1-2]3-4[5]6-198.
Contents: [Preface], 3-4; 'Lucile et Milcourt [. . .]', 5-198.
Textual revisions: Text identical to that of *An* II, 198 pp. re-edition (no.10) except preface has been reduced.
Library locations: MiU‡ (photocopy of entire book examined).
Sources: Hoefer; Saulnays; MMF, no.79.22.
Comments: The title page description 'Quatrième Édition' probably counts in 1779 original edition (no.6) as the first, since that edition is mentioned in a note on page 5. This would then indicate that all intervening re-editions are now located.

*Dolbreuse, ou l'homme du siècle, ramené à la vérité
par le sentiment et par la raison*

12.   *Dolbreuse*: 1777 edition (nonexistent)
'Dolbreuse, ou l'homme du siècle. A Paris, Berlin [*sic*], 1777. In-8.
[. . .] 1 frontispiece non signé' (Cohen, 6th ed).
Sources: Cohen, 3rd-6th eds; Lewine; Saulnays; Barroux; Bousquet; Didier.
Comments: All later sources drew upon Cohen or each other for this entry. Unfortunately they never sought to question its accuracy. Barroux repeats 'P. Berlin', which appears in Cohen, 4th-6th eds. However, this is an error that crept into Cohen with the 4th ed., since the 3rd ed. plainly

gives 'Belin', the publisher for the 1783, 1785, and 1786 editions of *Dolbreuse*. Thus, there was never an edition published in Berlin or by a publisher named Berlin. The date 1777 is found in Cohen 3rd ed. This date is erroneous as proved by two items of external evidence: first, the *An* II re-edition states 'Ce roman fut imprimé et parut pour la première fois, en l'année 1783' (i.13); second, Cioranescu (*Bibl*) notes that a *permission tacite* was obtained 16 August 1782. Two historical references in the 1783 and *An* II texts could not have appeared in a 1777 edition: first, a long episode concerning a pilgrimage to Ermenonville following the death of Rousseau, which occurred in 1778; second, a note (ii.84, 1783 edition) quoting an article published in the *Journal de Paris* dated 7 décembre 1781, which date and quotation have been verified as authentic. It is not possible to determine what date the Cohen entry actually refers to, but from the unsigned frontispiece notation, it would seem that the edition in question was one of the re-editions of 1785 or 1786, both of which contain unsigned frontispieces. The copy examined could well have had both volumes bound in one, as is the case with all the 8º editions examined for the present study, and the same careless examination that failed to reveal the frontispiece of volume ii could have misread the date. Whatever the case, a 1777 edition never existed.

13. *Dolbreuse*: 1783 original edition
DOLBREUSE, / OU / L'HOMME DU SIECLE, / Ramené à la Vérité par le Sentiment / & par la Raison. / [*double full rule*] / HIS TOIRE PHILOSOPHIQUE. / [*double full rule*] / Par M. LOAISEL DE TRÉOGATE. / [*half rule*] / Nous ne vivons que deux momens; / Qu'il en soit un pour la sagesse. / VOLTAIRE / [*half rule*] / PREMIERE PARTIE. / [*ornament* (6×15 mm)] / A AMSTERDAM; / Et se trouve A PARIS, / Chez BÉLIN, Libraire, rue Saint-Jacques, près / Saint Yves. / [*double three-quarter rule*] / M. DCC. LXXXIII.
2 frontispieces: Vol. i, signed 'De Lorge Peintre de L'empereur Inv. L. S. Berthet Sculp.'; Vol. ii, signed identically.

2 vols. 8º. pp.[i-iv]v-xii[1]2-182; [1]2-190.

Contents: Vol. i. 'Préface', v-xii; 'Dolbreuse [...]', 1-182. Vol. ii. 'Dolbreuse [...]', 1-190.
Library locations: BN†; Ars†; SteG; FU‡; NNC†; ICN; MH† (microfilm of BN copy).

Sources: *Journal du Paris*, 21 mars 1783, p.338 (an); *Journal de la librairie*, 29 mars 1783, article 8 (an); *Affiches, annonces et avis divers* (4°), 30 juillet 1783, pp.122-23 (rv); *Bibliothèque universelle des romans*, août 1783, pp.181-216 (rv and condensed version); *Journal de Paris*, 11 octobre 1783, pp.1171-72 (rv); *Journal encyclopédique*, 1783, vii, 2e partie, pp.279-86 (rv); *Mercure de France*, 1er novembre 1783, pp.13-24 (rv); *Année littéraire*, 1783, vii.270-80 (rv); *Journal de littérature, des sciences et des arts*, 1783, iv.244-59 (rv); *Journal de Monsieur*, 1783, vi.26-56 (rv); *Almanach littéraire ou étrennes d'Apollon*, 1785, p.136 (rv). Laporte, *Nouv suppl*, i.254 and ii.123; Ersch, *Fr lit*; Desessarts, *Siècles litts*; Fantin Des Odoards; Marc, p.183; Michaud; Pigoreau, p.242; Delcro, no.2684; Quérard, *Fr litt*; Rabbe; Levot; Hoefer; Cohen, 3rd-6th eds; Lewine; Mornet ed., *Nouvelle Héloïse*, i.369; Saulnays; Barroux; Cioranescu' *Bibl*; Bousquet; Morabito; MMF, no.83.33.
Comments: Cohen 3rd and 4th eds. carry a note that *Dolbreuse* also exists in a 2 vol. 18° edition 'sous la même date', but in the 5th and 6th eds, this reference to date has been eliminated, thus correcting the entry. The error might originally have arisen from misinterpreting the vague Pigoreau entry, which reads '1 vol. in-8, puis 2 vol. in-18'. Pigoreau knows full well the correct date of the 18° edition since he lists it for sale in his catalogue (p.40, no.414). Cioranescu notes that a *permission tacite* was obtained on 16 August 1782.

14.   *Dolbreuse*: 1783 condensed version
'Dolbreuse ou l'homme du siècle', *Bibliothèque universelle des romans*, août 1783, pp.181-216 (in section entitled 'Romans d'amour').
Library location: CtY‡ (other locations not researched).
Source: Saulnays, p.21.
Comments: The nature of the condensation is discussed above (p.79).

15.   *Dolbreuse*: 1785 re-edition
DOLBREUSE / OU / L'HOMME DU SIECLE, / Ramené à la Vérité par le Sentiment / & par la Raison. / [*double full rule*] / HISTOIRE PHILOSOPHIQUE. / [*double full rule*] / PAR M. LOAISEL DE TRÉOGATE. / [*three-quarter rule*] / Nous ne vivons que deux momens; / Qu'il en soit un pour sagesse. [*sic*] / VOLTAIRE. / [*three-quarter rule*] / PREMIERE PARTIE. / [*ornament* (26×27 mm)] / A PARIS, / Chez BÉLIN, Libraire, rue Saint-Jacques, près / Saint Yves. / [*double three-quarter rule*] / M. DCC. LXXXV.

2 frontispieces, both unsigned, identical to those in 1783 edition.

2 vols. 8°. pp.[i-iii]iv-viii[1]2-120; [1-3]4-128.

Contents: Vol. i. 'Préface', iii-viii; 'Dolbreuse [. . .]', 1-120. Vol. ii. 'Dolbreuse [. . .]', 3-128.

Textual revisions: Text identical to that of 1783 original edition (no.13).

Library locations: CLU† (photocopy of entire work examined); OClW‡; NPV.

Sources: Saulnays; MMF, no.83.33.

Comments: Mornet notes this re-edition in *Sentiment de la nature* (p.511, no.714) but not in *Nouvelle Héloïse*.

16.   *Dolbreuse*: 1786 re-edition

DOLBREUSE, / OU / L'HOMME DU SIECLE, / Ramené à la Vérité par le Sentiment / & par la Raison. / [*double full rule*] / HISTOIRE PHILOSOPHIQUE. / [*double full rule*] / PAR M. LOAISEL DE TRÉOGATE. / [*three-quarter rule*] / Nous ne vivons que deux momens; / Qu'il en soit un pour la sagesse. / VOLTAIRE. / [*three-quarter rule*] / PREMIERE PARTIE. / [*ornament* (22×45 mm)] / A PARIS, / Chez BÉLIN, Libraire, rue Saint-Jacques, près / Saint Yves. / [*double three-quarter rule*] / M. DCC. LXXXVI.

2 frontispieces, both unsigned, identical to those in 1783 edition.

2 vols. 8°. pp.[i-iii]iv-viii[1]2-120; [1-3]4-128.

Contents: Vol. i. 'Préface', iii-viii; 'Dolbreuse [. . .]', 1-120. Vol. ii. 'Dolbreuse [. . .]', 3-128.

Textual revisions: Text identical to that of 1783 original edition (no.13).

Library locations: BUR‡; Arras, *Cat*; Bibliothèque cantonale et universitaire du canton du Vaud, Lausanne (listed in MMF).

Sources: Saulnays; Barroux; Bousquet; MMF, no.83.33.

Comments: Close comparison of the 1786 re-edition to the similar appearing 1785 re-edition (no.15) reveals that type for the entire book was reset. Variations in the title pages other than date are evident from the transcriptions. Variations in type spacing, word division, catchwords, and typographical errors appear throughout the texts of both volumes of the two editions. Thus the 1786 re-edition is a completely new printing and qualifies as an independent re-edition. Mornet notes this re-edition in *Sentiment de la nature* (p.511, no.714) but not in *Nouvelle Héloïse*.

17.   *Dolbreuse*: 1790 German translation (unconfirmed existence) 'Trad. en Alem. Gera. 1790. 2T. 8' (Ersch, *Fr lit*).

Source: Ersch, *Fr lit*.

Comments: Fromm does not list this translation. However, the confirmation of Ersch's listing of the 1777 German translation of *Valmore* (no.38) argues in favour of the accuracy of this listing.

18.   *Dolbreuse*: 1792 Lille and Paris re-edition (unconfirmed existence) 'N. Ed. Lille et P. 1792, 2 vol. 18' (Ersch, *Fr lit*).

Sources: Ersch, *Fr lit*; Michaud; Delcro, no.2684; Quérard, *Fr litt*; Rabbe; Levot; Saulnays; MMF, no.83.33.

Comments: Sources prior to Saulnays list only one date for this re-edition. Ersch is probably the original source for all subsequent entries up to MMF. One might be tempted to conclude that Ersch made an error in converting from Revolutionary to Gregorian calendar the imprint (or publication) date of the *An* II (i.e., *1793-1794*) re-edition (no.19) and that this error has been perpetuated by later sources which used his data. But were Ersch to intend this reference to apply to an *An* II re-edition, the fact that he lists Lille as a place of publication suggests another re-edition separate from all the others listed here. The existence of such a re-edition is a possibility that cannot be overlooked. Saulnays's reference 'Lille et Paris, 1792-93' is probably intended to include both the 1792 and the *An* II reeditions, since he has no other reference to the latter. MMF repeats the 1792-1793 date, which came from Saulnays.

19.   *Dolbreuse*: *An* II re-edition

DOLBREUSE, / OU / L'HOMME DU SIECLE, / Ramené à la Vérité par le Sentiment / et par la Raison. / [*double full rule*] / HISTOIRE PHILOSOPHIQUE. / [*double full rule*] / Par le C. LOAISEL TRÉO GATE. / [*three-quarter rule*] / Nous ne vivons que deux momens; / Qu'il en soit un pour la sagesse. / VOLTAIRE. / [*three-quarter rule*] / PREMIERE PARTIE. / A PARIS, / Chez LE PRIEUR, Libraire, rue de Savoie, / No 12. / [*half rule*] / L'an second de la Rép. Franç. une et indivisible

2 frontispieces, both unsigned: Vol. i, similar to Vol. i frontispiece, 1783 edition; Vol ii, slightly altered version of frontispiece, Vol. ii, 1783 edition.

2 vols. 18°. pp.[i-iii]iv-xii[13]14-209; [1]2-204.

Novels

Contents: Vol. i. 'Préface', iii-xii; 'Dolbreuse [. . .]', 13-209. Vol. ii. 'Dolbreuse [. . .]', 1-204.

Textual revisions: Numerous minor revisions, additions, and omissions.

Library location: BN‡ (Double 49389-49390; the principal copy had been at the bindery for three years and was assumed lost at the time this *double* was examined).

Sources: *Journal de Paris*, 18 août 1794 (1er fructidor an II), p.2402 (an). Dessessarts, *Siècles litts*; Pigoreau, p.40, no.414 and p.242; Cohen, 5th-6th eds; Lewine; Saulnays; Monglond, *Fr rév*, iii(1933).160; Barroux; Bousquet; Morabito; MMF, no.83.33.

Comments: Monglond's format description of 12° is in error (see also nos 9 and 41). Lewine and MMF give format as 16°, but there is no other evidence for such an edition. See comments to no.18 concerning Saulnays's entry.

20.   *Dolbreuse*, 1799 re-edition (doubtful existence)
Library locations: none.
Sources: Saulnays; MMF, no. 83.33.
Comments: The MMF entry is based on Saulnays. Saulnays lists a date of 1799, but it is unclear which if any of the other data go with it. Since none of the sources he lists confirms this reference, there is every reason to believe it is in error.

Le Fils naturel

(doubtful attribution)

21.   *Le Fils naturel*: 1789 anonymously published original edition (doubtful attribution)
LE FILS / NATUREL. / [*full rule*] / Attache quelqu'attention au sujet: au style, / si peu que rien. / MONTAIGNE. / [*full rule*] / TOME PREMIER. / [*double half rule*] / A GENÈVE; / Et se trouve A PARIS, / Chez BUISSON, Libraire, rue Haute- / Feuille, hôtel de Coëtlosquet, no 20. / [*half rule*] / 1789.

2 vols. 18°. pp.[i-v]vi[vii]viii[1]2-252; [1]2-268.

Contents: Vol. i. 'Avertissement', v-vi; 'Errata', vii-viii; 'Le Fils naturel', 1-252. Vol. ii. 'Le Fils naturel', 1-268.
Library locations: BN†; Ars‡.

Sources: *Mercure de France*, 18 juillet 1789, pp.127-32 (rv); *Journal de Paris*, 21 juin 1789, pp.771-72 (rv). Gay, ii.314; Lewine, p.187; Assézat-Tourneux, v.5, n.2 and xx.100; Monglond, *Fr rév*, i(1930).603-604; Grieder, *Trans*; MMF, no.89.12.

Comments: Neither of the contemporary reviews names the author. MMF lists the *Feuille de correspondance* review under this 1789 edition, whereas the reference in that periodical is actually to the 1790 re-edition (no.23). There is no evidence of any contemporary attribtion to Diderot prior to the *An* v and 1797 re-editions (nos 24-27). All sources other than the two periodicals mention the attribution to Diderot. With the exception of the periodicals and Gay, all sources, including the BN *Cat*, declare that attribution to be false. Whatever the motivation may have been, the attribution of the *An* v and subsequent re-editions of the novel to Diderot was probably influenced somehow by the similarity between the titles of this work and Diderot's *drame*. Grieder attributes the work to Loaisel citing Mornet as her source but without specifying any reference to Mornet's publications (p.31, n.41). None of Mornet's publications consulted during research for this listing was found to contain any such attribution. Grieder most probably intended to cite Monglond, who does indeed attribute the work to Loaisel (see no.23). MMF classifies the work under 'auteurs inconnus'. Gay states that the work appeared in 1789 also under the title *Jules et Sophie*, but there is no other evidence for this. In fact he describes *Jules et Sophie* under another entry as being published in 1797, which coincides with the known facts. The MMF entry of a 1789 *Jules et Sophie* is based on Gay. Grieder mentions a *Jules et Sophie* reedition but gives no date for it. Monglond incorrectly gives format as 12°, probably basing his description on the same error in the BN *Cat*. Lewine gives format as 16°, but there is no other evidence for such an edition. He could have based his description on the *Journal de Paris*, which gives only 'petit format'.

22.   *Le Fils naturel*: 1789 English translation of anonymous French edition (doubtful attribution; unconfirmed existence)
'Julius; or, the Natural Son: translated from the French. 12mo. 2 vols. 5s. Ridgway. 1789' (*Monthly review*, 2nd series (August 1790), ii.462).
Sources: *Monthly review*, 2nd series (August 1790), ii.462-63 (rv). Summers, p.379; Grieder, *Trans*.
Comments: The *Monthly review* and Summers give no author for the work. Grieder attributes the French original to Loaisel (see no.21).

23. *Le Fils naturel*: 1790 re-edition by Loaisel (doubtful attribution; confirmed existence)

' "Le Fils naturel, par l'auteur de Dolbreuse, ou l'homme du siècle". Paris, 1790, 2 vol. in-12' (Monglond, *Fr rév*, i(1930).603-604); 'Le Fils naturel, 2 vol de 250 pag. chacun. Paris, 1790' (*Feuille de correspondance*, 1791, no.1069).

Library locations: None (but see comments).

Sources: Feuille de correspondance, 1791, no.1069 (rv). Monglond, *Fr rév*, i(1930). 603-604; MMF, no.89.12.

Comments: The *Feuille de correspondance* gives no author. Monglond provides the original and only basis for attributing this work to Loaisel. His entire comment, appearing in his description of the 1789 edition, reads as follows: 'Le Cat de la B.N. le classe sous le nom de Diderot, en faisant observer que cette attribution est erronée. M. G. Charlier m'a communiqué une édition, également anonyme, dont voici le titre: "Le Fils naturel, par l'auteur de Dolbreuse, ou l'homme du siècle". Paris, 1790, 2 vol. in-12. D'où il appert que ce roman doit être restitué à Loaisel de Tréogate'. Monglond seems not to have connected the 1797 re-editions under new titles (nos 25 and 26) with the editions of 1789 (no.21) and 1790 under the title *Le Fils naturel*. He must have assumed that the BN *Cat* attribution of its lone copy of the work to Diderot was based on evidence surrounding that anonymous 1789 edition. He might have been less certain in deciding to attribute the work to Loaisel had he been aware of the later title pages bearing Diderot's name. From the point of view of strictly bibliographical evidence, the attribution to Diderot has the greater claim to authenticity since it appears on later re-editions. In view of presently known evidence, this attribution to Loaisel must be considered highly doubtful. The MMF entry is based on Monglond but classifies the work under 'auteurs inconnus'. Monglond's description of format as 12° is undoubtedly in error here as well as in the case of his description of the 1789 edition (no.21). He also errs in describing as 12° every one of the BN 18° re-editions of Loaisel's works, all of which he seems to have examined personally (nos 9, 19, and 41). This plus the additional fact that all other editions and re-editions of *Le Fils naturel* are in 18° format argue strongly against this copy's being different.

24. *Le Fils naturel*: *An* v re-edition as *Jules et Sophie*, by Diderot (doubtful attribution; confirmed existence)

'Jules et Sophie, ou le fils natural, par DIDEROT. – Paris, an V, 2 tom. en 1 vol. in-18' (Le Mans, *Cat*, no.3269); '142 et 146p. avec deux gravures' (Assézat-Tourneux, v.5, n.2).

Library location: Le Mans, *Cat*.

Sources: Pigoreau, p.182; Delcro, no.5006; Assézat-Tourneux, v.5, n.2; Monglond, *Fr rév*, iv(1935).270; Grieder, *Trans*; MMF, n.89.12.

Comments: MMF lists no other locations and gives a description similar to the above without indicating a firsthand examination. The Assézat-Tourneux description is based on a firsthand examination of a copy in a private collection. Pigoreau and Delcro (Delcro cites Pigoreau as his source) make no comment on the attribution to Diderot. Assézat-Tourneux and Monglond (Monglond cites Assézat-Tourneux as his source) declare the attribution false as does MMF (see also no.21). Monglond does not connect this edition with the earlier editions under the title *Le Fils naturel* and seems unaware of the Assézat-Tourneux note in a later volume (xx.100) connecting *Jules et Sophie* with *Le Fils naturel*. Grieder gives no date for the *Jules et Sophie* re-edition.

25.   *Le Fils naturel*: 1797 3 volume re-edition as *Jules et Sophie* (re-issue of 1797 3 volume re-edition as *Le Chartreux*?), by Diderot (doubtful attribution)

JULES / ET SOPHIE, / OU / LE FILS NATUREL. / PAR DIDE ROT. / [*full rule*] / Attache quelqu'attention au sujet: au style, / si peu que rien. / MONTAIGNE. / [*full rule*] / TOME PREMIER. / A PARIS, / Chez TRAINETELLE, Relieur, rue et mai- / son Sorbonne, no 302 / MARCHAND, Md. de livres, sur le / Pont-Neuf, près le quai des Au- / gustins. / [*half rule*] / 1797.

2 frontispieces, both unsigned (Vol. i and Vol. ii only).

3 vols. 18°. pp.[i-iii]iv[5]6-144; [1-3]4-144; [1-3]4-152.

Contents: Vol. i. 'Avertissement', i-iii;; 'Le Fils naturel', 5-144. Vol. ii. 'Le Fils naturel', 3-144. Vol. iii. 'Le Fils naturel', 3-152.

Library location: CtY‡.

Sources: Gay, ii.746; Lewine, p.187; Assézat-Tourneux, v.5, n.2; Monglond, *Fr. rév*, iv(1935).270; Grieder, *Trans*; MMF, no.89.12.

Comments: Gay's description coincides with the above except for format, which he gives as 12°. There was no confirmation for a 12° edition. In Assézat-Tourneux and Monglond (Monglond cites Assézat-Tourneux as his source), title, imprint date, number of volumes, and format all coincide with the description above, but they list '3 gravures' – a distinct possibility since the two frontispieces in the copy examined were both single leaf inserts making the loss of a third quite easy. See no.26 regarding the question of re-issue versus re-edition. All sources except Gay point out that the attribution to Diderot is false (see also no.21). As with the *An* v re-edition (no.24), Monglond does not connect this re-edition with the earlier editions. Grieder gives no date for the *Jules et Sophie* re-edition.

26.   *Le Fils naturel*: 1797 3 volume re-edition as *Le Chartreux* (re-issue of 1797 3 volume re-edition as *Jules et Sophie?*), by Diderot (doubtful attribution; unconfirmed existence)

'Diderot. Le Chartreux, ou le Fils naturel. A Paris, 1797. 3 vol. in-18. 3 figures non signées' (Cohen, 6th ed, col. 305).

Sources: Cohen, 5th ed, col. 158 and 6th ed, col. 305; Lewine, p.146; Assézat-Tourneux, v.5, n.2 and xx.100; Monglond, *Fr rév*, iv(1935).270; MMF, no.89.12.

Comments: Cohen's and Lewine's entries are identical, and again Monglond cites Assézat-Tourneux. The MMF entry is based on Cohen. According to Assézat-Tourneux, the copies bearing the title *Le Chartreux* are merely re-issues of the 1797 *Jules et Sophie* re-edition (no.25). In the absence of an extant copy, there is insufficient information concerning order of publication and other essential criteria needed to distinguish between re-issue and re-edition, so this problem must remain unsolved for the moment. Cohen probably served as source of all subsequent references to *Le Chartreux*, but there is the possibility that the Assézat-Tourneux note is based on additional information. Cohen's description of the frontispiece as 'unsigned' seems to give evidence of firsthand knowledge. All sources note the attribution to Diderot and, with the exception of Cohen and Lewine, declare that attribution false (see also no.21). As with the *An* v re-edition (no.24), Monglond does not connect this re-edition with earlier editions.

27.   *Le Fils naturel*: 1799 English translation of French edition by Diderot (doubtful attribution; unconfirmed existence)

'The Natural Son; A Novel. Translated from the French of M. Diderot, Author of the Nun, James the Fatalist, & c. 12 mo. 2 vols. 7s. Boards. Longman. 1799' (*Monthly review*, 2nd series (September 1799), xxx.39).

Sources: *Monthly review*, 2nd series (September 1799), xxx.39-42 (rv).
Summers, p.441; Grieder, *Trans*.

Comments: Summers also gives Diderot as author but lists the imprint
date as 1798. Grieder attributes the French original to Loaisel (see
no.21).

Florello

28.   *Florello*: 1775 edition (nonexistent)
'Florello, histoire méridionale ou anecdote orientale. Paris, Moutard
1775 (?) in-8vo fig.' (Saulnays).
Sources: Saulnays; MMF, no.76.32.
Comments: MMF notes Saulnays's reference but gives no entry for this
edition. Saulnays's entry is part of a combined listing of all editions of
Florello. He does not explain the question mark after the date. No other
references were found to a 1775 edition. The following note to the *An* III
re-edition (no.41) rules out any printing for public distribution prior
to 1776: 'Cette nouvelle [*Valmore*] et la suivante [*Florello*], premiers
ouvrages de l'auteur, parurent pour la première fois en l'année 1776'
(p.5).

29.   *Florello*: 1776 original edition
FLORELLO, / HISTOIRE MERIDIONALE. / Par M. LOAISEL
DE TREOGATE, / ci-devant Gendarme du Roi. / [*double ornamental
full rule*] / Rura mihi & rigui placeant in vallibus amnes, / Flumina
amem Sylvasque inglorius. / VIRG. / [*double ornamental full rule*] /
PREMIERE PARTIE. / [*ornament* (44×56 mm)] / A PARIS, / Chez
MOUTARD, Libraire de la Reine, / rue du Hurepoix. / [*double ornamental three-quarter rule*] / M. DCC. LXXVI.
frontispiece, signed 'F. M. Quéverdo inv. L. L. Grand Sculp.'

8°. pp.[1*-3*]4*-16*[1]2-36[37-39]40-92.

Contents: 'Lettre à M. Coll.', 3*-16*; 'Florello, histoire méridionale',
1-36; 'Florello, histoire méridionale. Seconde Partie', 37-92 (title page,
p.37; text begins, p.39).

Library locations: Ars† (4 copies; G. D. 2097 (1)‡); BL *Cat*; Universitätsbibliothek Leipzig (Krauss and Fontius, no.4538).

Sources: *Catalogue hebdomadaire*, 1er juin 1776, article 3 (an); *Affiches,
annonces et avis divers* (4°), 5 juin 1776, p.90 (rv); *Journal des sciences*

et des beaux-arts, 15 juin 1776, pp.539-42 (rv); *Journal encyclopédique*, 1er juillet 1776, p.158 (rv); *Mercure de France*, juillet 1776, premier volume, pp.103-106 (rv); *Année littéraire*, 1777, i.288 (an); *Journal des sçavans*, août 1777, p.575 (an). Laporte, *Suppl.* ii.81; Nyon, *Cat La Vallière*, iii.156; Ersch, *Fr lit*; Desessarts, *Siècles litts*; Fantin Des Odoards; Marc, p.183; Michaud; Arnault; Delcro, no.3562; Quérard, *Fr litt*; Rabbe; Levot; Hoefer; Mornet ed, *Nouvelle Héloïse*, i.369; Saulnays; Dufrenoy, ii.213, 324; Barroux; Cioranescu, *Bibl*; Godenne, *Nouvelle*; Bousquet; Morabito; MMF, no.76.32.

Comments: The description in the BL *Cat* is so confusing, that a query was sent to resolve the matter. Their copy is indeed identical to the edition described here. It was bound together with three other totally unrelated contemporary novels, including one story from Baculard d'Arnaud's *Epreuves du sentiment*. The catalogue listing attempts to describe the entire bound volume and is inaccurate on several points. Barroux probably was misled by the BL *Cat* entry in formulating his description of *Florello*, which reads 'Florello, histoire méridionale P.1776 (t. IV des *Epreuves du sentiment*, P.1772-81, par Baculard d'Arnaud)'. Ersch gives format as 12°, but there is no other evidence for such an edition. He also describes the work as in 2 volumes, evidently taking the 2 'parties' as separate volumes, which they are not. Several later sources repeat the same error.

30. *Florello*: 1780 German translation (unconfirmed existence)
'Trad. en Allem. Ib. [Breslau] 1780. 8' (Ersch, *Fr lit*).
Source: Ersch, *Fr lit*.
Comments: Fromm does not list this translation, but since Ersch's reference to the German translation of *Valmore*, also published in Breslau and in the same format, has been confirmed, there is every reason to believe that this reference to a German translation of *Florello* is accurate as well.

Florello: An III re-edition combined with *Valmore*: see nos 40-42.

31. *Florello*: An III separate re-edition (nonexistent)
'Réimprimé in-18 en l'an III (1795)' (Desessarts, *Siècles litts*).
Sources: Desessarts, *Siècles litts*; Michaud; Rabbe; Hoefer.
Comments: Desessarts's reference to a re-edition of *Florello* is separate from his listing of an undated, 18° re-edition of *Valmore* (see no.39).

But since he does not mention the combined *An* III re-edition (no.41) as such, the separate references to *Valmore* and *Florello* probably apply to that combined re-edition. Hoefer's references are based on Desessarts, and Rabbe's are based on Michaud. Michaud gives no data other than date (1795) and could be referring either to the combined re-edition or to separate re-editions of *Valmore* and of *Florello*. As with *Valmore*, there is no convincing evidence of any separate re-edition of *Florello*.

Florello: 1802 Russian translation: see no.42.

Héloïse et Abeilard, ou les victimes de l'amour
(confirmed existence)

32. *Héloïse et Abeilard*: 1803 original edition (confirmed existence)
'Heloïse et Abeilard, ou les Victimes de l'Amour, Roman historique, galant et moral; par J. M. Loaisel Tréogate, auteur de Valrose, ou les Orages de l'amour, etc.' (*Journal typographique et bibliographique*, 20 mai 1803 [30 floréal an XI], p.254). 'Paris, Barba, 1803. 3 vol. in-12. fig.' (*Lefilleul*, mars 1877, p.20). '1 plate after Huot by Noël' (Lewine).
Sources: *Bibliothèque française*, mars 1803 (ventôse an XI), p.208 (an); *Journal de Paris*, 11 mai 1803 (21 floréal an XI), p.1483 (an); *Journal typographique et bibliographique*, 20 mai 1803 (30 floréal an XI), p.254 (an); *Nouvelle bibliothèque des romans*, Ve année, xii.196 (an). Ersch, *Fr lit*; Marc, p.183; Michaud; Pigoreau, p.242; Arnault; Delcro, no.3924; Quérard, *Fr litt*; Rabbe; Levot; Hoefer; *Lefilleul*, mars 1877, p.20; Gay, ii.460; Lewine; Cohen, 6th ed; Thieme-Becker, xviii(1925). 162, article 'Huot, François'; Saulnays; Monglond, *Fr rév.* vi(1949).363; Barroux; Cioranescu, *Bibl*; Bousquet; Morabito.
Comments: The listing in *Lefilleul* confirms the existence of this work although no extant copies have been located. The description of the title taken from the *Journal typographique* is probably the most accurate of any, since the description it gave of *Valrose* in another issue (see no.43) was a verbatim transcition. The *Lefilleul* description coincides but is less complete. There is full agreement among all sources on place of publication and publisher. *Lefilleul* lists the imprint date in the Gregorian calendar only. The accuracy of *Lefilleul* as regards imprint dates is evident in the instance of *Valrose*, for which Gay cites a *Lefilleul* description giving the true imprint date of *An* VIII. However, Lewine

gives 'An xi. (1803)' for the date of *Héloïse et Abeilard*. So also does Cohen, but his source is undoubtedly Lewine, since they both give precisely the same information and since Cohen lacked any entry for *Héloïse et Abeilard* in the editions preceding publication of Lewine. Lewine also lists the artist and engraver for the plate, thus making it seem he had examined the actual book or at least had the record of a visual examination, since no other source contains information regarding the plate. Thus, there is no agreement on what the actual imprint date might be. Thieme-Becker lists *Héloïse et Abeilard* among the books for which François Huot designed engravings. The source of this information was undoubtedly Lewine through Cohen, since Cohen is the only one of Thieme-Becker's listed sources which mentions *Héloïse et Abeilard*. Noël is tentatively identified by Thieme-Becker as C. F. Noël. An attempt was made to track down further information on this work through sources treating these illustrators but to no avail. In fact among the works on illustrators and illustrated books listed below under 'Sources consulted', no further mention at all was found of *Héloïse et Abeilard*. Gay cites as source 'Catal. de Dresde, No 795'. The BN has no such catalogue in its collections either of bookseller catalogues (Q 10) or of library sale catalogues (delta). Krauss and Fontius do not list the work thus discounting the theory that Gay's reference was to the catalogue of the Dresden Library (Sachsische Landesbibliothek). This work's erotic content, which *Lefilleul* suggests in the short descriptive comment 'Roman galant, très-curieux', may have had an influence on its disappearance, as could also have been the case with *Valrose*. The *Journal de Paris* curiously and suggestively misprints the title as '[. . .] roman historique, *érotique* & moral [. . .]'.

Lucile et Milcourt

See nos 9-11.

Soirées de mélancolie

(confirmed attribution)

33. *Soirées de mélancolie*: 1777 anonymously published original edition (confirmed attribution)

SOIRÉES / DE / MÉLANCOLIE. / PAR M. L***. / [*three-quarter rule*] / …Est quaedam flere voluptas. / OVIDE. Elégie. / [*three-quarter rule*] / [ornament (31 × 45 mm)] / A AMSTERDAM, / Chez ARKSTÉE ET MERKUS, Libraires. / [*double half rule*] / M. DCC. LXXVII.

8°. pp.[i]ii-xiv[xv-xvi][1]2-160.

Contents: [Advertisement], facing title page; 'Avertissement', i-xiv; 'Table des Articles', xv; 'Errata', xvi; 'La Vision', 1-12; 'L'Innocence protégée du Ciel', 13-32; 'Le Remords', 33-44; 'Nisa', 45-56; 'Les Regrets', 57-66; 'Le Crime puni', 67-74; 'Le Songe', 75-94; 'L'Empire de la Beauté', 95-130; 'Le Vieux Laboureur', 131-143; 'A Ma Julie', 144-150; 'Le Port', 151-157; 'Au Lecteur', 158-160.

Library locations: Ars† (3 copies, catalogued under 'Tréogate' in Ars, *BL*; 8° B. L. 22591‡); Troyes, *Cat*.

Sources: *Année littéraire*, 1777, i.288 (an); *Journal des sciences et des beaux-arts*, 1er mars 1777, pp.452-53 (rv); *Journal encyclopédique*, 15 avril 1777, pp.350-51 (rv); *Catalogue hebdomadaire*, 10 mai 1777, article 17 (an); *Journal de Paris*, 26 mai 1777, p.1 (an); *Journal de Paris*, 8 juin 1777, p.1 (rv); *Mercure de France*, août 1777, pp.96-100 (rv); *Affiches, annonces et avis divers* (4°), 15 octobre 1777, p.166 (rv); *Almanach littéraire ou étrennes d'Apollon*, 1778, p.129 (rv). Laporte, *Suppl*, i.134 and ii.196; Nyon, *Cat La Vallière*, iii.288; Desessarts, *Siècles litts* and *Dict*; Fantin Des Odoards; Delcro, no.8344; Quérard, *Fr litt*; Rabbe; Quérard, *Fr litt*, xi(1854).257; Levot; Hoefer; Weller, ii.204; Barbier, iv.512e; Mornet ed., *Nouvelle Héloïse*, i.367; Saulnays; Barroux; Cioranescu, *Bibl*; Bousquet; Morabito; Didier; MMF, no.77.47.

Comments: There is no doubt concerning the attribution of this work to Loaisel. Facing the title page is an advertisement for *Valmore* and *Florello* described as being 'du même auteur'. The 'Avertissement' mentions *Valmore* and *Florello* by name (pp.i and xii) with the clear implication that these two works are by the author of the *Soirées de mélancolie*. A statement in the section 'Au lecteur' settles the matter clearly: 'J'ai mieux soigné mon style que je n'avois fait dans Valmore & Florello' (p.158). An advertisement on p.31 of *Aux âmes sensibles* (1780), published under the name 'M. de Tréogate', carries the *Soirées de mélancolie* among the other works 'du même auteur'. Both the *Année littéraire* and the *Journal encyclopédique* give Loaisel as author. According to the title page, the book was published in Amsterdam by Arkstée et Merkus. Weller lists this edition as carrying a false place of publication in the imprint and gives Paris as the true place. The actual existence of the publisher Arkstée et Merkus was long held in doubt. It was listed by Gustave Brunet as an 'imprimeur imaginaire' or a 'libraire supposé'.[19] However, J.-P. Belin later discovered a piece of correspondence from Arkstée et Merkus addressed to Malesherbes, dated 1758 and thus established its actual existence.[20] Based on present knowledge then, one must conclude that place of publication and publisher were indeed those printed on the title page. Most of the bibliographies and reference works cited above which list place of publication give 'Amsterdam (Paris)'. *La Valliére* gives 'Paris, Moutard' as place and publisher. Although the sereferences would seem to suggest the possibility of another 1777 edition, there are very logical explanations for their referring all to the Amsterdam, Arkstée et Merkus edition. Many of these sources are based on announcements and reviews in periodicals. All references in periodicals except the *Année littéraire* carry the notation 'A Amsterdam', and all except the earlier one in the *Journal de Paris* indicate further that the book was also *for sale* 'A Paris, chez Moutard'. Since announcements in periodicals were much more concerned with indicating distribution outlets than with giving publication data strictly speaking, the references to Moutard certainly need not refer to the imprint and probably are intended to indicate no more than the location where the book could be purchased in Paris. On the other hand, if the bibliographies and reference works in question based their references on actual examination of copies of the *Soirées*, they could easily have chosen to cite in addition to – or, in the case of La Vallière, in place of – the actual imprint, the advertisement of *Valmore* and *Florello* facing the title page. The advertisement begins, 'On trouve chez Moutard, Libraire-Imprimeur de la Reine [...]'. With imprecision of distinction between booksellers and publishers being so common and widespread, there is indeed no firm evidence here to suspect that there ever existed another 1777 edition.

34. *Soirées de mélancolie*: 1778 edition (nonexistent)
'Les Soirées de mélancolie. Amsterdam et P.1778. 8' (Ersch, *Fr lit*).
Source: Ersch, *Fr lit*.

[19] *Imprimeurs imaginaires et libraires supposés* (Paris 1866), pp.19-20.
[20] *Le Commerce des livres prohibés à Paris de 1750 à 1789* (Paris 1913; reprint, New York), p.50.

Comments: Since Ersch does not list any other editions of the *Soirées de mélancolie*, he is undoubtedly referring here to the original 1777 edition (no.33). There are no other references to support a 1778 edition.

35. *Soirées de mélancolie*: *An* III anonymously published re-edition (confirmed attribution; spurious additions)
SOIRÉES / DE / MÉLANCOLIE / Nouvelle Edition, avec gravures. / [*full rule*] / TOME PREMIER. / [*full rule*] / A PARIS, / Chez LOUIS, Libraire, rue / Severin, No. 29. / [*three-quarter rule*] / L'an III.
2 frontispieces: Vol. i, signed 'Flotte Inv. et del. Carrée Sculp.'; Vol. ii, signed 'Le Barbier, Pic. Reg. del C. S. Gaucher dir.'

2 vols. 18°. pp.[1]2-186[187-188]; [1]2-154[155-156]1**-6** [Note: the first page of each *conte* is unnumbered; this has not been indicated in the pagination formula.]

Contents: Vol. i. 'La Vision', 1-21; 'L'Innocence protégée', 22-56; 'Les Regrets', 57-72; 'Azoline', 73-107; 'La Mélancolie', 108-114; 'Les Albigeoises', 115-124; 'Laure et Gauvin', 125-145; 'Le Remords', 146-166; 'Nisa', 167-186; 'Table', 187. Vol. ii. 'Le Songe', 1-35; 'L'Empire de la Beauté', 35-98; 'Le Vieux Laboureur', 99-122; 'A Ma Julie', 123-134; 'Le Port', 135-145; 'La Folle de St.-Joseph', 146-154; 'Table', 155; 'Catalogue de livres en petit format qu'on trouve chez Louis [. . .]', 1**-6**.
Textual revisions: Loaisel's text is practically identical to the 1777 original edition (no.33). Spurious additions are discussed below.
Library location: CtY‡.
Sources: *Mercure français*, 30 décembre 1794 (10 nivôse an III), pp.226-28. Desessarts, *Siècles litts*; Marc, p.183; Hoefer; Saulnays; Monglond, *Fr rév*, iii(1933).161; Barroux; Bousquet; MMF, no.77.47.
Comments: The *Mercure* does not identify Loaisel as the author of this edition, but does speak of the work as if it were a re-edition. It also gives format incorrectly as 16°, which is repeated by Monglond, citing the *Mercure* review as his source. The catalogue contained in the back of *Valmore et Florello* (no. 41) lists the *Soirées de mélancolie* with Loaisel indicated as author (p.247). As is evident from the description of the contents, the *conte* 'Le Crime puni' has been omitted, and five new pieces added. The five new pieces, however, were not written by Loaisel. 'Azoline', 'La Mélancolie', 'Les Albigeoises', and 'Laure et Gauvin' were first published in 1791 in a volume entitled 'Azoline ou la

rose d'amour, nouvelle turque; suivi des Albigeoises. Avec figure & musique gravées. Par M. Mercier, Musque de M. Pollet'. The imprint reads 'A Chypre. Et A Paris, chez Pollet [. . .], 1791'. The Mercier in question is Calude-François-Xavier Mercier de Compiègne. All evidence supports his authorship of the four pieces contained in *Azoline*. A review of *Azoline* appearing in the *Almanach littéraire ou étrennes d'Apollon* of 1792 (p.231) confirms 1791 as the year of distribution (an excerpt appears in the same periodical, p.77). The texts of Mercier de Compiègne's four works as published in *Azoline* are identical to those published in the *An* III *Soirées de mélancolie*.[21] *Azoline* is listed in the catalogue published at the end of the *An* III *Soirées de mélancolie* (p.2**) proving that the bookseller Louis knew of Mercier de Compiègne's work. But there is no way to determine whether he was familiar with the content of *Azoline* or indeed whether it was he or Loaisel who was actually responsible for the addition of the pieces by Mercier de Compiégne to the new edition of the *Soirées de mélancolie*. 'La Folle de St.-Joseph' was published in letter 45 of *Ainsi finissent* (ii.56-64). The letter opens with the statement that it is enclosing 'une lettre qui a courru Paris manuscrite' and which had been sent to the Chevalier de . . . . This enclosed letter contains the short story 'La Folle de Saint-Joseph'. According to Barbier (ii.478) and Quérard, *Fr litt* (ii.348-49 and iii.455), 'La Folle de Saint-Joseph' is by the chevalier de Grave (Pierre Marie, marquis de Grave, 1755-1823) and was circulated and printed elsewhere besides in Loaisel's works. It appears in Grimm's *Correspondance littéraire* of June 1786 and in the *Année littéraire* of the same year.[22] It is also contained in a collection of tales about 'fous' and 'folles' entitled *Les Folies sentimentales, ou l'égarement de l'esprit par le cœur* (Paris: Royez, 1786; 2 copies at Ars – 8° B. L. 20311, 8° B. L. 20312). This volume was awarded a *permission tacite* on 19 July 1786 (see Cioranescu, *Bibl*, no.21976, an entry on 'La Folle par amour' of Cubières-Palmezeaux, one of the stories included in the volume) and was reviewed as early as 26 October 1786 (*Journal général de France*, p.512). The tale next turns up in *Nouvelles folies sentimentales, ou folies*

21 a microfilm of *Azoline* was obtained from the Bibliothèque municipale de Reims, the location having been furnished by the authors of MMF. This is the only copy so far located of *Azoline* of of its three re-editions, published between 1792 and 1795 under the title *Les Trois nouvelles*. The NjP and PU copies of the 4th edition, listed in the *NUC*, are both missing. See also Quérard, *Fr litt*, vi.62 and 64.

22 Friedrich Melchior Grimm *et al*, *Correspondance littéraire, philosophique et critique*, ed. Maurice Tourneux (Paris 1877-1882); xiv.385-88. *Année littéraire* (1786), v.280-86. Both references were found in Etienne, p.343, n.4.

par amour (Paris: Royez, 1786; copies at BN – Y² 8552, Ars– 8º B. L. 20313, and BL) as one of two tales from the first volume which were being reprinted, according to the editor, because of typographical errors in the first edition. These two volumes of 'folies' were published as part of the *Bibliothèque choisie de contes, de facéties et de bons mots* (copies in BN and BL) but also seem to have appeared separately. The bibliographical details are too complicated to discuss here. Grimm identifies the author as 'M. Le Chevalier de Grave', and the *Folies sentimentales* carry 'M. le ch de G.' on the title page, but the other publications do not name the author. Loaisel's text differs from all the afore-mentioned but is definitely closer to the *Folies* and *Nouvelles folies* than to either Grimm or the *Année littéraire*. No information was found concerning earlier printed or manuscript editions. But there is good reason to believe that Loaisel did indeed obtain the story from a manuscript, as he claims in the voice of Le Chevalier de . . . at the beginning of letter 45. At the end of the text on the last page of volume ii of *Ainsi finissent* appears the following statement, presumably by the publisher Poinçot: 'Il y a plus de deux ans que ce Recueil est rédigé et livré au Libraire qui en a fait l'acquisition; on croit devoir en prévenir les Lecteurs' (ii.247). If true, this statement places the latest possible date for completion of composition of *Ainsi finissent* in late 1785, thus prior to any of the known published versions of 'La Folle de Saint-Joseph'. The statement of Le Chevalier de . . . in letter 45 concerning the source of the story and the general announcement in the 'Préface de l'éditeur' concerning the inclusion of 'citations de morceaux connus' in the letters provide ample acknowledgement for this borrowed material to remove any possible grounds for a charge of plagiarism (see no. 2 for further discussion of this matter). In the case of the *An* iii re-edition of the *Soirées de mélancolie*, since the work was published anonymously, no direct claim was made that Loaisel was the author of either 'La Folle de St.-Joseph' or of the pieces by Mercier de Compiègne, even though the implication is there in the title. Strictly speaking this is not a case of plagiarism either. The frontispieces are new with this re-edition, there having been none in the original edition.

Valmore

36.   *Valmore*: 1775 edition (doubtful existence)
'Valmore, anecdote françoise, Paris 1775 in-8vo' (Ars, *BL*).

Library location: Ars, *BL* (copy missing).
Sources: Saulnays; MMF, no.76.33.
Comments: MMF notes Saulnays's reference but gives no entry for this edition. Saulnays probably bases his listing on the Ars catalogue entry, which plainly shows one copy of an edition dated 1775 and assigned a call number. This copy was not present, however, when the inventory was conducted to assign new call numbers. The two copies dated 1776 (see following entry) were both present at that time and no additional copies were found. As was the case with *Florello*, the note to the *An* III re-edition rules out a printing for public distribution before 1776 (see no. 28). In view of this fact and since there is no confirmation of a 1775 edition from an independent source, it seems most likely that the entry of a 1775 date was an error made during the original cataloguing of the Ars collection entry of a 1775 and that, therefore, the existence of this edition is highly doubtful.

37. *Valmore*: 1776 original edition
VALMORE, / ANECDOTE FRANÇOISE. / Par M. LOAISEL DE TREOGATE, / Gendarme du Roi. / [*double ornamentel full rule*] / Funera quos manent beati! OVID. / [*double ornamental full rule*] / [*ornament (57×50 mm)*] / A PARIS, / Chez MOUTARD, Libraire de la Reine, / rue du Hurepoix. / [*double ornamental three-quarter rule*] / M. DCC. LXXVI.
frontispiece, signed 'F. M. Quéverdo inv. L. L. Grand Scul.'

8°. pp.[1-5]6-96.

Contents: 'Valmore, anecdote françoise', 5-96.
Library locations: Ars†; BL, *Cat*; Universitätsbibliothek Leipzig (Krauss and Fontius, no. 4539); ICU‡.
Sources: *Catalogue hebdomadaire*, 13 avril 1776, article 12 (an); *Journal des sciences et des beaux-arts*, 1er mai 1776, pp.277-79 (rv); *Journal encyclopédique*, 1er juillet 1776, p.158 (rv); *Journal des sçavans*, juillet 1776, p.510 (an); *Mercure de France*, janvier 1777, premier volume, pp.97-99 (rv); *Almanach littéraire ou étrennes d'Apollon*, 1777, p.210 (rv); *Année littéraire*, 1777, i.288 (an). Laporte, *Suppl* i.134 and ii.217; Nyon, *Cat La Vallière*, iii.116; Ersch, *Fr lit*; Desessarts, *Siècles litts*; Michaud; Arnault; Delcro, no. 8907; Quérard, *Fr litt*; Rabbe; Levot; Hoefer; Cohen, 3rd-6th eds; Lewine; Mornet ed., *Nouvelle Héloïse*,

i.367; Saulnays; Barroux; Cioranescu, *Bibl*; Godenne, *Nouvelle*; Bousquet; Morabito; MMF, no.76.33.

38.   *Valmore*: 1777 German translation (confirmed existence)
'Valmore, eine französische geschichte. Von Loaisel v Tréogate. Übers. v. Johann Gottlieb Valkelt. – Breslau: Gutsch 1777' (Fromm).
Library location: Niedersächsischen Staats-und Universitätsbibliothek Göttingen. Sign.: 8° Fab.Rom. V, 460 (location furnished by Deutsche Staatsbibliothek in East Berlin).
Sources: Ersch, *Fr lit*; Fromm; Barroux.

Valmore: *An* III re-edition combined with *Florello*: see nos 40-42.

39.   *Valmore*: *An* III separate re-edition (nonexistent)
'1795 in-12mo fig. in-18mo fig.' (Saulnays).
Sources: Desessarts, *Siècles litts*; Michaud; Rabbe; Saulnays.
Comments: Desessarts's reference to an undated, 18° re-redition of *Valmore* 'avec fig.' is separate from his listing of a dated re-edition of *Florello* (see no.31). But since he does not mention the combined *An* III re-edition (no.41) as such, the separate references to *Valmore* and *Florello* probably apply to that combined re-edition. Rabbe's entry is based on Michaud, who gives no data other than date (1795) and could be referring either to the combined re-edition or to separate re-editions of *Valmore* and *Florello*. Saulnays does not indicate his sources for the 12° format, which does not appear in any of the other sources listed above, but he most probably took this item from some descriptions of the combined *An* III re-edition. As with *Florello*, there is no convincing evidence of any separate re-edition of *Valmore*.

Valmore: 1802 Russian translation: see no.42.

Valmore et Florello

40.   *Valmore et Florello*: 1776 edition (nonexistent)
'Valmor [*sic*] et Florello (1776), 1 vol. in-18' (Pigoreau, p.242).
Source: Pigoreau, p.242.
Comments: Pigoreau lists no other editions of either *Valmore* or *Florello*. He is probably indicating the original date of publication while other-

wise describing the *An* III re-edition (no. 41). Since there is no confirmation of such an edition, it may be reasonably concluded that Pigoreau's description is inaccurate.

41.   *Valmore et Florello*: *An* III original combined edition
VALMORE / ET / FLORELLO. / NOUVELLES. / PAR LOAISEL-TRÉOGATE. / [*ornament* (6×14 mm)] / A PARIS, / Chez LEPRIE UR, Libraire, rue de / Savoie, no. 12. / [*full rule*] / L'An troisième de la République française, / une et indivisible.
frontispiece, unsigned, similar to that of *Valmore*, 1776 original edition.

18°. pp.[1-5]6-239[240-241]242-248.

Contents: 'Valmore, nouvelle française', 5-128; 'Florello, nouvelle américaine', 129-239; 'Catalogue des livres en petits formats in-18. Qui se trouvent chez Leprieur [...]', 241-248.
Textual revisions: Both texts contain numerous minor revisions, additions, and omissions.
Library locations: BN‡; Universitätsbibliotek Leipzig (Krauss and Fontius, no. 4565); NNC† MH† (microfilm of BN copy).
Sources: Ersch, *Fr lit*; Michaud; Quérard, *Fr litt*; Rabbe; Saulnays; Monglond, *Fr rév*, iii(1933).444; Dufrenoy, ii.233, 324; Barroux; Godenne, *Nouvelle*; Cioranescu, *Bibl*; Bousquet; Morabito; MMF, nos 76.32, 76.33.
Comments: Ersch's description of format as 12° is repeated by Quérard and Saulnays. He is almost certainly referring to this 18° edition and has made an error in format since he makes no other mention of this edition. There is no other independent evidence for a 12° edition. Saulnays and Quérard most probably got their 12° format description from Ersch, as they did with the *Lucile et Milcourt An* II re-edition of *La Comtesse d'Alibre* (no.9). Monglond's 12° description is his own error, since he based it on a personal examination of the BN copy described above (see nos 9 and 19). For the possibility that references to separate re-editions of *Valmore* and *Florello* actually apply to this combined re-edition, see nos 31 and 39.

42.   *Valmore et Florello*: 1802 Russian translation (unconfirmed existence)
'Moscou, 1802, in-12mo' (Michaud).
Sources: Michaud; Arnault; Rabbe.

Comments: As with the *An* III French edition (no.41), Michaud may be referring either to a separate translation of *Valmore* or to a combined *Valmore et Florello* translation. Since Arnault and Rabbe are based on Michaud, there is no other independent evidence for this edition.

Valrose, ou les orages de l'amour

43. *Valrose*: *An* VIII original edition
VALROSE, / OU / LES ORAGES DE L'AMOUR. / PAR J. M. LOAISEL TRÉOGATE, / Auteur de DOLBREUSE, de LUCILE / et MILCOURT, etc. etc. / TOME PREMIER. / [*half rule*] / A PARIS, Chez LE PRIEUR, Libraire, rue Saint- / Jacques, N.o [*sic*] 278, à côté de l'hôtel de Lyon. / [*half wavy line*] / AN VIII.
2 frontispieces: Vol. i, signed 'Binet del. Bovinet Sculp.'; Vol. ii, signed identically.

2 vols. 12°. pp.[i-v]vi-xiv[xv]xvi-xxii[23]24-228; [1-5] 6-226.

Contents: Vol. i. 'Avis de l'Éditeur', v-xiv; 'Préface de l'Auteur', xv-xxii; 'Valrose, ou les orages de l'amour', 23-228; Vol. ii. 'Valrose, ou les orages de l'amour', 5-226.
Library location: Leningrad‡ (microfilm copy examined).
Sources: *Journal typographique et bibliographique*, 21 mars 1800 (30 ventôse an VIII), p.189 (an); *Journal général de la littérature de France*, germinal an VIII, p.111 (an); *Décade philosophique*, 30 avril 1800 (10 floréal an VII), p.247 (an); *Bibliothèque française*, mai 1800 (floréal an VIII), p.12 (an); *Journal de Paris*, 15 août 1800 (27 thermidor an VIII), p.1617 (an). Desessarts, *Siècles litts*; Ersch, *Fr lit*; Marc, p.183; Michaud; Pigoreau, p.242; Arnault; Delcro, no.8909; Quérard, *Fr litt*; Rabbe; Levot; Hoefer; Cohen, 3rd-6th eds; Gay, iii.1300; Lewine; Saulnays; Monglond, *Fr rév*, iv(1935).1126 and v(1937).345; Barroux; Cioranescu, *Bibl*; Bousquet; Morabito; Didier; MMF, no.00.103.
Comments: The Leningrad copy location was furnished by professor Richard Frautschi. *Valrose* is a completely rewritten version of *Ainsi finissent* with such extensive changes, omissions, and additions that it should be considered a separate work (the general nature of the revisions is discussed above, pp.92-93). Cioranescu's listing of the imprint date as 'an VII (1799)' undoubtedly comes from his own conversion of a Gregorian calendar date given in his source. Monglond's first entry is

under 1799 and cites Quérard, Delcro, and Pigoreau as his sources. His second entry lists *Valrose* as an anonymous work, his source being the *Décade* announcement of 10 floréal an VIII (he erroneously cites the issue of 10 prairial an VIII in which there is no mention of *Valrose*), which itself omits any mention of authorship, although the full title is given confirming that it is indeed Loaisel's work. Gay correctly identifies Binet as the artist of the frontispieces, taking his description from a Lefilleul catalogue of 1878. Cohen states that the frontispieces are unsigned, an error repeated by Lewine. No explanation other than error can account for Didier's listing 1779 as the publication date.

3

Plays

~~~

Adélaïde de Bavière

Performances (total: 19)

2 juillet 1801 (13 messidor an IX) – 1er octobre 1801 (9 vendémiaire an x): Théâtre de l'Ambigu-Comique: 19 performances.
Sources: *Courrier des spectacles* (perf an). *Courrier des spectacles*, no.1586 (3 juillet 1801 [14 messidor an IX]), p.2 (rv); *Portefeuille français*, 1802, p.247 (rv); *Almanach des spectacles de Paris, pour l'an 1809*, p.179 (an); *Annuaire dramatique, ou étrennes théâtrales*, 1813, pp.235-36 (an). Babault, ii.380; Goizet, *Dict*, p.28; Douay, *Rép Paris*, ix, année 1801, f.17v; Duval, iv.6; Wicks and Schwietzer, i.1; Barroux; Bousquet.
Comments: Goizet, Douay, and Duval all indicate 'musique de Darondeau', a detail they could well have taken from the review in the *Courrier des spectacles* (where, however, the name is spelled 'Darando'). The *Annuaire dramatique* carries this play as being in the repertoire of the Ambigu-Comique until 1813, but no performances were announced in the *Courrier des spectacles* or later in the *Journal de l'Empire* after the ones noted above.

44. *Adélaïde de Bavière*: *An* IX (1801) original edition
ADÉLAÏDE DE BAVIÈRE, / DRAME / EN QUATRE ACTES, EN PROSE, / A SPECTACLE. / Représenté, pour la première fois, sur le théâtre de l'Ambigu- / Comique, le 13 messidor an IX. / PAR J. -M. LOAISEL TRÉOGATE. / [*quarter rule*] / A PARIS. / SE VEND AU THÉÂTRE. / [*double quarter rule*] / AN IX. – 1801.

8°. 43 pp.
Library locations: Ars†; BL, *Cat*; CtY‡; IaU.
Sources: Ersch, *sec suppl*; Delandine, p.38; Quérard, *Fr litt*; Lacroix, *Bibl Soleinne*, no.3451; Levot; Goizet, *Dict*, p.28; Tourneux, iii(1900),

no.18827; Duval, iv.6; Monglond, *Fr rév*, v(1937).757-58; Saulnays; Barroux; Cioranescu, *Bibl*; Bousquet; Morabito.

Comments: Quérard, Levot, Duval, and Saulnays all give Barba as the publisher. No such indication was found in any of the copies examined. It is entirely possible that Quérard got his data from an advertisement which named Barba as the bookseller. Levot and Saulnays undoubtedly got this information from Quérard, and so probably did Duval. Goizet gives 45 pages, but no such copy was found or described elsewhere.

45. *Adélaïde de Bavière*: 1801 Dutch translation
ADELAIDE VAN BEIJEREN, / TOONEELSPEL. / IN VIER BEDRIJVEN. / NAAR HET FRANSCHE / VAN / J. M. LOAISEL TREOGATE.
frontispiece, signed 'R. Vinkeles, inv et sculp.'
In *Spectatoriaale schouwburg, behelzende eene verzameling der beste zedelijke tooneelstukken, bij een gebraqt uit alle de verscheiden taalen van europa*, xxviii.145-210. Amsterdam 1801.

8°.

Library locations: BL, *Cat*; CtY‡; NN; IaU; (additional locations not researched).
Sources: Worp; Barroux.

Les Amans siciliens, ou les apparences trompeuses
(unpublished?; confirmed attribution)

Performances (total: 1)

19 janvier 1799 (30 nivôse an VII): Théâtre des Amis des Arts, et des Élèves de l'Opéra-Comique, ci-devant Molière, rue Martin: 1 performance
'Les Amans siciliens, ou les apparences trompeuses' (*Journal des théâtres, de littérature et des arts*, no.53 (21 janvier 1799 [2 pluviôse an VII]), p.210); 'Comédie en deux acts et en prose' (*Courrier des spectacles*, no.698 (20 janvier 1799 [1er pluviôse an VII]), p.2).
Sources: *Courrier des spectacles* (perf an); *Journal des théâtres, de littérature et des arts* (perf an). *Courrier des spectacles*, no.698 (20 janvier 1799 (1er pluviôse an VII), p.2 (rv); *Journal des théâtres, de littérature*

et des arts, no.53 (21 janvier 1799 [2 pluviôse an VII]), p.210 (rv); *Mercure de France*, 29 janvier 1799 (10 pluviôse an VII), p.60 (rv); *Revue des théâtres*, an VIII, p.124 (an); *Almanach des spectacles* (an IX) xlv, 1ère partie, p.130 (an); *Annuaire dramatique, ou étrennes théâtrales*, 1813, p.236 (an). Rabbe; Levot; Goizet, *Dict*, p.90; 'fiche Lecomte'; Douay, *Rép Paris*, viii, année 1799, f.21; Duval, ii.31; Saulnays.

Comments: None of the reviews either analyses the play or names the author. They all agree that the play was a total 'chute' and drop their discussion of it at that. The *Almanach des spectacles* and the *Annuaire dramatique* both attribute the play to Loaisel, although the latter mistakenly lists the performances as having been at the Théâtre des Jeunes Artistes. Goizet, Douay, and Duval all accept Loaisel as author with the 'fiche Lecomte' giving only 'L.-T.' Arthur Pougin erroneously attributes this play to Chazel[22a] undoubtedly confusing it with a play by Chazel given the next day, 20 January, since that is the date he gives for the *Amans siciliens* (Douay lists the Chazel play on the same folio with the *Amans siciliens*). Overall, the evidence strongly suggests that the attribution to Loaisel is correct.

Les Amans siciliens: editions (unpublished?)
No editions were located, Goizet and the 'fiche Lecomte' both note that the play was not printed, which seems quite logical given the reception it received from the public and critics.

L'Amour arrange tout

(confirmed attribution)

Performances (total: 59)
22 juillet-4 novembre 1790: Théâtre des Beaujolais: 59 performances
Sources: *Affiches, annonces et avis divers ou journal général de France* (8°) (perf an). *Almanach des spectacles* (an IX) xlv, 1ère partie, p.130 (an). Desessarts, *Siècles litts*; Rabbe; Goizet, *Dict.*, p.106; Douay, *Rép Paris*, vii, année 1788, f.5; Duval, ii.38; Barroux; Bousquet.
Comments: Rabbe's date of 1789, repeated by Saulnays, has no meaning either as date of first performance or of publication. There was a sort of 'reprise' in April 1789, after a cessation of performances since 8

[22a] 'Le théâtre révolutionnaire en 1791: le Théâtre Molière', *Bulletin de la société de l'histoire du théâtre* (1903), 2e année, no. 6, p.20.

December 1788, but the date 1789 has no other significance for this work. Douay gives 'Juin 20, 1788' for the date of the first performance, but the daily theatre announcements in the *Affiches, Annonces* and the date given on the title page of the printed play confirm 22 July 1788 as the correct date.

46. *L'Amour arrange tout*: 1788 anonymously published original edition (confirmed attribution)
L'AMOUR / ARRANGE TOUT, / COMÉDIE / EN UN ACTE ET EN PROSE, / Représentée, pour la première fois, à Paris, le 22 / Juillet 1788, sur le Théâtre de Monseigneur / LE COMTE DE BEAUJOLOIS, au / Palais Royal. / [*three-quarter rule*] / Prix 1 liv. 4 sols. / [*three-quarter rule*] / [*ornament* (15×15 mm)] / A PARIS, / Chez CAILLEAU, Imprimeur-Libraire, / rue Gallande, No.64. / [*double three-quarter rule*] / 1788.

8°. 35 pp.
Library locations: BN‡; Ars†; BL† (microfilm copy examined).
Sources: *Affiches, annonces et avis divers ou journal général de France* (8°), 14 octobre 1788, supplément, p.2872 (an). Quérard, *Fr litt*; Lacroix, *Bibl Soleinne*, no.3425; Levot; Hoefer; Goizet, *Dict*, p.106; Barbier, i.139a; Duval, ii.38; Saulnays; Brenner, p.128; Barroux; Cioranescu, *Bibl*; Bousquet; Morabito.
Comments: There is no evidence regarding authorship in the printed edition. However, all sources cited above for both performances (except the daily performance announcements in the *Affiches, Annonces*) and the edition attribute the work to Loaisel. In addition, the review of *Lucile et Dercourt* in the *Almanach général de tous les spectacles de Paris et des provinces*, 1791 (p.85) names Loaisel as author of both that work and *L'Amour arrange tout*. The agreement among the three contemporary sources – the *Almanach général*, the *Almanach des spectacles*, and Desessarts – is quite adequate justification for considering the attribution to Loaisel correct.

Belzors

(unpublished?; doubtful attribution)

Performances (total: 9)
7 janvier 1801 (17 nivôse an IX) – 11 février 1801 (22 pluviôse an IX):

Théâtre des Jeunes-Élèves, rue de Thionville: 9 performances
'Belzors, com. en 3 a. et en pr.' (Goizet, *Dict*, p.311).

Sources: *Courrier des spectacles* (perf an). Goizet, *Dict*, p.311; 'fiche Lecomte'; Douay, *Rép Paris*, ix, année 1801, f.22; Wicks and Schweitzer, i.9.

Comments: The *Courrier des spectacles* gives no review of this play nor does it identify the author. The other sources cited above attribute the play to Loaisel except Duval, who gives no author. The Wicks and Schweitzer attribution appears only with the index to volume iii and not on the page where the play is listed. The lack of any information on authorship from a contemporary source leaves the attribution of this play in considerable doubt.

Belzors: editions (unpublished?)
No editions were located. Goizet and the 'fiche Lecomte' both note that the play was not published.

La Bisarrerie de la fortune, ou le jeune philosophe

Performances (total: 52)

16 avril 1793 – 5 juillet 1793: Théâtre du Marais (also performed at the Théâtre de la rue Feydeau by the actors of the Marais): 23 performances
Sources: *Affiches, announces et avis divers ou journal général de France* (8°) (perf an). *Affiches, annonces et avis divers ou journal général de France* (8°), 18 avril 1793, supplément, pp.1654-55 (rv); *Chronique de Paris*, 19 avril 1793, p.4 (rv); *Mercure français*, 25 mai 1793, pp.154-55 (rv); *Spectacles de Paris et de toute la France* (1794) xliii, 1ère partie, p.271 (rv); *Almanach des muses*, 1794, p.229 (an); *Annuaire dramatique, ou étrennes théâtrales*, 1813, p.235 (an). Desessarts, *Siècles litts*; Babault, ii.380 and v.55-57; Goizet, *Dict*, p.329; Douay, *Rép Paris*, viii, année 1793, f.28; Duval, ii.106; Saulnays; Barroux; Bousquet.

Comments: The title is given in the sources as *La (Les) Bisarrerie(s)* or *La (Les) Bizarrerie(s)*. All printed editions give only *La Bisarrerie*.

22 juillet 1794 (4 thermidor an II) – 16 août 1794 (29 thermidor an II): Théâtre de la République: 9 performances
Sources: *Journal de Paris* (perf an); *Journal des théâtres et des fêtes nationales* (perf an); *Affiches, annonces et avis divers ou journal général de France* (8°) (perf an). *Décade philosophique*, 7 août 1794 (20 thermidor

an II), pp.99-104 (rv); *Journal des théâtres et des fêtes nationales*, no.1 (18 août 1794 [1er fructidor an II]), p.7 (an), no.15 (1er septembre 1794 [15 fructidor an II]), pp.116-18 (rv), and no.21 (7 septembre 1794 [21 fructidor an II]), pp.164-67 (rv); *Almanach des spectacles* (an VIII) xliv.248 (an) and (an IX) xlv, 1ère partie, p.130 (an); Goizet, *Dict*, p.329; Douay, *Rép Paris*, viii, année 1794, f.3.

13 août 1796 (26 thermidor an IV) – 2 septembre 1796 (21 fructidor an IV): Théâtre de la rue Martin: 7 performances
Sources: Affiches, annonces et avis divers ou journal général de France (8°) (perf an).

2 mars 1800 (11 ventôse an VIII) – 18 mai 1800 (29 floréal an VIII: Théâtre de la Gaîté: 13 performances
Sources: Courrier des spectacles (perf an). *Courrier des spectacles*, no. 1094 (3 mars 1800 [12 ventôse an VIII]), p.2 (rv); *Almanach des muses*, 1801, p.350 (an); *Almanach des spectacles* (an IX) xlv, 2e partie, p.63 (an). Rabbe; Levot; Douay, *Rép Paris*, ix, année 1800, f.23; Monglond, *Fr rév*, iv(1935).1104.
Comments: Monglond mistakenly gives *An* VII and lists the play as anonymous, basing his reference on the anonymous announcement in the *Almanach des muses*.

26 janvier 1801 (6 pluviôse an IX) – 2 juin 1801 (13 prairial an IX): Théâtre de la Gaîté: 4 performances
Source: Courrier des spectacles (perf an).

20 septembre 1802 (3e jour complémentaire an X) – 29 novembre 1802 (8 frimaire an XI): Théâtre de la Cité (also performed at the Théâtre des Etrangers, ce-devant Marais by the actors of the Cité): 6 performances
Sources: Courrier des spectacles (perf an). *Courrier des spectacles*, no.2030 (27 septembre 1802 [5 vendémiaire an XI]), p.2 (rv).

47. *La Bisarrerie de la fortune*: 1784 edition (nonexistent)
Sources: Barroux; Bousquet.
Comments: Bousquet's reference is based on Barroux's inferring of a 1784 edition because of a suspected German translation in that year. The existence of a 1784 German translation (no.48) is highly doubtful, but there is no evidence whatsoever for a 1784 French edition.

48. *La Bisarrerie de la fortune*: 1784 German translation (doubtful existence)

'Der Glückwechsel oder der liebenswürdige Sonderling. – Tubingen: Cotta, 1784' (Fromm).

Library locations: None (see comments).

Sources: Fromm; Barroux.

Comments: In addition to searching all the libraries listed above under 'Sources consulted', a search request for all unlocated German translations listed by Fromm was sent to the Deutsche Staatsbibliothek in East Berlin. After a thorough inquiry on their part, they reported no locations for this translation in the libraries of either the German Democratic Republic or the Federal Republic of Germany. Barroux's reference to German translations evidently came from Fromm, since the two are identical. Fromm's source for this reference could not be determined, thus adding to the difficulty of solving the puzzle that it creates. For if the date of this reference is correct, the German version would be the first to have been published. This raises a further problem. Fromm's title makes no mention of a translator nor of Loaisel as author as do the other titles he lists. This German version may not, then, be by Loaisel and could be an entirely different play. Were it to be identical and not by Loaisel, then *La Bisarrerie* is a plagiarism. However, such a radical conclusion – and the consequences for the history of *La Bisarrerie* and for Loaisel's reputation – requires a good deal more justification than Fromm's lone reference. Indeed, it hinges on the accuracy of a single digit, the '8' in the '1784' date of publication. So one must also, and perhaps more logically, envision the possibilities of inaccuracies in Fromm's reference. As with his erroneous reference to the Augsburg translation – 1788 for 1794 (see no.52) – this date of 1784 could again be the date of the first volume of a multivolume collection in which the *Bisarrerie* translation had a later date. Or it could simply be an error, typographical or other. A date of 1794, for example, would fit into the publication history of *La Bisarrerie* as otherwise known. In fact, a 1794 date, also for a Tübingen translation, is listed by Ersch (see no.53). Since Ersch doesn't mention the publisher 'Cotta', it is evident that Fromm had additional or different sources. Even so, given the existing evidence, and until additional evidence to the contrary is discovered, one must tentatively opt for the most logical solution to the puzzle: Fromm's date must be in error and should read '1794'.

49. *La Bisarrerie de la fortune*: 1788 German translation (nonexistent) see no.52.

50.   *La Bisarrerie de la fortune*: 1793 original edition
LA BISARRERIE / DE LA FORTUNE, / OU / LE JEUNE PHILO
SOPHE, / COMÉDIE EN CINQ ACTES / ET EN PROSE, / Repré
sentée pour la première fois au Théâtre du / Marais, à Paris, le 16 avril
1793. / PAR LE C. LOAISEL TRÉOGATE. / [*half rule*] / Prix, 1 liv.
10 sols. / [*half rule*] / [*ornament* (17×45 mm)] / A PARIS, / Chez la
Citoyenne TOUBON, sous les galeries du / Théâtre de la République,
à côté du passage vîtré. / [*quarter rule*] / 1793.

8°. 112 pp.

Library locations: Ars† (4 copies; G. D. 8° 3350 (6)‡); MH†; MiU†
(photocopy of title page examined; pagination verified by query).
Sources: *Journal des spectacles*, no.108 (18 octobre 1793 [27 vendémiaire
an II]), p.859 (an); *Almanach des muses*, 1794, p.229 (rv). Ersch, *Fr
lit*, and suppl; Babault, ii.55-57; Quérard, *Fr litt*; Lacroix, *Bibl Soleinne*,
no.2452; Levot; Hoefer; Quérard, *Supercheries*, ii.802b; Goizet, *Dict*,
p.329; Taylor, *Bibl* ms, no.406; Tourneux, iii(1900), no.19084; Duval,
ii.106; Saulnays; Monglond, *Fr rév*, ii(1931).1061; Barroux; Cioranescu,
Bibl; Bousquet.
Comments: Tourneux comments 'L'ex. de la bibliothèque de l'Opéra
porte de nombreuses corrections très probablement autographes'.
Barroux repeats the remark. Tourneux cites the Opéra copy as belonging
to the 'Coll. Taylor'. The Opéra no longer has a separate 'Collection
Taylor', although it is a known fact that part of his collection was given
to the library (Rondel, 'Conférence bibliographie dramatique', p.20)
In fact, no copy at all of *La Bisarrerie* could be located there. The
manuscript catalogue of the baron Taylor's collection lists a copy of
La Bisarrerie (in 'T.111' of the collection), which is evidently the 1793
Toubon edition since, although no date is given, its reference on '*Cn*.
Loaisel-Tréogate' could only have come from the title page of that
edition. The Taylor sale catalogue lists no *Bisarrerie*, although there are
numerous groupings of works not broken down by title.[23] Thus, there
is still hope that this copy may be unearthed some day in the far recesses
of the Bibliothèque de l'Opéra. For a discussion of Quérard's remarks
in *Supercheries*, see no.57. The undated Cordier edition (no.51) may
actually have preceded this one.

[23] *Catalogue de la bibliothèque dramatique de feu le baron de Taylor ... dont la vente aura
lieu le lundi 27 novembre au mercredi 13 décembre 1893* (Paris 1893).

51.   *La Bisarrerie de la fortune*: undated Cordier edition
LA BISARRERIE / DE LA FORTUNE, / OU / LE JEUNE PHILO
SOPHE, / COMÉDIE. / EN CINQ ACTE [*sic*] EN PROSE. / [*double
ornamental full fule*] / PAR J. M. LOAISEL TRÉOGATE. / [*double
ornamental full rule*] / REPRÉSENTÉE pour la premiere [*sic*] fois, à
Paris, / ce 14 Mai 1793. / [*ornament* (25×23 mm)] / A PARIS, / CHEZ
CORDIER, rue & maison de Sorbonne / No. 382.

8°. 60 pp.

Textual revisions: Text is identical to that of 1793 Toubon edition
(no. 50).
Library location: Ars† (2 copies; Rf 18643‡).
Sources: Goizet, *Dict*, p.329; Saulnays.
Comments: The title page notation of the first performance in Paris as
occuring on '14 mai 1793' is erroneous. In fact, no performance at all
was announced in the *Affiches, annonces* for that date. There was no
way of determining the date of publication of this edition, although it
undoubtedly preceded the *An* III re-edition (no.54), which contains
many textual revisions. It may actually have preceded the 1793 Toubon
edtion (no. 50), which lists Cordier in the colophon as the printer.

52.   *La Bisarrerie de la fortune*: 1794 German translation, Augsburg
Der Glükwechsel [*sic*], / oder / der liebenswürdige Sonderling. / [*double
ornamental half rule*] / Ein / Lustspiel in fünf Aufzügen. / Aus dem
Französischen des / Loaisel Treogate / frey übersezt. / [*ornament*
(15×22 mm)] / [*double full rule*] / 1794.

8°. 112 pp.

In *Deutsche Schaubühne*, Sechsten Jahrgange, Eilfter Band, Nach der
Ordnung zister Band. Augsburg 1794.
Library location: BL‡ (examination based on photocopies of title pages;
pagination taken from BL, *Cat*).
Sources: Fromm; Barroux.
Comments: Fromm, the BL, *Cat*, and Barroux (Barroux's information
came from the other two sources) all give a publication date of 1788.
This date was obviously taken from the title page of the first volume in
the *Deutsche Schaubühne* and has no significance for *Der Glükwechsel*,
which is located in volume 71 dated 1794, as described above.

53.   *La Bisarrerie de la fortune*: 1794 German translation, Tubingue

(unconfirmed existence)

'Trad. en Allem Tubingue. 1794. 8' (Ersch, *Fr lit*).

Library locations: None (see comments to no.48).

Sources: Ersch, *Fr lit*.

Comments: There is a strong possibility that Fromm's listing of a 1784 translation, also published in Tübingen, is an erroneous reference to this 1794 edition. If that conclusion is correct, then the publisher for this edition is Cotta, as listed by Fromm. The publication of this edition, although unconfirmed, seems quite logical. It could have either preceded, coincided with, or followed the 1794 Augsburg edition (no. 52) and have been designed to be sold separately, whereas the Augsburg edition was part of a series. The popularity of *La Bisarrerie* in France in 1794 – that is, the publicity given by the performances at the Théâtre de la République – could have led to a demand or anticipation of demand for the play outside the country (for a discussion of this play's popularity see above, pp.88-89).

54. *La Bisarrerie de la fortune*: *An* VII re-edition

LA BISARRERIE / DE LA FORTUNE, / OU / LE JEUNE PHILO SOPHE, / COMÉDIE / EN CINQ ACTES, EN PROSE, / Repré sentée pour la première fois au Théâtre du Marais, / à Paris, le 16 Avril 1793, reprise au Théâtre français / de la République, rue de la Loi. / PAR J. M. LOAISEL TRÉOGATE. / [*double full rule*] / SECONDE ÉDITION, / Revue et corrigée par l'Auteur, avec un nouveau / dénouement. / [*double full rule*] / A TROYES, / Au Magasin général des Piéces [*sic*] de Théâtre, / Chez GOBELET, Imprimeur-Libraire, près la / Maison Commune, no. 206. / ET A PARIS, / Chez BARBA, Libraire, Maison du Petit-Dunkerque, / Quai Conti, vis-à-vis le Pont-neuf. / [*quarter rule*] / AN VII.

8°. 72 pp.

Textual revisions: Numerous minor revisions in addition to the new denouement.

Library locations: BN†; Ars†; Troyes, *Cat*; BL, *Cat*; CtY‡; NN†; PU.

Sources: Delandine, p.113; Lacroix, *Bibl Soleinne*, no. 2543; Lacroix, *Bibl Pixerécourt*, p.360; Goizet, *Dict*, p.329; Monglond, *Fr rév*, ii(1931). 1061; Saulnays; Barroux; Cioranescu, *Bibl*; Morabito.

Comments: Goizet incorrectly gives the date of publication as *An* VIII. He also notes that this revised version was the one performed at the

Théâtre de la République, but this claim cannot be supported. The one available review of that *reprise* does not give any details that permit determining which version was actually used.

55. *La Bisarrerie de la fortune*: 1803 Dutch translation
DE JONGE FILOSOOF, / OF / DE GRILLIGHEDEN VAN DE FORTUIN / BLYSPEL. / NAAR HET FRANSCH. / Volgens de tweede, verbeterde en vermeerderde Uitgave. / VAN / J. M. LOAISEL TREOGATE.

8°. 116 pp.

frontispiece, signed, 'D.A. v.d. Wart, del. J. E. Marerts, Sc.'
In *Zedelyk schouw-tooneel der menschelyke hartstochten en Daaden. of tooneel-stukken van vernuft en smaak*, xi. Amsterdam 1803.
Library location: BN‡; (additional locations not researched).
Sources: Worp; Barroux; Morabito.

56. *La Bisarrerie de la fortune*: 1808 German translation (unconfirmed existence)
'Der Glückwechsel, oder der liebenswürdige Sonderling – Lustpiel, Nach d. Franz. v. Th. Hell (d.i. Karl Theodor Winkler). – Leipzig: Hinricks 1808' (Fromm).
Library locations: None (see comments to no.48).
Sources: Fromm; Barroux.
Comments: It was not possible to find Fromm's source. He seems to have enough particulars about this edition to remove almost all doubt about its being a separate translation different from the others listed and to argue strongly for its actual existence.

57. *La Bisarrerie de la fortune*: 1823 plagiarised re-edition as *Les Coups du sort*, by 'Mowinsky'
LES COUPS DU SORT, / COMÉDIE EN CINQ ACTES ET EN PROSE, / PAR A. MOWINSKY.
Trans. G. Baer, in *Chefs-d'œuvre du théâtre polonais*: vol. xxiii of *Chefs-d'œuvre des théâtres étrangers*. Paris 1823; pp.407-514.
8°.
Library locations: CtY‡; (additional locations not researched).
Sources: Quérard, *Fr litt*, vi(1834).352; Lacroix, *Bibl Soleinne*, no.5114; Hoefer, xxvii(1858).195; Quérard, *Supercheries*, ii.802b; Duval, ii.188; Horn-Monval, viii.77, no.937.

Comments: All sources, except Quérard's *Supercheries* refer to the *Chefs-d'œuvre* collection with no mention of any connection between Loaisel and the *Coups du sort*. In his *Supercheries*, Quérard repeats a charge brought against Loaisel originally by Nicolas Brazier that *La Bisarrerie* is a plagiarism: 'Les Bizarreries de la Fortune ne sont autre chose qu'une comédie polonaise, *les Coups du Sort*, de Mowinski'.[24] Quite to the contrary, it now appears that it was Loaisel who was plagiarised and not vice versa. Brazier's charge seems based solely on the supposed 'Polish translation' published in 1823. In fact, no original Polish version has been located, and it seems quite certain that none ever existed. 'A. Mowinsky' is the pseudonym for Ignace Krasicki, a fact acknowledged in the *Chefs-d'œuvre du théâtre polonais* by the combined statements of G. Baer in the 'Notice' to *Les Coups du sort* (p.409) and Alphonse Denis in the preface, 'Coup d'œil sur la littérature dramatique en Pologne'. The 'Notice' also notes that the play was written in 1781. Modern literary historians agree that it was Krasicki who wrote three plays published in 1780 under the name of his secretary, Michala Mowinskiego.[25] But none of these three plays nor any of the others written by Krasicki bears any resemblance to *Les Coups du sort*. Furthermore, close examination of the texts reveals that the text of *Les Coups du sort* definitely matches the text of the *An* VII re-edition (no.54) of *La Bisarrerie* closer than that of the 1793 original edition (no.50). Were Loaisel to have plagiarised his text, it is highly unlikely that his revisions should be closer to the original than his first version. It seems, therefore, that '*Les Coups du sort*, par A. Mowinsky' is a hoax perpetrated by the 'translator' G. Baer (and Alphonse Denis?).

Le Château du Diable

Performances (total: 228)

5 décembre 1792 – 20 décembre 1793 (30 frimaire an II): Théâtre de Molière: 77 performances

[24] *Histoire des petits théâtres de Paris depuis leur origine,* new ed. (Paris 1838), ii.12-13; *Chronique des petits théâtres de Paris,* ed. Edmond Antoine Poinsot [pseudonym: Georges d'Heylli] (Paris 1883), i.357-58.

[25] Paul Cazin, *Le Prince-évêque de Varmie, Ignace Krasicki, 1735-1801* (Paris 1940), p.215; Mieczyslaw Piszczkowski, *Ignacy Krasicki: monografia litteracka* (Krakow 1969), p.434.

Sources: *Affiches, annonces et avis divers ou journal général de France* (8°) (perf an). *Chronique de Paris*, 8 décembre 1792, p.1370 (rv); *Spectacles de Paris* (1793), xlii.281-83 (rv); *Almanach des muses*, 1794, p.238 (an); *Almanach des spectacles* (an VIII), xliv.247 (an) and (an IX), xlv, 1ère partie, p.130 (an): *Annuaire dramatique, ou étrennes théâtrales*, 1813, p.235 (an). Desessarts, *Siècles litts;* Rabbe; Goizet, *Dict*, p.475; Douay, *Rép Paris*, viii, année 1792, f.20; Duval, ii.149; Barroux; Bousquet.

20 mars 1796 (30 ventôse an IV) – 9 avril 1797 (20 germinal an V): Théâtre de la rue Martin (=Théâtre de Molière): 61 performances
Sources: *Affiches, annonces et avis divers ou journal général de France* (8°) (perf an); *Courrier des spectacles* (perf an).

9 février 1798 (20 pluviôse an VI) – 4 avril 1798 (14 germinal an VI): Théâtre de l'Émulation (=Théâtre de la Gaîté): 9 performances
Sources: *Courrier des spectacles* (perf an). *Courrier des spectacles*, no.353 (9 février 1798 [21 pluviôse an VI]), p.2 (rv).

7 janvier 1800 (17 nivôse an VIII) – 21 mars 1800 (30 ventôse an VIII): Théâtre de Molière: 22 performances
Source: *Courrier des spectacles* (perf an).

11 octobre 1800 (19 vendémiaire an IX) – 7 décembre 1800 (16 frimaire an IX): Théâtre de Molière: 17 performances
Sources: *Courrier des spectacles* (perf an). *Courrier des spectacles*, no.1317 (12 octobre 1800 [20 vendémiaire an IX]), p.2 (rv).

24 novembre 1802 (3 frimaire an XI) – 26 mars 1803 (7 germinal an XI): Théâtre des Variétés nationales et étrangères, salle Molière: 29 performances
Source: *Courrier des spectacles* (perf an).

19 mars 1804 (28 ventôse an XII) – 25 novembre 1804 (4 frimaire an XIII): Théâtre du Marais: 12 performances
Source: *Courrier des spectacles* (perf. an).

8 décembre 1805 (17 frimaire an XIV): Théâtre de Molière: 1 performance
Source: *Courrier des spectacles* (perf an).

58.   *Le Château du Diable*: 1793 original edition
LE CHÂTEAU / DU DIABLE, / COMÉDIE HÉROÏQUE, / EN QUATRE ACTES ET EN PROSE, / Représentée pour la première fois à Paris, sur / le Théâtre de Molière, le 5 décembre 1792. / PAR LE C.

LOAISEL TRÉOGATE. / [*three-quarter rule*] / Prix, 1 liv. 4 sols. / [*three-quarter rule*] / [*ornament* (28×47 mm)] / A PARIS, / Chez la Citoyenne TOUBON, sous les galeries du / Théâtre de la République, à côté du passage vitré. / [*quarter rule*] / 1793.

8°. 60 pp.

Library locations: BN†; Ars†; BL, *Cat*; IaU‡; MH†.

Sources: *Almanach des muses*, 1794, p.238 (an). Ersch, *Fr lit*; Fantin Des Odoards: Quérard, *Fr litt*; Lacroix, *Bibl Soleinne*, no.3432; Levot; Goizet, *Dict*, p.475; Tourneux, iii(1900), no.19107; Duval, ii.149; Saulnays; Monglond, *Fr rév*, ii(1931).729; Barroux; Cioranescu, *Bibl*; Bousquet.

Comments: Lacroix, *Bibl Soleinne*, gives the date 1792 but as the date the play entered the repertory of the Théâtre Molière and not as the date of publication.

59. *Le Château du Diable*: 1801 German translation, by Kotzebue
Des / Teufels Lustschloss. / [*quarter rule*] / Eine natürliche Zauber-Oper / in drei Aufzügen. / [*ornamental quarter rule*] / Erschien 1801. / [*ornamental quarter rule*]
In *Theater von August v. Kotẓebue*, xiv.113-176. Leipzig: Eduard Kummer; Vienna: Ignaz Klang, 1841.

16°.

Library location: CtY‡; (additional locations not researched).

Sources: Douay, *Rép prov*, vii, lettre 'C', année 1801; Rabany, p.472.

Comments: Douay indicated that Frederic Reichard composed the music and that the work was performed for the opening of the Théâtre de la Patrie (?) in Berlin in 1801. Rabany provides no further details on the performance but does observe that the play 'paraît imitée d'ailleurs du *Château du diable*, "comédie héroique" en quatre actes par Loaisel de Tréogate (Paris, 1792)'. A comparison of the texts confirmed that this is indeed the case. He gives place and date of publication as Leipzig, 1802, but either he is referring to another edition or this in an error, since it conflicts with the information on the title page described above. No attempt has been made to locate or describe other editions of this adaptation.

60. *Le Château du Diable*: *An* x – 1802 re-edition
LE CHATEAU / DU DIABLE, / COMÉDIE HÉROÏQUE / EN

QUATRE ACTES ET EN PROSE / Par J. M. LOAISEL TRÉO
GATE. / Représentée, pour la première fois, sur le théâ- / tre de Molière,
le 5 décembre 1792. / Nouvelle Edition, revue et corrigée. / [*quarter rule*] /
A PARIS, / Chez BARBA, libraire, Palais du Tribunat, galerie derrière /
le Théâtre Français de la République, no.51. / [quarter rule] / N [*sic*]
X. (1802).

8°. 47 pp.

Textual revisions: Numerous minor revisions and additions.
Library locations: Ars† (3 copies; Rf18641‡); MiU† (photocopy of
entire text examined).
Sources: Goizet, *Dict*, p.475; Saulnays.
Comments: An advertisement on page 2 of the *An* VII re-edition of
La Bisarrerie (no.54) confirms that this re-edition of *Le Château du
Diable* was 'corrigée par l'auteur', a significant detail lacking on the
title page, as shown in the description above.

Le Combat des Thermopyles, ou l'école des guerriers

Performances (total: 7)

2 août 1794 (15 thermidor an II) – 14 août 1794 (27 thermidor an II):
Théâtre de la Cité-Variétés: 4 performances
Sources: Affiches, annonces et avis divers ou journal général de France
(8°) (perf an). *Almanach des spectacles* (an VIII), xliv.151, 247 (ans) and
(an IX), xlv, 1ère partie, p.130 (an); *Annuaire dramatique, ou étrennes
théâtrales*, 1813, p.236 (an). Desessarts, *Siècles litts*; Rabbe; Goizet,
Dict, p.537; Duval, ii.162; Douay, *Rép Paris*, viii, année 1794, f.19;
Barroux; Bousquet.
Comments: Only Goizet, Duval, Douay, and Barroux give an exact date
for the first performance. Goizet gives the correct opening date, but
Duval, Douay, and Barroux take the incorrect one given on the title
page of the printed play (see no.61). Duval in his volume of 'Auteurs'
(xiii.107) inexplicably gives a date of 1799, having no significance for
the play, which was not performed after 31 March 1798. The actual
opening date as confirmed by announcements in the *Affiches, annonces*
was as shown above.

20 mars 1798 (30 ventôse an VI) – 31 mars 1798 (10 germinal an VI):
Théâtre de la Cité: 3 performances

Plays

Sources: *Courrier des spectacles* (perf an). *Courrier des spectacles*, no.393 (21 mars 1798 [1er germinal an VI]), p.2 (rv).

61. *Le Combat des Thermopyles*: *An* III original edition
LE COMBAT / DES THERMOPYLES, / OU / L'ÉCOLE DES GUERRIERS, / FAIT HISTORIQUE EN TROIS ACTES ET EN PROSE, / Par LOAISEL, Citoyen Français. / Représenté pour la premiere [*sic*] fois, à Paris, sur le / Théâtre de la CITÉ-VARIETÉS [*sic*], le cinq / thermidor, l'an second de la République Française. / [*half rule*] / Prix, 1 liv. 10 sols. / [*half rule*] / [*ornament* (20×30 mm)] / A PARIS, / Chez la Citoyenne TOUBON, sous les g leries [*sic*] du Théâtre / de la République, à côte du passage vi ré [*sic*]. / [*full rule*] L'an III de la République française une et indivisible.

8°. 58 pp.

Library locations: BN†; Ars†; BL, *Cat*; IaU‡; InU.

Sources: *Almanach des muses*, 1796, p.280, Quérard, *Fr litt*; Lacroix, *Bibl Pixerécourt*, p.361; Lacroix, *Bibl Soleinne*, nos 2470 and 3433; Levot; Hoefer; Goizet, *Dict*, p.537; Tourneux, iii(1900), no.19458; Duval, ii.162; Saulnays; Monglond, *Fr rév*, iii(1933).211; Cioranescu, *Bibl*; Barroux; Bousquet; Morabito.

Comments: Goizet and Duval list the year of publication as 'An II'. Since they do not mention the *An* III edition, and since there is no other evidence for an *An* II edition, they undoubtedly are referring to the *An* III edition having perhaps confused the year of the first performance with the date of publication. As pointed out in the comments on the first run of performances, the actual date of the first performance was 2 août 1794 (15 thermidor an II) and not 'le cinq thermidor an II' as printed on the title page. This error could easily have arisen by the printer's misreading the date on the copy had it been written in characters, '15', with a weak '1' in the tens digit position.

La Fontaine merveilleuse, ou les époux musulmans

Performances (total: 20)

13 septembre 1799 (27 fructidor an VII) – 26 octobre 1799 (3 brumaire an VIII): Théâtre de l'Ambigu-Comique: 20 performances
Sources: *Courrier des spectacles* (perf an). *Courrier des spectacles*, no.935

(14 septembre 1799 [28 fructidor an VII]), pp.2-3 (rv); *Mercure de France*, 16 septembre 1799 (30 fructidor an VII), pp.272-76 (rv); *Almanach des spectacles* (an VIII), xliv.165 (rv) and 247 (an); *Revue des théâtres*, an VIII, p.135 (rv); *Almanach des spectacles* (an IX), xlv, 1ère partie, p.130 (an) and 2e partie, p.53 (an), Desessarts, *Siècles litts*; Rabbe; Douay, *Rép Paris*, viii, année 1799, f.18*v*; Barroux; Bousquet.
Comments: Rabbe and Douay confuse the exact terminology of the genre, the former speaking of a 'pantomime tragique', the latter of a 'pantomime dialoguée'. The printed edition (no.62) and the performance announcements in the *Courrier des spectacles* read clearly 'pantomime-féerie'. Duval lists a 'Fontaine merveilleuse. 1799' in his volume of 'Auteurs' under the article on Loaisel (xiii.107) but has no entry for this work in the volumes of plays. Bousquet incorrectly lists the play as performed in 1798, probably a result of his own conversion to the Gregorian calendar.

62.   *La Fontaine merveilleuse*: *An* VII original edition
LA FONTAINE / MERVEILLEUSE, / OU / LES ÉPOUX MUSUL
MANS, / PANTOMIME-FÉERIE en cinq Actes, à grand / Spectacle,
mêlée de Dialogue, de Combats, / Chants et Danses; / Réprésentée,
pour la première fois, à Paris, sur / le Théâtre de l'Ambigu-Comique,
au mois / de Fructidor an 7; / Par J.-M. LOAISEL-TRÉOGATE; /
Musique nouvelle du Cen OTHON, Ballets du / Cen AUMER, Artistes
du Théâtre des Arts; / Décors du Cen MOENCH. / [*ornament* (19 mm
diameter)] / A PARIS, et se vend / A l'Imprimerie A PRIX-FIXE,
rue des Coutures- / Saint-Gervais, près l'égoût de la Vieille rue / du
Temple, no.446. / [*quarter rule*] / AN VII.

8°. 48 pp.

Library locations: BN‡; Ars†; BL† (microfilm copy examined).
Sources: Delandine, p.257; Quérard, *Fr litt*; Lacroix, *Bibl Soleinne*,
no.3451; Levot; Monglond, *Fr rév*, iv(1935).1094-95; Saulnays;
Barroux; Cioranescu, *Bibl*; Bousquet; Morabito.

La Forêt périlleuse, ou les brigands de la Calabre

Performances (total: 259)
7 mai 1797 (18 floréal an V) – 31 janvier 1798 (12 pluviôse an VI): Théâtre
de la Cité: 23 performances

Sources: *Courrier des spectacles* (perf an). *Courrier des spectacles*, no.122 (8 mai 1797 [19 floréal an v]), pp.2-3, (rv), no.125 (11 mai 1797 [22 floréal an v]), pp.3-4 (rv), and no.182 (7 juillet 1797 [19 messidor an v]), p.2 (rv); *Vérités à l'ordre du jour*, an VI, p.145 (rv); *Almanach des spectacles* (an VIII), xliv.152 and 247 (ans), and (an IX), xlv.130 (an); *Annuaire dramatique, ou étrennes théâtrales*, 1813, p.236 (an). Desessarts, *Siècles litts*; Babault, ii.380; Rabbe; Douay, *Rép Paris*, année 1797, f.12; Duval, iv.109; Saulnays; Barroux; Bousquet.

Comments: Saulnays gives 17 mai 1797 as the date of the first perform-ance, obviously having found that erroneous date on the title page of one of the editions he lists (see comments to no.63 for a discussion of the title page error). Douay again gives the wrong date, but this time he is off only by one day, 'Mai 8, 1797'. There is much variance among sources on the genre of the play, the terms 'comédie', 'drame', or 'mélodrame' all being employed. Duval lists this play also under the title 'La Forêt noire ou les Brigands de la Calabre'. Such was the title announced in the *Courrier des spectacles* of 7 mai 1797 (18 floréal an v) for the first performance, and this is undoubtedly Duval's source. The title was corrected in the next issue of the *Courrier des spectacles*.

7 juillet 1799 (19 messidor an VII) – 13 décembre 1799 (22 frimaire an VIII): Théâtre de la Cité: 19 performances
Source: *Courrier des spectacles* (perf an).

21 avril 1800 (1er floréal an VIII): Théâtre des Victoires nationales, rue du Bacq.: 1 performance
Source: *Courrier des spectacles* (perf an).

23 janvier 1801 (3 pluviôse an IX) – in repertory until end 1812: Théâtre de l'Ambigu-Comique: 54 performances in 1801; 162 thereafter
Sources: *Courrier des spectacles* (perf an); *Courrier de l'Europe et des spectacles* (perf an); *Journal de l'Empire* (perf an). *Almanach des spectacles de Paris pour l'an 1809*, p.180 (an); *Annuaire dramatique, ou étrennes théâtrales*, 1805-1814 (*Forêt périlleuse* carried as one of the plays in the repertory of the Ambigu-Comique); *Courrier de l'Europe et des spectacles*, no.1456 (14 juin 1811), p.2 (rv).

63. *Le Forêt périlleuse*: 1797 original edition
LA / FORÊT PÉRILLEUSE / OU LES / BRIGANDS DE LA CALABRE, / DRAME EN TROIS ACTES, EN PROSE. / PAR J. M. LOAISEL-TÉOGATE. [*sic*] / Représenté pour la première fois,

sur le théâtre / de la Cité, à Paris, le 18 floréal de l'an V, / (17 mai 1797.) / [*quarter rule*] / A PARIS. / CHEZ la citoyenne TOUBON, sous les galleries [*sic*] du / théâtre de la République, à côté du passage vitré. / [*double quarter rule*] / 1797.

8°. 72 pp.

Library locations: Ars†; BL, *Cat*; DLC; PU‡.

Sources: *Journal général de la littérature de France*, an VI, p.54 (an). Fantin Des Odoards; Delandine, p.258; Quérard, *Fr litt*; Lacroix, *Bibl Soleinne*, no.3433; Levot; Hoefer; Tourneux, iii(1900), no.19488; Monglond, *Fr rév*, iv(1935).250-51; Barroux; Cioranescu, *Bibl*; Bousquet.

Comments: The title page carries the incorrect Gregorian calendar date '17 mai', which should read '7 mai', probably a typographical error. This error continues to appear on title pages of several of the succeeding editions. Fantin Des Odoards, obviously confusing two of Loaisel's titles, lists the play as 'Soirées de la forêt périlleuse'. Quérard's description is based on the 1816 edition, so he gives the genre as 'mélodrame' and publisher as 'Fages', neither of which is correct for the 1797 edition he lists first. Levot repeats exactly the same ambiguous description.

64. *La Forêt périlleuse*: 1798 re-edition

LA / FORÊT PÉRILLEUSE / OU LES / BRIGANDS DE LA CALABRE, / DRAME EN TROIS ACTES, EN PROSE. / PAR J. M. LOAISEL-TRÉOGATE. / Représenté pour la première fois, sur le Théâtre / de la Cité, à Paris, le 18 Floréal de l'an V, / (17 Mai 1797.) / [*ornament* (49×51 mm)] / A MARSEILLE, / Chez JEAN MOSSY, Imprimeur-Libraire, à la / Canebière. / [*three-quarter rule*] / 1798.

8°. 40 pp.

N.B. A cancellans imprint pasted over the original on the PU copy reads 'A PARIS, / Chez DELAVIGNE, tenant Cabinet de lecture, / rue Bourg-l'Abbé, no.34, passage de l'Ancre,'. The original imprint date is left visible.

Textual revisions: Text is identical to that of the 1797 edition (no.63).

Library locations: Ars‡; PU† (photocopy of entire work examined).

Source: Saulnays.

Comments: The actors listed in this edition are those of the Théâtre de la Cité as listed in the 1797 edition (no.63) and confirmed by the review in the *Courrier des spectacles*, no.182 (7 juillet 1797 [19 messidor an v]), p.2. No evidence was discovered to suggest that this edition was connected with a performance of the play at Marseille. Saulnays's listing lacks the date. The error in the Gregorian calendar date for the first performance, '17 mai' for '7 mai', appears again as in the 1797 edition.

65. *La Forêt périlleuse*: 1799 English translation, by Turnbull (confirmed existence)
'Rudolph; or, The Robbers of Calabria. A melodrama in three Acts, as performed at the Boston Theater. 18mo, pp.141. Boston, 1799' (Wegelin, p.76).
Sources: Wegelin, p.76; Sabin.
Comments: Sabin lists and describes only the 1807 edition, but adds the following comment: 'Editions of Boston 1799, 1813, and 1826, and Hallowell, 1813, are listed in the Catalogue of the Harris Collection, 1886, but no copies are found in that collection as now located at [Boston University]'. These references from a collection catalogue testify to the probable existence of the editions. The confirmation of the Wegelin reference provides additional assurance of the existence of the 1799 edition, especially in view of the fact that the pagination described is different from that of the 1807 edition (no.69), thus testifying to the existence of another, separate edition. The date may be questioned in light of Hill's statement that the first performance at the Boston Theatre was on 13 May 1807 (see no.69). However, the play might well have been published before being performed, or a prior performance might have gone unnoticed.

66. *La Forêt périlleuse*: 1800 Dutch translation (unconfirmed existence)
'De struikroovers van Kalabrien, of de onveilige vildernis, 1800, d. M. G. Englemann' (Worp).
Source: Worp.
Comments: Worp's listings are confirmed in two cases out of four. There is no reason to doubt his reliability.

67. *La Forêt périlleuse*: *An* x (1802), 40 pp. re-edition
LA FORÊT / PÉRILLEUSE, / OU / LES BRIGANDS DE LA CALABRE, / DRAME, / EN TROIS ACTES, EN PROSE, / PAR

J. M. LOAISEL-TRÉOGATE. / Représenté, pour la première fois, à Paris, / sur le Théâtre de la Cité, le 18 Floréal, an / V (17 Mai 1797); et repris sur le Théâtre / de l'Ambigu-Comique, le 3 Pluviôse an [*sic*] IX / (23 Janvier 1800.) / Nouvelle Edition, revue et corrigée par l'Auteur. / [*ornament (6×27 mm)*] / A PARIS, / Chez FAGES, Libraire, boulevard Saint- / Martin, No 26, vis-à-vis le Théâtre des Jeunes / Artistes, et rue Meslé, No. 25. / [*double half rule*] / AN X. (1802.)

8°. 40 pp.

N. B. Partial cancellans imprints bearing the names of different book-sellers have been pasted over the originals on the CtY and MiU copies and read as follows: 'Chez BARBA, Libraire, palais du Tribunat, galerie derrière / le Théâtre de la République, no.51.' (CtY); 'Chez ROULLET, Libraire, Palais du / Tribunat, galerie Noire, près le Théâtre de la / République, no.3.' (MiU). The original imprint dates are left visible.

Textual revisions: Moderate number of minor revisions.
Library locations: BN†; Ars† (2 copies; RF 18649‡); CtY†; MiU† (photocopy of title page examined); IaU; MH.
Sources: Quérard, *Fr litt*; Levot; Saulnays; Barroux: Cioranescu, *Bibl*; Bousquet; Morabito.
Comments: It was not possible to determine with certainty which of the *An* x (1802) re-editions – 40 pp. or 32 pp. – was published first (see no.68). As in earlier editions, the Gregorian calendar date for the Cité first performance is incorrect as printed on the title page. Also in error is the Gregorian calendar date for the opening performance at the Ambigu-Comique, which should read '23 janvier 1801'. These errors will be repeated in subsequent editions. Saulnays incorrectly lists this as the first edition. According to the notarial act reprinted on page 2 of this edition, Loaisel sold to Fages the exclusive rights to print and sell this play. Future editions except that of Lévy all carry Fages's name on the imprint. The actors listed in this edition are different from those in the 1797 and 1798 editions and are thus evidently those of the Ambigu-Comique, suggesting that this was the text used for the performances in that theatre.

68. *La Forêt périlleuse: An* x (1802), 32 pp. re-edition
LA FORÊT / PÉRILLEUSE, / OU / LES BRIGANDS DE LA CALABRE, / DRAME / EN TROIS ACTES, EN PROSE, / PAR

Plays

J. M. LOAISEL-TREOGATE; / Représenté, pour la première fois, à Paris, / sur le Théâtre de la Cité, le 18 Floréal an V / (17 Mai 1797), et repris sur le Théâtre de / l'Ambigu-Comique, le 3 Pluviôse an IX / (23 Janvier 1800.) / Nouvelle Édition, revue et corrigée par l'Auteur. / A PARIS, / Chez FAGES, au Magasin de Pièces de Théâtre, / Boulevard Saint-Martin, No. 25, vis-à-vis le / Théâtre des Jeunes Artistes. / [*quarter rule*] / AN X. (1802.)

8°. 32 pp.

Textual revisions: Text is identical to that of *An* x (1802), 40 pp. (no.67) except that scene i of act III is omitted. Some minor changes are made in stage and scenery directions, and act III is divided into eight rather than fifteen scenes.

Library location: Ars‡.

Sources: see no.67; except for Cioranescu, who lists only the 40 pp. edition, sources do not specify pagination and could thus refer equally well to either edition.

Comments: As in the 40 pp. re-edition of this date (no.67), the Gregorian calendar dates for the first performance at the Cité and the opening at the Ambigu-Comique are incorrect as printed on the title page. The actors listed include alternates for the principal roles, not listed in the 40 pp. edition of the same date. This would seem to indicate that the 32 pp. edition was printed *later*, after the play had become established in its own right and alternates were appearing with some regularity. Also, the fact that the text of the 32 pp. edition serves as the basis for all subsequent Fages reeditions suggests that since it is the preferred text, it is the later of the two to have been published.

69. *La Forêt périlleuse*: 1807 re-edition of English translation by Turnbull

Rudolph, / OR THE / ROBBERS OF CALABRIA; / A MELO DRAME, / IN THREE ACTS. / WITH MARCHES, COMBATS AND CHORUSSES, / AS PERFORMED AT THE BOSTON THEATER. / [*ornamental three-quarter rule*] / BY JOHN D. TURN BULL, / of the Boston Theater – Author of the Maid of Hungary. / [*ornamental full rule*] / COPY RIGHT SECURED ACCORDING TO LAW. / [*double full rule*] / PRINTED BY B. TRUE, 75 STATE-STREET, BOSTON. / [*quarter dotted rule*] / 1807.

18°. 47 pp.

Library locations: CtY‡; DLC; ICU; MB; MH; MWA; NN†; PU; RPB; (locations from Hill).
Sources: Wegelin, p.76; Hill, no.307; Sabin.
Comments: *La Forêt périlleuse* is not acknowledged as the original version, but a comparison of the texts revealed that *Rudolph* is indeed a translation of Loaisel's work. Hill states that *Rudolph* was 'first played at the Boston Theater, May 13, 1807' and mentions no editions prior to 1807. However, see no.65, where the Sabin entry is also discussed. Wegelin refers to 'several' re-editions but specifies no dates.

70.   *La Forêt périlleuse*: 1809 re-edition
LA FORÊT / PÉRILLEUSE, / OU / LES BRIGANDS DE LA CALABRE. / MÉLODRAME / EN TROIS ACTES ET EN PROSE, / Par J. M. LOAISEL-TRÉOGATE; / Représenté, pour la première fois, à Paris, sur / le Théâtre de l'Ambigu-Comique; le 23 / Janvier 1800. / [*ornament* (35 × 30mm)] / A PARIS, / Chez FAGES, au Magasin de Pièces de Théâtre, / boulevard Saint-Martin, No.29, vis-à-vis la / rue de Lancry. / [*quarter rule*] / 1809.

8°. 32 pp.

Textual revisions: Text is identical to that of *An* x (1802), 32 pp. (no.68).
Library location: Ars‡ (2 copies; G. D. 8° 10820‡).
Comments: The information printed on the title page regarding the first performance is incorrect. The Gregorian calendar date for the Ambigu-Comique opening, now standing alone, was erroneous beginning with the *An* x (1802) editions (nos 67 and 68). Furthermore, the error is introduced with this edition of designating the Ambigu-Comique opening as the first Paris performance, which it of course was not. These two errors will be repeated in future editions.

71.   *La Forêt périlleuse*: 1812 re-edition
LA FORÊT / PÉRILLEUSE, / OU / LES BRIGANDS DE LA CALABRE, / MÉLODRAME / EN TROIS ACTES ET EN PROSE, / Par J. M. LOAISEL-TRÉOGATE; / Représentée [*sic*] pour la pre- / mière fois, à Paris, / sur le Théâtre de l'Ambigu-Comique, le / 23 Janvier 1800. / [*wavy half line*] / A PARIS, / CHEZ FAGES, Libraire, au Magasin des Pièces de / Théâtre, boulevard Saint-Martin, no. 29, / vis-à-vis la rue de Lancry. / [*wavy quarter rule*] / 1812.

8°. 32 pp.

Textual revisions: Text is identical to that of *An* x (1802), 32 pp. (no.68).

Library location: BN‡ (currently available on microfiche; see no.84)

Sources: Tourneux, iii(1900), no.18806; Duval, iv.109; Monglond, *Fr rév*, iv(1935).250-51; Barroux; Bousquet; Morabito.

Comments: Errors regarding the first performance information are identical to those in the 1809 re-edition (no.70).

72.   *La Forêt périlleuse*: 1813 Boston re-edition of English translation by Turnbull (unconfirmed existence)

'Boston, 1813' (Sabin).

Sources: Wegelin, p.76; Hill, no.307; Sabin.

Comments: Only Sabin gives the date and place of publication, but he has taken these data from a library collection catalogue, thus strongly supporting the actual existence of this re-edition (see no.65). Hill and Wegelin refer to 'several' re-editions, but neither specifies dates.

73.   *La Forêt périlleuse*: 1813 Hallowel re-edition of English translation by Turnbull (unconfirmed existence)

'Hallowell, 1813' (Sabin).

Sources: Wegelin, p.76; Hill, no.307; Sabin.

Comments: same as no.72.

74.   *La Forêt périlleuse*: 1816 re-edition

LA FORÊT / PÉRILLEUSE, / OU / LES BRIGANDS DE LA CALABRE, / MÉLODRAME / EN TROIS ACTES ET EN PROSE, / Par J. M. LOAISEL-TRÉOGATE; / Représenté pour la première fois, à Paris, sur le / Théâtre de l'Ambigu-Comique, le 23 Janvier 1800. / [*ornament* (30✕30 mm)] / A PARIS, / CHEZ FAGES, LIBRAIRE, au Magasin de Pièces de Théâtre, / boulevart [*sic*] St.-Martin, no. 29, vis-à-vis la rue de Lancry. / [*wavy quarter rule*] / DE L'IMPRIMERIE DE CUSSAC, RUE D'ORLEANS S.-HONORÉ, No.13. / [*double quarter rule*] / 1816.

8º. 32 pp.

Textual revisions: Text is identical to that of *An* x (1802), 32 pp. (no.68)

Library locations: BN‡; NIC† (photocopy examined).

Sources: Quérard, *Fr litt*; Levot; Saulnays; Barroux; Bousquet; Morabito.

Comments: Errors regarding the first performance information are identical to those in the 1809 re-edition (no.70).

75. *La Forêt périlleuse*: 1826 re-edition of English translation by Turnbull (unconfirmed existence)
'Boston, 1826' (Sabin).
Sources: Wegelin, p.76; Hill, no.307; Sabin.
Comments: same as no.72.

76. *La Forêt perilleuse*: 1831 English translation? (unpublished?)
'*The Brigands of Calabria; or the Forest of Saint Euphemia* (The City of London Theater, 31/10/1831)' (Nicoll, iv.621).
Source: Nicoll, iv.621.
Comments: No other information was found regarding this play. Nicoll lists neither an author nor a translator. He does not, in fact, indicate that it is a translation, but he fails to do so also in the case of the [1866?] English Translation by Suter (no.79). The play is listed here because of the similar sounding title, but it certainly cannot be counted among the translations of Loaisel's works until more evidence is discovered. This reference obviously appears to refer to a performance, not to an edition.

77. *La Forêt périlleuse*: 18[62?] Lévy re-edition
Printed across the top of the first page are:
price: 'Chaque pièce, 20 centimes'
series title and issue number: 'Théâtre Contemporain illustré. 505e livraison.'
imprint: 'Michel Lévy frères, Editeurs. Rue Vivienne, 2 bis.'
Illustration (top third of first page), signatures illegible.
Title (located on first page between illustration and 'distribution'):
LA FORÊT PÉRILLEUSE / OU / LES BRIGANDS DE LA CALA BRE / DRAME EN TROIS ACTES, EN PROSE / PAR / J. M. LOAISEL-TRÉOGATE / REPRÉSENTÉ POUR LA PREMIERE FOIS, A PARIS, SUR LE THÉÂTRE DE LA CITÉ, LE 17 MAI 1797, ET REPRIS, SUR LE THÉÂTRE DE / L'AMBIGU-COMI QUE, A DIVERSES ÉPOQUES.

30×21 cm. 8 pp.

Textual revisions: Text is identical to that of *An* x (1802), 40 pp. (no.67).
Library locations: BN†; Ars‡' BL, *Cat.*
Sources: Lorenz, iii.297; Saulnays; Morabito.
Comments: The exact date of publication could not be confirmed.

The BL, *Cat* gives 1852-1867 as the suspected inclusive dates of publication for the entire series of the 'Théâtre contemporain illustré'. Lorenz gives 1862 for the *Forêt périlleuse* 'livraison', as does Saulnays, this being as close as one can get to accuracy. The format could not be determined with any certainty, so only overall dimensions are given. There are no water marks or chain lines in the paper. The first and last leaves are conjugate as are the second and third. The date of the first performance at the Théâtre de la Cité is still incorrect as with the *An* x (1802) editions (nos 67 and 68).

78.   *La Forêt périlleuse*: 18[??] Lévy re-issue
Identical to the preceding entry except for the information printed across the top of the page, which is changed as follows: price: 'Prix 30 centimes'; series and issue number: omitted; imprint: 'Calmann Lévy, Éditeur, Ancienne Maison Michel Lévy Frères, Rue Auber, 3, et Boulevard des Italiens, 15, A La Librairie Nouvelle'.
Library location: Ars† (2 copies; G. D. 49152‡).
Comments: Aside from the changes to page 1 noted above, this copy was printed from the same type-setting as the copy described in no.77, thus making them both part of the same edition. The copy described in this entry qualifies as a re-issue since it was printed at a later date than the copy described in no.77. The later publication date can be deduced from the imprints, which show the passage of the publishing house between printings from Michel to Calmann Lévy.

79.   *La Forêt périlleuse*: [1866?] anonymously published English translation (attribution to Suter confirmed)
THE / BRIGANDS OF CALABRIA. / A Romantic Drama, / IN ONE ACT. / THOMAS HAILES LACY, / 89, STRAND, LONDON.

12°. 18 pp.

In *Lacy's acting edition of plays, dramas, farces, extravaganzas. etc. etc. as performed at the various theatres,* lxv. London.
Library locations: BL, *Cat*, xxxi.1062; CtY‡ (additional locations not researched).
Source: Nicoll, v.588.
Comments: Nicoll states that the author of this play is William E. Suter. That attribution is confirmed by the American edition listed in the

following entry. Nicoll further gives the opening performance in London as at The Grecian Saloon on '12/2/66'. There is no information on date of publication, the '[1866?]' date above being taken from the BL, *Cat.* No mention is made by Nicoll or in the printed play that this is a translation of Loaisel's work, which a comparison of the texts definitely shows that it is.

80.   *La Forêt périlleuse*: undated American edition of English translation by Suter.
AMES AND HOLGATES' / SERIES OF / STANDARD AND MINOR DRAMA. / NUMBER 14. / [*half rule*] / The Brigands of Calabria. / A Romantic Drama / IN ONE ACT, BY / WILLIAM E-SUTER, ESQ. / Author of 'Lady Audley's Secret,' 'Give me my wife,' / 'John Wopps,' &c. &c. / [. . .] / AMES AND HOLGATE, Publishers, / CLYDE, OHIO.
12°. 13 pp.
Library location: CtY‡; (additional locations not researched).
Comments: There is no way to be certain that this edition came after the British edition (no.79), since neither is dated. But since Suter was British, it might be presumed that a British publication would precede an American one.

81.   *La Forêt périlleuse*: 1871 English translation, by W. E. Lane
THE ROBBERS OF CALABRIA. / A DRAMA, IN ONE ACT. —ADAPTED BY W. E. LANE.
In *The British drama, illustrated*, v.225-32. London John Dicks, 1871.
Library locations: BL, *Cat* xxxi.1062; RPB‡; (other locations not researched).
Comments: A comparison of texts revealed that this is a translation of *La Forêt périlleuse*. The *NUC* reference (cccxiv, p.398, col. 2) gives no locations for the Lane translation but instead mistakenly equates it with the Suter translation (no.79). The two are definitely different.

82.   *La Forêt périlleuse*: 1879 re-issue (?) of English adaptation by W. E. Lane (confirmed existence)
'The Brigands of Calabria. Adapted by W. E. Lane. A Reissue. London, [1879?] 8°. [Dicks' Standard Plays. no.150.]' (BL, *Cat*, xxxi.1062).
Library location: BL, *Cat*, xxxi.1062.

Comments: The determination that this copy is a re-issue was made by the BL.

83.   *La Forêt périlleuse*: 1975 re-edition
La Forêt périlleuse ou les brigands de la Calabre, Drame, en trois actes, en prose. In Morabito.
Text: Text appears to be that of Lévy (nos 77 and 78) or Fages, *An* x (1802), 40 pp. (no.67). There are major errors in transcription of the first few scenes of act III (pp.42-46).
Library locations: not researched.

84.   *La Forêt périlleuse*: 1975 microfiche re-edition
La Forêt périlleuse ou les brigands de la Calabre, mélodrame en 3 actes en prose: microfiche no.5372 in *Le Théâtre de la Révolution et de l'Empire, 132 pièces de théâtre sélectionées et présentées par Marc Régaldo*. Micro-éditions Hachette. Paris 1975.
Text: 1812 re-edition (no.71).
Library locations: not researched.

Le Grand chasseur, ou l'isle des palmiers
(confirmed attribution to Pixerécourt as co-author)

Performances (total: 16)
6 novembre 1804 (15 brumaire an XIII) – 23 décembre 1804 (2 nivôse an (XIII): Théâtre de l'Ambigu-Comique: 16 performances
Sources: *Courrier des spectacles* (perf an). *Courrier des spectacles*, no.2810 (7 novembre 1804 [16 brumaire an XIII]), p.4 (rv); *Annuaire dramatique, ou étrennes théâtrales*, 1813, p.236 (an). Babault, ii.380; Rabbe; Pixeré-court, 'Tableau chronologique', no.53; Douay, *Rép Paris*, ix, année 1804, f.20; Duval, iv.118; Saulnays; Wicks and Schweitzer, i.31; Barroux; Bousquet.
Comments: Duval gives an incorrect revolutionary calendar date, '19 Brumaire'. The *Annuaire dramatique* carries this play as being in the repertory of the Ambigu-Comique until 1813, but no performances were announced in the *Courrier des spectacles* or later in the *Journal de l'Empire* after the ones noted above. Pixerécourt gives 27 performances in Paris and 4 in the provinces, indicating also that the play was performed 'en société'.

85. *Le Grand chasseur*, 1804 original edition, by Loaisel and [Pixeré-court] (confirmed attribution to Pixerécourt as co-author)
LE / GRAND CHASSEUR, / OU / L'ISLE DES PALMIERS, / MÉLODRAME / EN TROIS ACTES, EN PROSE, / ET À GRAND SPECTACLE. / PAR MM. LOAISEL-TRÉOGATE, / Et ***. / Représenté, pour la première fois, à Paris, sur / le Théâtre de l'Ambigu-Comique, le 15 bru- / maire, an XIII. (6 novembre 1804). / [*ornament* (9×19 mm)] / A PARIS, / CHEZ FAGES, au Magasin de Pièces de Théâtre [*sic*], / Boulevard Saint-Martin, No.25, vis-à-vis le / Théâtre des Jeunes Artistes. / [*double half rule*] / AN XIII. (1804).
8°. 48 pp.
Library locations: BN‡; Ars†; BL, *Cat*; PU†; MH†.
Sources: Ersch, *sec suppl*; Fantin Des Odoards; Delandine, p.273; Quérard, *Fr litt*; Pixerécourt, 'Tableau chronologique', no.53; Lacroix, *Bibl Soleinne*, no.2535; Levot; Virely, no.24; Duval, iv.118; Monglond, *Fr rév*, vi(1949).843-44; Saulnays; Barroux; Cioranescu, *Bibl*; Bousquet; Morabito.
Comments: The review of the first performance in the *Courrier des spectacles* names only Loaisel as author. The first source to identify Loaisel's collaborator as Pixerécourt was Quérard, *Fr litt*. Pixerécourt's listing of the work in his 'Tableau chronologique' confirms the attribution to him as co-author. Lacroix's Soleinne catalogue lists the play as belonging to the following collection: '2535. Théâtre de René-Charles Guilbert de Pixerécourt. Paris, Barba, s.d., 10 vol. in-8. . .'. There is no way of knowing, however, whether this 10 volume collection was a publisher's edition or simply bound together and labelled at the owner's direction. Virely lists only this separate 1804 edition. Ersch gives 1805 as the year of publication. Since he does not elsewhere mention the 1804 edition, and since there is no other evidence for an 1805 edition, he undoubtedly is referring to the 1804 edition and has erred in the date of publication. On page 2 appears the date of the censor's *permission*, 'le 28 thermidor, an 12' (16 août 1804).

La Loi singulière, ou malheur et constance
(unconfirmed attribution)

Performances (total: 42)
13 avril 1811 – 4 décembre 1811: Théâtre de l'Ambigu-Comique: 42

performances

Sources: *Courrier de l'Europe et des spectacles* (perf an); *Journal de l'Empire* (perf an). *Courrier de l'Europe et des spectacles*, no.1390 (14 avril 1811), pp.3-4 (rv) and no.1407 (25 avril 1811), p.4 (rv); *Journal de l'Empire*, 15-16 avril 1811, pp.3-4 (rv); *Almanach des muses*, 1812, p.303 (an); *Opinion du parterre*, 1812, p.403 (an); *Mémorial dramatique ou almanach théâtrale*, 1812, p.181 (rv); *Annuaire dramatique, ou étrennes théâtrales*, 1812, p.221 (an) and 1813, p.326 (an). Duval, iv.158; 'fiche Lecomte'; Douay, *Rép Paris*, x, année 1811, f.18; Wicks and Schweitzer, i.43.

Comments: None of the contemporary sources except the *Annuaire dramatique* names Loaisel as author. The name under which the play was published, 'La Glehenaye', is the one given in the *Courrier de l'Europe et des spectacles* (no.1390), the *Almanach des muses*, the *Opinion du parterre*, and the *Mémorial dramatique*. Douay lists Loaisel as author citing the *Annuaire dramatique* as source. The 'fiche Lecomte' and Wicks and Schweitzer both attribute the play to Loaisel but without explaining why. Duval simply lists the play under 'De La Glehenay'. There is some basis for hypothesising that the name printed on the title page of the play is indeed a pseudonym used by Loaisel, as will be discussed in the comments to the next entry. The *Annuaire dramatique* carries this play as being in the repertory of the Ambigu-Comique in both 1812 and 1813, but no performances were announced in the *Journal de l'Empire* during 1812. Performance statistics were not compiled for the year 1813.

86. *La Loi singulière*: 1811 original edition (unconfirmed attribution)
LA LOI SINGULIERE, / OU / MALHEUR ET CONSTANCE, / MÉLODRAME / EN TROIS ACTES, EN PROSE, A GRAND SPECTACLE, / PAR M. L. T. DE LA GLEHENAYE; / Musique de MM. QUAISAIN et LANUSSE; / Ballets de M. MILLOT; décors de M. MOENCH; / Représenté, pour la première fois, à Paris, sur le / Théâtre de l'Ambigu-Comique, le 13 Avril 1811. / [*ornamental half rule*] / DE L'IMPRIMERIE DE HOCQUET ET Cie., / RUE DU FAUBOURG MONTMARTRE, No. 4. / PARIS, / BARBA, Libraire, Palais-Royal, derriere [*sic*] le / Théâtre Français, no.51. / [*quarter rule*] / 1811.

8°. 53 pp.

Library locations: BN‡; Ars†; MH.

Sources: Quérard, *Fr litt*; Lacroix, *Bibl Soleinne*, no.3451; Duval, iv.158; 'fiche Lecomte'; Monglond, *Fr rév*, ix(1963).507; Saulnays.

Comments: The only library catalogue which attributes the work to Loaisel is that of the Ars *fonds* Rondel. The author card catalogue (not the bound ms catalogue) of the Rondel collection cites Lacroix, *Bibl Soleinne* as the authority for the attribution. It is, however, only in the *Table des pièces* (published by Charles Brunet in 1914) of the Soleinne catalogue that the attribution is made and not in the catalogue itself. On the other hand, the card for the Douay collection copy of the second edition (no.87) G. D. 8° 690 (12) bears a *cancelled* attribution to Loaisel on the back of the card listing the play under La Glehenaye. In summary then, one contemporary source (the *Annuaire dramatique*) attributes the play to Loaisel as do three modern sources, which fail to disclose their evidence (Lecomte, Brunet, and Wicks and Schweitzer). Barbier, Georges d'Heylli's *Dictionnaire des pseudonymes*,[26] and Quérard's *Supercheries* fail to mention the work. Examination of the pseudonym may help to shed some additional light upon this problem. In the first place, the full name on the title page reads 'M. L. T. de la Glehenaye'. The initials 'L. T.' certainly suggest 'Loaisel Tréogate'. Loaisel had long since dropped the 'de' preceding 'Tréogate'. He might have taken on the new surname to disguise his identity in making a comeback. In fact, the name 'La Glehenaye' has considerable significance in regard to Loaisel. A village named 'La Gléhennaye', spelled with two 'n's is located approximately 12 kilometres due east of Loaisel's childhood home in Brittany. Moreover, the same name seems to have been intended for a character in *Ainsi finissent* referred to in the cryptic but suggestive form of the 'Comte de la Glehen. . .' (ii.164). Although far from conclusive on its own right, this evidence, when combined with the secondary source evidence cited previously, makes a moderate case in favour of Loaisel's authorship.

87.   *La Loi singulière*: 1811 second edition (unconfirmed attribution) Title page is identical to that of no.86.

8°. 50 pp.

Textual revisions: Many revisions and some omissions.
Library locations: Ars† (2 copies; G. D. 8° 690 (12)‡); MiU.
Sources: see no.86; except for the 'fiche Lecomte', which lists both the

[26] 3rd ed. (Paris 1887).

50 pp. and the 53 pp. editions, sources do not specify pagination and could thus refer equally well to either edition.

Comments: Although the type was not reset for the title page, the entire text was printed from a new type setting, thus resulting in two distinct editions. The title pages of the 50 pp. copies show evidence of more type wear than those of the 53 pp. copies, suggesting that the 53 pp. edition (no. 86) was the original.

Lucile et Dercourt
(unpublished?; confirmed attribution)

Performances (total: 18)

2 mai 1790 – 10 novembre 1790: Théâtre des Beaujolais: 18 performances 'Lucile et Dercourt, comédie en prose et en deux actes, par M. de Tréogate' (*Almanach général de tous les spectacles de Paris et des provinces*, 1791, p.85).

Sources: *Chronique de Paris* (perf an). *Almanach général de tous les spectacles de Paris et des provinces*, 1791, p.85 (rv); *Almanach des spectacles* (an IX), xlv, 1ère partie, p.130 (an); *Annuaire dramatique, ou étrennes théâtrales*, 1813, p.236 (an). Desessarts, *Siècles litts*; Rabbe; Levot; Douay, *Rép Paris*, viii, année 1790, f.13; Duval iii.68; Saulnays.

Comments: All sources, four of which are contemporary, give Loaisel as author, making the attribution as certain as possible in the absence of a published edition. Desessarts and Saulnays give a date of 1789, and Duval gives 1 May 1790; however, the daily theatre announcements in the *Chronique de Paris* clearly give the date of the first performance as 2 May 1790, and the *Almanach général* indicates that the play was first performed in 1790. There were no announcements found of any play by this name in 1789.

Lucile et Dercourt: *editions* (*unpublished?*)
No editions were located nor were any source references found to editions.

Raoul de Montfort
(unpublished?; unconfirmed attribution)

Performances (total: ?)
dates unknown: Théâtre de Molière (or Théâtre de la Cité): number of performances unknown

'Raoul de Montfort, melodrame en 3 actes par Loaisel-Tréogate' ('fiche Lecomte').

Sources: Almanach des spectacles (an VIII), xliv.247 (an); *Annuaire dramatique, ou étrennes théâtrales*, 1813, p.236 (an); 'fiche Lecomte'.

Comments: The *Almanach des spectacles* attributed the play to Loaisel in the *an* VIII issue but removes it from the list of his works in the following year ((an IX) xlv, 1ère partie, p.130), thus seeming to disavow the former listing, although it might equally well have been an oversight. The *Annuaire dramatique* gives Loaisel as author. The play was performed at the Théâtre de Molière, according to the *Almanach*, or the Théâtre de la Cité, according to the *Annuaire*. No daily performance announcements were discovered for a play under this name at any theatre in Paris for the period covered by this survey. Lecomte evidently has another source since the information 'melodrame en 3 actes' was lacking in both of the contemporary sources discovered. Thus, additional evidence must exist on this play, but until it is discovered, the attribution remains unconfirmed.

Raoul de Montfort: editions (unpublished?)
No editions were located nor were any source references found to editions.

Roland de Monglave

Performances (total: 43)

28 janvier 1799 (9 pluviôse an VII) – 26 mars 1799 (6 germinal an VII): Théâtre de l'Ambigu-Comique: 23 performances
Sources: Courrier des spectacles (perf an). *Courrier des spectacles*, no.707 (29 janvier 1799 [10 pluviôse an VII]), p.3 (rv); *Journal des théâtres, de littérature et des arts*, no.62 (30 janvier 1799 [11 pluviôse an VII]), pp.246-47 (rv) and no.64 (1er février 1799 [13 pluviôse an VII]), p.254 (rv); *Mercure de France*, 8 février 1799 (20 pluviôse an VII), pp.122-24 (rv); *Almanach des spectacles* (an VIII), xliv.164 (rv) and 247 (an); *Revue des thèâtres*, an VIII, p.134 (rv); *Almanach des muses*, 1800, p.322 (an); *Almanach des spectacles* (an IX), xlv, 1ère partie, p.130 (an) and 2e partie, p.56 (an); *Annuaire dramatique, ou étrennes théâtrales*, 1813, p.236 (an). Desessarts, *Siècles litts*; Rabbe; Duval, iv.231; Douay, *Rép Paris*, viii, année 1799, f.18; Barroux; Bousquet.

Comments: The *Almanach des spectacles* (an IX), xlv, 2e partie, p.56 gives the genre as 'pantomime dialoguée', which Rabbe repeats. Desessarts incorrectly gives 1798 as the year of first performance, evidently converting *An* VII as such. Duval in an obvious mistake has written 'an IX (1799)'.

19 juin 1799 (1er messidor an VII) – 18 août 1799 (1er fructidor an VII): Théâtre de la Gaîté: 6 performances
Sources: *Courrier des spectacles* (perf an). *Courrier des spectacles*, no.849 (20 juin 1799 [2 messidor an VII]), pp.2-3 (rv).

19 janvier 1803 (29 nivôse an XI) – 26 mai 1803 (6 prairial an XI): Théâtre de la Porte Saint-Martin, ci-devant Salle de l'Opéra: 13 performances
Sources: *Courrier des spectacles* (perf an). *Courrier des spectacles*, no.2146 (20 janvier 1803 [30 nivôse an XI]), p.3 (rv).

8 décembre 1805 (17 frimaire an XIV): Théâtre Molière: 1 performance
Source: *Courrier des spectacles* (perf an).

88. *Roland de Monglave*: *An* VII original edition
ROLAND / DE MONGLAVE, / DRAME EN QUATRE ACTES, / En prose, à spectacle. / Représenté, pour la première fois, à Paris, sur le / Théâtre de l'Ambigu-Comique, le 9 pluviôse, / l'an 7 de la ré publique. / PAR J. M. LOAISEL-TRÉOGATE, auteur / de la Bizar rerie de la Fortune, du Château du / Diable, etc. / [*ornamental half rule*] / A PARIS, / Chez BARBA, Libraire, au Magasin des Pièces / de théâtres, quai de l'Unité, vis-à-vis le Pont-neuf. / [*double half rule*] AN VII.

8°. 50 pp.
Library locations: BN†; Ars†; BL, *Cat*; NN‡.
Sources: Quérard, *Fr litt*; Lacroix, *Bibl Soleinne*, no.3451; Tourneux, iii(1900), no.18799; Duval, iv.231; Monglond, *Fr rév*, iv(1935), 1095; Saulnays; Barroux; Cioranescu, *Bibl*; Bousquet; Morabito.
Comments: Tourneux incorrectly gives pagination as 30 pp. even though he cites the BN copy. Cioranescu's Gregorian calendar equivalent date is wrong (i.e., '1790'). Saulnays's entry is too confused to warrant serious consideration, but he does cite an *An* VII edition.

89. *Roland de Monglave*: 1800 Dutch translation (unconfirmed existence)
'Roland van Monglave, of de zegepraal der onschuld, 1800, d. M. G. Engleman' (Worp).

Source: Worp.

Comments: Worp's listings are confirmed in two cases out of four. There is no reason to doubt his reliability.

90.   *Roland de Monglave*: *An* XI (1803) re-edition
ROLAND / DE MONGLAVE, / DRAME EN QUATRE ACTES, / EN PROSE, A SPECTACLE. / Représenté, pour la première fois, à Paris, sur / le théâtre de l'Ambigu-Comique, le 9 pluviose [*sic*] / an 7. / Par J. M. LOAISEL THÉOGATE [*sic*], auteur de la Bisarrerie / de la Fortune, du Château du Diable, etc. / [*half rule*] / A PARIS, / Chez BARBA, Libraire, Palais du Tribunat, galerie derrière / le théâtre Français de la République, no. 51. / [*quarter rule*] / AN XI. (1803)
8°. 44 pp.

Textual revisions: Text is identical to that of *An* VII edition (no.88) except that only the 'dénouement plus simple' (IV.ix in *An* VII edition) is kept rather than offering a choice between two, as in the *An* VII edition.
Library locations: BN†; Ars†; CtY‡; MiU.
Sources: Saulnays; Monglond, *Fr rév*, iv(1935).1095; Barroux; Bousquet; Morabito.
Comments: Bousquet's entry is an obvious misprint, reading '1903'. Saulnays's confused entry does list an *An* XI (1803) edition.

Virginie

(unpublished?; confirmed attribution)

Performance (total: 26)

30 juin 1790 – 21 février 1791: Théâtre Français comique et lyrique, rue de Bondy: 26 performances
'Virginie, drame en prose et en trois actes, par M. de Tréogate' (*Almanach général de tous les spectacles de Paris et des provinces*, 1791, p.118).
Sources: *Chronique de Paris* (perf an). *Almanach général de tous les spectacles de Paris et des provinces*, 1791, p.118 (rv); *Almanach des spectacles* (an IX) xlv, 1ère partie, p.130 (an); *Annuaire dramatique, ou étrennes théâtrales*, 1813, p.236 (an). Desessarts, *Siécles litts*; Rabbe; Levot; Douay, *Rép Paris*, viii, année 1790, f.10v; Duval, iii.395; 'fiche Lecomte'; Saulnays.

Comments: The attribution of this play to Loaisel is as firmly established as possible in the absence of a printed edition. The review in the *Almanach général* not only names Loaisel as author but also refers in a general manner to his other plays. Two other contemporary sources, the *Almanach des spectacles* and the *Annuaire dramatique,* confirm the attribution to Loaisel. All later sources concur, with the 'fiche Lecomte' giving only 'par L. de T.' The *Chronique de Paris,* in the daily theatre announcements, the *Almanach des spectacles,* and the 'fiche Lecomte' refer to *Virginie* as a 'comédie' (the *Annuaire dramatique* lists no genre), thus leaving this item of the description undecided. The *Annuaire dramatique* lists the theatre as 'Th des Jeunes Artistes'; however, this is not a discrepancy but in fact the name of the company that after 1794 occupied the same building in which the company of the Théâtre Français comique et lyrique had performed before. Desessarts's reference, repeated by Saulnays, to a 'Virginie, com en 5 actes, 1789, non-imprimée' cannot be reconciled with the other references. He does not mention the 1790, 3 act play and may have wrongly attributed another *Virginie* to Loaisel.

91. *Virginie: An* II original edition (doubtful existence)
Source: Douay, *Rép Paris,* viii, année 1790, f.10*v*.
Comments: Douay's notation 'an II imp' seems to indicate a printed edition, but there was no other evidence to support this claim. In fact, no other source references to editions were found nor were any editions located.

Le Vol par amour

Performances (total: 31)

2 novembre 1795 (11 brumaire an IV) – 12 août 1796 (26 thermidor an IV): Théâtre de l'Ambigu-Comique: 31 performances
Sources: *Affiches, annonces et avis divers ou journal général de France* (8°) (perf an). *Almanach des spectacles* (an VIII), xliv.247 (an) and (an IX), xlv, 1ère partie, p.130 (an) and 2e partie, p.56 (an); *Annuaire dramatique, ou étrennes théâtrales,* 1813, p.236 (an). Desessarts, *Siècles litts*; Rabbe Douay, *Rép Paris,* viii, année 1795, f.11*v* and année 1796, f.15*v*; Duval, iii.396; Barroux; Bousquet.
Comments: The date of the first performance may be considered firmly

established as given above. It is listed as such on the title page of the published play and so listed in the theatre announcements of the *Affiches, annonces*. Thus, Duval's listing of '23 Brumaire an IV (14 novembre 1795)' is erroneous as is Douay's '21 Brumaire v (11 novembre 96)' (Douay, année 1796). The theatre for the first performance has been given in several modern sources as the Théâtre de la Cité.[27] The only contemporary source to list the Cité is the *Annuaire dramatique*, but since it fails to mention any performances at the Ambigu-Comique, this listing is undoubtedly a mistake. It is probably the source for subsequent references to the Cité. The *Affiches, annonces* show no performance at the Cité, and the *Almanach des spectacles* lists only the Ambigu-Comique. The title page of the printed play does not list a theatre for the first performance. The best evidence available, thus, does not support any performances at the Cité.

92. *Le Vol par amour*: 1796 original edition
LE VOL PAR AMOUR, / COMÉDIE / EN DEUX ACTES, EN PROSE, / REPRÉSENTÉE pour la première fois à / Paris, le 11 Brumaire de l'an 4eme. / de l'Ere républicaine, 2 novembre / 1795, (vieux style.) / PAR J. M. LOAISEL TRÉOGATE. / [*ornament* (18 ×36 mm)] / A PARIS, / Chez la Citoyenne TOUBON, sous les Galeries / du Théâtre de la République, à côté du / Passage vîtré. / [*quarter rule*] / 1796.

8° 52 pp.

Library locations: Ars† (3 copies; G. D. 8° 19213‡); BL† (microfilm copy examined).

Sources: Quérard, *Fr litt*; Lacroix, *Bibl Soleinne*, no.3433; Levot; Duval, xiii.107; Tourneux, iii(1900), no.19471; Monglond, *Fr rév*, iii(1933).516; Gay, iii.1396; Saulnays; Barroux; Cioranescu, *Bibl*; Bousquet; Morabito.

Comments: Saulnays gives a publication date of 1795 in addition to 1796, but there is no other evidence for such an edition.

---

[27] Ars, *Rondel*, xi.104 (in the description of Rf 18646); Barroux; Douay; Louis Henry Lecomte, *Le Théâtre de la Cité, 1792-1907*: vol.ix of his *Histoire des théâtres de Paris* (Paris 1910), p.110.

4

Poems

A m. le chevalier de Parny, après avoir lu
ses Poésies érotiques

93. *A m. Le chevalier de Parny*: 1802 publication in *Nouvel almanach des muses*
'A M. Le Chevalier de Parny, Après avoir lu ses Poésies érotiques. 1782.' In *Nouvel almanach des muses pour l'an grégorien 1802*, pp.196-97.
Library locations: Ars†; CtY†; (additional locations not researched).
Comments: This poem was discovered during the *depouillement* for works originally published in periodicals.

Aux âmes sensibles

94. *Aux âmes sensibles*: 1780 original edition
AUX AMES / SENSIBLES, / ÉLÉGIE, / PAR M. DE TREOGATE. / [*double ornamental full rule*] / Ut multa luctuosa dolor invenit. / PLINE. / [*double ornamental full rule*] / [*ornament* (32×60 mm)] / A PARIS, / Chez L. JORRY, Imprimeur-Libraire, rue de / la Huchette, près du Petit-Châtelet; / Et les Marchands de Nouveautés. / [*double half rule*] / M. DCC. LXXX.

8°. pp.[1-2]3-20[21]22-30[31-32].

Contents: [Preface], 3-20; 'Aux Ames sensibles, élégie', 21-30; [Advertisement] 'On trouve chez BELIN [. . .], les Ouvrages suivants du même Auteur', 31.
Library locations: BN‡; IEN; MH† (microfilm of BN copy).
Sources: *Affiches, annonces et avis divers* (4°), 31 mai 1780, p.86 (rv). Laporte, *Nouv suppl.* i.254 and ii.8; Ersch, *Fr lit*; Desessarts, *Siècles litts*

and *Dict*; Michaud; Rabbe; Levot; Saulnays; Barroux; Cioranescu, *Bibl*; Bousquet; Morabito.

Comments: On page 30 after the end of the text appears the date of the censor's authorisation, '18 janvier 1780'. Saulnays notes a copy existing in the Ars *fonds* Rondel, but none was found there.

95.   *Aux âmes sensibles*: 1975 re-edition
Aux âmes sensibles, élégie. In Morabito.
Library locations: not researched.

See also 'Works published in periodicals' in section 5 below.

5

Miscellaneous works

~~~~~~~~~~~~

Articles in *Histoire des hommes*, by Delisle de Sales
(unconfirmed attribution)

'De Louis I, surnommé le Débonnaire'. In *Histoire des hommes, ou histoire nouvelle de tous les peuples du monde, partie de l'histoire moderne, France*, tome ii, pp.49-87. Paris 1779. [BN – G. 14623 (2)]
'Histoire de Philippe II'. In *Histoire des hommes, ou histoire nouvelle de tous les peuples du monde, partie de l'histoire moderne, Espagne*, tome ii, pp.185-237. Paris 1783. [BN – G. 14622]
Library location: BN†.
Sources: Ersch, suppl; Michaud; Arnault; Quérard, *Fr litt*; Rabbe; Levot; Saulnays.
Comments: The articles and indeed the entire *Histoire des hommes* were published anonymously. All source references attributing the articles to Loaisel are probably based on Ersch. Barbier (ii.754-55) lists as the collaborators of Delisle de Sales only Ch.-Jos. Mayer and L.-S. Mercier, stating further 'L'histoire de France est de L.-S. Mercier'. Quérard (*Fr litt*, ii.456) also lists only Mayer and L.-S. Mercier as collaborators. The BN *Cat* lists only these three names as authors. It is highly likely, however, that there were many minor collaborators, since this entire work is over fifty volumes in length. Loaisel could have been one of them, but the only definitely independent evidence so far discovered for this attribution is Ersch's listing.

Works published in periodicals
(unconfirmed existence)

'Poésies fugitives et autres pièces et vers insérées dans le Mercure et autres feuilles périodiques, etc. etc.[. . . .] Beaucoup d'extraits et de morceaux de prose, insérés dans le journal Encyclopédique et autres journaux des tems' (Desessarts, *Siècles litts*).

Sources: Desessarts, *Siècles litts*; Ersch, suppl; Michaud; Arnault; Rabbe; Quérard, *Fr litt*; Levot; Hoefer; Saulnays.

Comments: There seems little doubt that all these similarly phrased references are based only on Desessarts's original remarks. The 'extraits' to which he refers are most probably those that appeared in the reviews. The only poem located in a periodical was *A m. le Chevalier de Parny*. A thorough *dépouillement* of the *Mercure* and *Journal encyclopédique*, following the procedures outlined above under 'Sources consulted', uncovered no works attributed to Loaisel other than the extracts in reviews. His works could have been among the many anonymous pieces, or they could have escaped identification in the *tables* of the individual issues. Saulnays's remark that Loaisel's *œuvre* is 'éparse dans le *Mercure de France* ancien, comme dans le *Journal encyclopédique*' (p.7) cannot in any way be supported or refuted since Saulnays claims that most of the articles are anonymous.

[178?] *Projet de discipline militaire*

(nonexistent? unpublished? or anonymously published?)

This work, announced in a note appearing in *Dolbreuse* (1783 ed., i.52-54), was discussed above on page 79. The same note is reprinted verbatim in the 1785 and 1786 re-editions, thus still referring to the work as a future publication. The work might well have been abandoned either in the composition stage or before publication. If it was actually completed and published, no trace of it has been discovered. Secondary sources mention no such work, unless it be included among those supposedly appearing in periodicals. That possibility must be kept open as well as anonymous publication, or existence in manuscript form. But since the same note as reprinted in the *An* II re-edition of *Dolbreuse* (i.67-69) drops the paragraph mentioning this 'projet', it would appear most probable that Loaisel actually abandoned the work.

ca. 1786 Political – philosophical work

(nonexistent? unpublished? or
anonymously published?)

This work, announced in *Ainsi finissent* in the 'Préface de l'éditeur'
(i.13-14) and in a note by 'l'éditeur de ces Lettres' (ii.126), was discussed above on pp.82-84. No copies of this work have been located,
leaving the same alternatives regarding its existence as for the *Projet
de discipline militaire*, discussed in the preceding entry. In *Valrose*, all
mention of the work is omitted.

Appendices

A

Chronology of Loaisel de Tréogate*

⚘

1744 24 November: marriage of Loaisel's parents, Vincent Joseph Loaisel and Anne Marie de La Cour

1745 3 September: birth of Loaisel's sister Françoise Mathurine Marie

1746 16 October: birth of Loaisel's brother Alexandre Marie

1747 2 December: birth of Loaisel's brother Gobrien Mathurin Joseph

1752 17 August: birth of Joseph Marie Loaisel in the parish of St Guyomard in Brittany

1754 18 April: birth of Loaisel's sister Emilie Judith

1754-
1771 Death of both of Loaisel's parents

1773 31 May: Loaisel enters the Gendarmerie

1775 10 April: Loaisel is given a 'congé de retraite' from the Gendarmerie

1776 *Valmore, anecdote françoise*
Florello, histoire méridionale

1777 *Soirées de mélancolie*

1779 *La Comtesse d'Alibre, ou le cri du sentiment, anecdote françoise*

1780 *Aux âmes sensibles, élégie*

1781 14 June: death of Loaisel's sister Emilie Judith

1782 Composition of the poem *A m. le Chevalier de Parny, après avoir lu ses Poésies érotiques*

1783 *Dolbreuse, ou l'homme du siècle, ramené à la vérité par le sentiment et par la raison, histoire philosophique*

1787 *Ainsi finissent les grandes passions; ou les dernières amours du Chevalier de ...*

1788 21 July: marriage to Marie Opportune Prout in Paris
22 July: first performance of *L'Amour arrange tout, comédie en un acte et en prose* (Théâtre des Beaujolais)

* Works whose authenticity or existence is in any doubt have been included only when conforming to criteria discussed in the listing.

1789 5 July: birth of Loaisel's son, Alexandre Prosper

1790 2 May: first performance of *Lucile et Dercourt, comédie en prose et en deux actes* (Théâtre des Beaujolais)

29 May: birth of Loaisel's daughter, Angélique Eulalie

30 June: first performance of *Virginie, drame en prose et en trois actes* (Théâtre Français comique et lyrique, rue de Bondy)

1792 5 December: first performance of *Le Château du Diable, comédie héroïque, en quatre actes et en prose* (Théâtre de Molière)

1793 16 April: first performance of *La Bisarrerie de la fortune, ou le jeune philosophe, comédie en cinq actes et en prose* (Théâtre du Marais)

1794 22 July: opening of *La Bisarrerie de la fortune* at the Théâtre Français de la République

2 August: first performance of *Le Combat des Thermopyles, ou l'école des guerriers, fait historique en trois actes et en prose* (Théâtre de la Cité-Variétés)

1795 4 September: Loaisel awarded an 'encouragement' of 2000 *livres* by decree of the Convention

2 November: first performance of *Le Vol par amour, comédie en deux actes, en prose* (Théâtre de l'Ambigu- Comique)

1797 7 May: first performance of *La Forêt périlleuse ou les brigands de la Calabre, drame en trois actes, en prose* (Théâtre de la Cité)

1799 19 January: first (and only) performance of *Les Amans siciliens, ou les apparences trompeuses, comédie en deux actes et en prose* (Théâtre des Amis des Arts, et des Elèves de l'Opéra-Comique, ci-devant Molière, rue Martin)

28 January: first performance of *Roland de Monglave, drame en quatre actes* (Théâtre de l'Ambigu-Comique)

13 September: first performance of *La Fontaine merveilleuse, ou les époux musulmans, pantomime-féerie en cinq actes, à grand spectacle, mêlée de dialogue, de combats, chants et danses* (Théâtre de l'Ambigu-Comique)

1800 16 February: death of Loaisel's first wife, Marie Opportune Prout

Valrose, ou les orages de l'amour

1801 23 January: opening of *La Forêt périlleuse* at the Théâtre de l'Ambigu-Comique

2 July: first performance of *Adélaïde de Bavière, drame en quatre actes, en prose, à spectacle* (Théâtre de l'Ambigu-Comique)

1802   Publication of poem *A m. le Chevalier de Parny, après avoir lu ses Poésies érotiques* in *Nouvel almanach des muses pour l'an grégorien 1802*

1803   *Héloïse et Abeilard, ou les victimes de l'amour, roman historique, galant et moral*

1804   10 October: marriage to Jeanne Sophie Delaville
       6 November: first performance of *Le Grand chasseur ou l'isle des palmiers, melodrame en trois actes, en prose, et à grand spectacle* (Théâtre de l'Ambigu-Comique)

1812   11 October: death of Joseph Marie Loaisel de Tréogate in Paris

B

Chronological list of editions and translations*

Dates	Original editions	Re-editions	Translations
1776	Valmore		
	Florello		
1777	Soirées de mélancolie		
			Valmore (German)
1779	La Comtesse d'Alibre		
1780	Aux âmes sensibles		
			Florello (German)
1781			La Comtesse d'Alibre (English)
1783	Dolbreuse		
		Dolbreuse (Bibliothèque des Romans)	
1785		Dolbreuse, 2nd ed	
1786		Dolbreuse, 3rd ed	
1787	Ainsi finissent		
1788	L'Amour arrange tout		
1789		Ainsi finissent, 2nd ed	
1790			Dolbreuse (German)
1792		Dolbreuse, 4th ed	
1793	Château du Diable		
	Bisarrerie de la fortune		
1793		Bisarrerie de la fortune 2nd ed (Date?)	

* Works or editions whose authenticity or existence is in any doubt have been included only when conforming to criteria discussed in the listing.

Dates	Original editions	Re-editions	Translations
(An II)		Dolbreuse, 5th ed Lucile et Milcourt, 2nd ed of La Comtesse d'Alibre Lucile et Milcourt, 3rd ed of La Comtesse d'Alibre	
1794			Bisarrerie de la fortune (German – 2 separate editions)
(An III)	Combat des Thermopyles		
		Soirées de mélancolie, 2nd ed Valmore et Florello	
1796	Vol par amour		
1797	Forêt périlleuse		
1798		Forêt périlleuse, 2nd ed	
(An VII)	Roland de Monglave Fontaine merveilleuse		
		Bisarrerie de la fortune, 3rd ed	
1799			Forêt périlleuse (English)
(An VIII)	Valrose		
1800			Forêt périlleuse (Dutch) Roland de Monglave (Dutch)
1801	Adélaïde de Bavière		Adélaïde de Bavière (Dutch)

Dates	Original editions	Re-editions	Translations
			Château du Diable (German)
(An x)		Lucile et Milcourt, 4th ed of La Comtesse d'Alibre	
1802	A m. le chevalier de Parny (published)		
		Château du Diable, 2nd ed	
		Forêt périlleuse, 3rd ed	
		Forêt périlleuse, 4th ed	
			Valmore et Florello (Russian)
1803	Héloïse et Abeilard		
		Roland de Monglave, 2nd ed	Bisarrerie de la fortune (Dutch)
1804	Grand chasseur		
1807			Forêt périlleuse (English)
1808			Bisarrerie de la fortune (German)
1809		Forêt périlleuse, 5th ed	
1812		Forêt périlleuse, 6th ed	
1813			Forêt périlleuse (English-Boston)
			Forêt périlleuse (English-Hallowell)

Chronological list of editions and translations

Dates	Original editions	Re-editions	Translations
1816		Forêt périlleuse, 7th ed	
1826			Forêt périlleuse (English)
18[62?]		Forêt périlleuse, 8th ed	
[1866?]			Forêt périlleuse (English)
18??			Forêt périlleuse (English)
1871			Forêt périlleuse (English)

C

A m. le chevalier de Parny,
après avoir lu ses Poésies érotiques
1782

Jeune Parny, ce n'est plus un mystère,
D'Apollon tu reçus le jour:
Apollon chérissait les bosquets de Cythère,
Et dans ces lieux Cypris devint ta mère
Sous le myrthe où naquit l'Amour.

A ton berceau le dieu venait sourire,
Tes doigts déjà préludaient sur sa lyre;
Il t'enseignait à moduler des tons.
Bientôt, abandonné dans l'amoureux empire
Tu surpris les échos du charme de tes sons:
D'un cœur brûlant tu peignis le délire,
Et ses tourmens et ses doux abandons.
Apollon t'entendit, sa voix resta muette.
De tes accens il connut le pouvoir,
De ton triomphe on le vit s'émouvoir,
Et son silence accusa sa défaite.

Mais de l'amour d'un père, heureux enchantement!
J'ai vu par tes accords les muses entraînées,
Quitter sa cour et son trône éclatant,
Te couronner de fleurs au Pinde moissonnées,
De mille dons combler leur jeune amant,
Et, sans punir leur fuite téméraire,
Le dieu lui-même admirant tes chansons,
Vient, m'a-t-on dit, modeste et solitaire,
Prendre à son tour de tes leçons.

LOAISEL DE TRÉOGATE

Réponse
aux vers précédens

Des parens que vous me donnés,
Hélas! mes soins infortunés
N'ont point obtenu la tendresse:
Apollon ne m'écoute plus;
Vénus, la cruelle Vénus
Ne m'a pas rendu ma maîtresse.
Par eux, enfin, déshérité,
Je cesse d'aimer et d'écrire.
A leur arrêt je dois souscrire,
Car c'est vous qu'ils ont adopté.

PARNY

D

Descriptive summaries of the novels*

～～～※～～～

Ainsi finissent les grandes passions

This epistolary novel is primarily a psychological study of the Chevalier de . . . during his affair with Mme de V. . . as told in the Chevalier's letters to Mme de V. . . and to the Comte de P. . . , a retired friend of the Chevalier living in the country. Numerous digressions on a variety of topics central among the preoccupations of late eighteenth-century thought are interspersed throughout, usually, but not always, when the story provides an appropriate pretext.

Unhappy with his dull, lonely existence in Paris, the Chevalier is suddenly brought to life when he meets Mme de V. . . , a widow of two years, who is just now returning to society. Having previously experienced disillusionment in love, he proposes that they establish an 'amitié', which he sees as the highest and most rewarding type of relationship. But he soon develops desires of a more physical nature, declares his love, and is ecstatic to receive an *aveu* from Mme de V. . . . Their feelings persist, becoming more certain and more intense, but Mme de V. . . rejects the idea of marriage preferring instead a voluntary union based solely on 'l'inclination'. After a short separation necessitated by the Chevalier's required presence at the court of Versailles, the couple leaves Paris for the nearby estate of Mme de V. . .'s uncle at Gur. . . .

For a brief period, they live a veritable *idylle* enjoying walks in the lush countryside, a 'bal champêtre' with the local villagers, and visits to the virtuous families of local *gentilshommes*. A fire which totally destroys the *hameau* of Gur. . . brings the *idylle* to an end, causing Mme de V. . . to fall into a state of melancholy and the Chevalier to begin worrying about the future. As Mme de V. . . begins to show signs of ennui, the Chevalier wishes for the security of marriage but knows that Mme de V. . . will never consent. He agrees to let her invite some

* Summaries are based on first editions.

202

friends from Paris for a visit to cheer her up. Among them is the Vicomte de ..., a vain and pompous but good looking *Officier aux Gardes*. Although he at first inspires only the scorn of Mme de V..., little by little, he mends his ways sufficiently to win her affections. This *galanterie* destroys the delicate balance of what remained of her relationship with the Chevalier.

One day the Chevalier, who has grown exceedingly jealous, stalks out after an argument with Mme de V... and takes off into the woods to calm himself and gather his thoughts. Temporarily lost, he comes upon a rustic *pavillon* where he meets the Comte de la Gleh..., an old gentleman, somewhat of a recluse but very wise as to the ways of the world. After a long wide-ranging discussion, the Chevalier comes away resigned to his situation. To his surprise, Mme de V... is waiting for him and extremely upset. But after their reconciliation and the departure of the guests, including the Vicomte de..., Mme de V... soon returns to her state of ennui.

The death of an uncle calls Mme de V... to Strasbourg leaving the Chevalier behind at Gur... to suffer the tribulations of separation. He is greatly worried that she will be unfaithful to him and writes her of his fears only to apologise after receiving her assurances of fidelity. Then begin the first signs of the Chevalier's 'folie' or 'délire'. As Mme de V... prolongs her stay in Strasbourg, the Chevalier pleads for her to return, and again suspecting her of infidelity, begs her to tell him the truth, preferring to fill his present emotional void with some sort of feeling inspired by her and her alone, even if that feeling be despair.

The Chevalier is informed by a relative in Strasbourg that Mme de V... is indeed enjoying the company of a certain Marquis de R..., Colonel of the regiment of *Dragons* stationed there. Seeking some sort of consolation, the Chevalier returns to the *pavillon* of the old Comte de la Gleh... only to find that he has died. He writes Mme de V... of his regrets over her infidelity but then yields to her pleadings for a reconciliation.

Their reunion in Paris is, however, a great disappointment. Mme de V... has become vain and taken on an air of false frivolity, but the Chevalier continues to love her, feeling that he is to blame because he has ceased to please her. He continues to accept his fate and remains in love even after the Marquis de R... comes to Paris and seduces Mme de V.... But this episode causes a severe recurrence of the Chevalier's temporarily forstalled 'délire'. When he discovers a note from the

Marquis to Mme de V... confirming the full extent of the affair, he flees to the Jardin des Tuileries where he faints. He ends up at the Bois de Vincennes where he decides to commit suicide by jumping from the Château tower. But the view of a tranquil countryside inspires in him the will to live. Resigned to his suffering, the Chevalier decides his future will be devoted to relationships founded solely on 'amitié'. Several months later, he refuses the reconciliation offered by Mme de V..., who has in the meantime been deserted by two other lovers, although he has never ceased to love her.

La Comtesse d'Alibre

This sentimental and 'sombre' story of ill-fated love and adultery, narrated in the third person, takes place in rural Provence. The ageing Chevalier de Saint-Flour returns to his decaying château, having become discouraged by life at court, where he never received the recognition and rewards deserved for his thirty years of service to the king. Unable to provide for his daughter, Lucile, who had been raised during his long absence by her aunt, the Chevalier is delighted when his old commander, the Comte d'Alibre, a rich neighbour of Italian origin, becomes attracted to Lucile and proposes marriage. Lucile, however, admits that she has long been in love with Milcourt, the son of an old enemy of Saint-Flour. The Chevalier at first opposes his daughter's wishes but finally consents. When he suddenly disappears, leaving behind a letter explaining his desire to spare the young lovers the burden of a dying father, Lucile becomes frantic in her distress, feeling herself responsible for her father's actions. After days of searching, she finally locates him tilling the earth in the field of one of his tenant farmers as a final effort to fulfil his duty to humanity. In the belief that she might restore happiness to her father in his last years, Lucile sacrifices her love for Milcourt and marries the Comte d'Alibre, whom she has grown to detest. Unfortunately, the Chevalier de Saint-Flour dies almost immediately thereafter. Before long, the Comte d'Alibre learns of his wife's undying love for Milcourt, and when cruelty fails to change her mind, he abandons her, setting out to seek riches in the *Levant*.

In the meantime, Milcourt, who has been fighting in Italy, has received word of the marriage. After first seeking death in frenetic fighting on the battlefield, he flees into the forest to savour his torments amidst a hostile nature but finally decides to return to Saint-Flour in hopes that Lucile might still love him. On the way to Lucile's château, he encounters a ferocious she-wolf, which he kills with three deep thrusts of his sword into the monster's heart. Following the exchange of several letters and a threat of suicide, Milcourt finally persuades Lucile to see him again, and eventually they succumb to their passionate desires. This brief idyllic episode ends in despair when their love bears fruit. Although Lucile feels an enormous guilt toward society, Milcourt sees their actions as perfectly innocent according to the laws of nature. He convinces Lucile to flee with him once the child is born so that they might properly fulfil their duties as parents. But before they can leave, the Comte d'Alibre unexpectedly returns, whereupon Lucile's guilt feelings provoke a confession. The outraged Comte throws his wife and the fruit of her adultery into a dimly lit dungeon to starve to death. Milcourt murders the Comte but discovers Lucile too late to prevent her death and the death of the child, Lucile's attempts to nourish the infant with her own blood having failed. In the dark of night, Milcourt removes his wife's remains from the local cemetery and transfers them to a tomb on his own land by the ocean shore hidden from the world. There, he too soon expires and is interred next to his beloved by a faithful servant sworn forever to secrecy.

Dolbreuse

This psychological and philosophical memoir novel recounts the life of Dolbreuse, the narrator, from birth through marriage to his childhood sweetheart, Ermance, to her death and his withdrawal into the monastery of Roga. Children of neighbouring Breton nobles, the two were born on the same day and become inseparable from the time they are put into the care of the same wet nurse. They are less attracted to the values of the old romances of chivalry, with which their fathers had hoped to inspire them, than to the ideas they gather from their own readings of the tragedies of Racine and particularly of *La Nouvelle Héloïse*, which was to become their *livre de chevet*. Ermance, who is a veritable paragon of virtue and the stronger spiritual and intellectual force of the two, persuades Dolbreuse to delay the marriage they both so ardently desire and to which their parents wholeheartedly consent.

Dolbreuse enters the army inspired both by his father's tales of their noble warrior ancestors and by Ermance's insistence that a new kind of love, 'l'amour héroïque', will lead him on to noble actions so as to return fully worthy of marriage. But life in a peacetime provincial garrison was to lead Dolbreuse to boredom and the temptation of infidelity. He returns faithful, however, three years later. Finally Ermance consents to marriage, only to have the long awaited event further postponed by a brief period of mourning for their deceased fathers. Their simple wedding ceremony, held in an old chapel on the estate of a relative, is followed by a practically immediate consummation in the natural setting of an idyllic corner of the countryside.

After a brief period of marital bliss in the country, Dolbreuse leaves Ermance to seek favour and position at court. Disgusted and disappointed by the life at court, he withdraws and starts frequenting the society gathering around 'un Vieux Seigneur de la Cour' in his estate at Versailles. There he meets the charming young widow, la Marquise de ***, and after much moral turmoil, finally succumbs to her seductive advances. She persuades him to accompany her to Paris, 'cette nouvelle Sybaris', which he had so scrupulously avoided up to then. Soon abandoned by la Marquise de ***, Dolbreuse falls prey next to an *actrice* and then to numerous *courtisanes*, whom he both criticises and defends and of whom he finally tires. Having become a fully fledged *libertin*, he turns his attentions to ladies of the highest social status, but in spite of a series of *galanteries*, he remains subject to an incurable *ennui*.

The turning point in Dolbreuse's descent into total corruption and degradation comes with his elaborately conceived and executed seduction of the young, naive Comtesse de ***, which he tells as a story within a story. With the help of the Baronne de ***, Dolbreuse lures the Comtesse to a love nest in a country retreat, where he achieves his victory only to find that overwhelming feelings of remorse and guilt follow closely behind a moment's ecstasy. The Comtesse, even more upset than her seducer, returns to her country home leaving Dolbreuse to deal with his own anxiety.

Dolbreuse is also troubled by financial problems, having accumulated considerable debts. After exhausting the money he received from Ermance under false pretences, he turns unsuccessfully to gambling and even sells all his possessions but still remains in debt. Amidst these tribulations, the husband of the Comtesse de *** arrives to demand satisfaction. Dolbreuse is moved to repentence at the very moment he is in a position to finish off his adversary. The Comte refuses to kill Dolbreuse, who offers his life as penance for his actions, but rather leaves him to suffer the even worse punishment of remorse and self-incrimination. When a letter from the Comte arrives announcing that the Comtesse is near death, Dolbreuse flees to their lodgings and faints when he sees the house draped in mourning. Before he can recover from the shock, he is recognised by the authorities and imprisoned for failure to pay his debts. But prison comes to him practically as a relief and marks the end of his dissolution. There he receives word that the Comtesse still lives and that she and the Comte have pardoned him. His thoughts turn once again to Ermance.

Ermance arrives to bail out Dolbreuse, having been informed of his unfortunate misconduct. After a reconciliation, Ermance decides that Dolbreuse should return to the salubrious influence of the country, and they find themselves once again together in Brittany. During the first night home, however, Dolbreuse departs to seek reclusion and atonement in the monastery of Roga. Following much thought and prayer, he returns to Ermance feeling once again worthy to take his place as her husband.

The couple settles down to an idealised patriarchal country life fully worthy of 'le siècle d'or'. Their lives are filled with benevolent and pious works, readings of Voltaire and Rousseau, and contemplation amidst nature, ruins, and tombs. Soon, Ermance gives birth to a daughter, whom they raise according to Jean-Jacques's principles. A year after Rousseau's death, they decide to make a pilgrimage to his tomb on the Ile des Peupliers. Later they meditate on the injustices he suffered and on the unwarranted *libelles* that were issued following his death. Soon afterwards Ermance becomes melancholic. One night after a long discussion of their memories and present happiness, Ermance faints. Her sleep is troubled by disturbing dreams of death. She becomes ill in the days following and finally succumbs, but fully prepared to meet death. Not content with an ordinary funeral and burial for his wife, Dolbreuse removes her corpse from the coffin, cremates it in the forest at night, and places the remains in a crystal urn. Every morning thereafter, at daybreak, he steals away to the concealed ruins of an old château, there to offer his prayer to 'l'Eternel' and to contemplate the sun's rays reflecting off the urn, which he rests atop the remains of a column. When his daughter dies from sorrow, Dolbreuse retreats once again into the monastery of Roga after burying the urn along with the remains of his ancestors. In the monastery he composes his memoirs leaving instructions that they not be published until after his death.

Florello

The story of Florello, narrated in the third person, takes place in the exotic New World setting of the Orinoco valley. The wise old Kador, a 'noble savage' of unknown background, has been living alone peacefully for a number of years in this isolated, idyllic environment. One day he discovers a young Englishman, Florello, whom he befriends. After a series of romanesque adventures and cruel disappointments, Florello had set out from England for Peru, full of hatred for man and society. During a storm at sea, a sailor had rudely shoved him overboard. Once safe on land, Florello had been passively awaiting death, having lost all will to live. Now, thanks to Kador's advice and instruction, Florello acquires a new outlook on life deciding to build a new happiness out of his past misfortunes and settles down to live with Kador. When the venerable wise man finally dies, Florello buries him beside the river vowing to continue living according to the principles instilled in him by his mentor.

One day Florello ventures forth farther than usual from his *cabane* and sees a native hunter killing a tiger. Returning later to the same spot, he catches his first view of a native woman. This beautiful creature, named Eurimale, awakens amorous desires and weakens Florello's resolve to live forever the solitary life. She is frightened and flees but is more calm during their second meeting. At their third meeting, the two yield to their natural desires and make love, the first of many such encounters. This blissful situation is upset when Eurimale's father, Thoal, discovers the two together. Thoal becomes enraged both because of his hatred for Europeans, who had killed his wife, and because he has already promised Eurimale to a young savage, Orabski, the tiger-hunter whom Florello had seen earlier. Thoal nearly kills Florello in his rage but is moved to compassion by the young Englishman's virtuous resolution either to wed Eurimale or die at her father's hands. Finally, overcome by pity for his daughter, who protests at her betrothal to the wild and hateful Orabski, Thoal consents to her marriage with Florello. The three visit Florello's *cabane*, where Thoal stays while the young couple, during a tour of the surroundings, again experience the ecstasy of love. Florello later leaves Eurimale and Thoal in the *cabane* while he searches for a meal of exotic delicacies. Upon his return he finds Thoal dying of wounds and Eurimale gone – results of Orabski's vengeance.

Florello goes temporarily mad and sets out during a raging storm in pursuit of Orabski and Eurimale. He finally spots them and cries out to his beloved, but Orabski sends a giant boulder crashing down upon him. When Florello regains consciousness, still crazed by anger and grief, he hurls himself upon a young, innocent savage and kills him, mistaking him for Orabski. Overcome with grief and guilt at the discovery of this error, Florello returns to his *cabane* and tears at his flesh attempting to kill himself. He quickly realises the shamefulness of this act and resolves simply to sequester himself and let death come from the hands of nature.

He chooses as a fitting tomb wherein to await his death, the hollow interior of a giant tree growing deep in the heart of a dark forest. Eurimale, who has escaped from Orabski, discovers him here but too late to save him. As Florello dies, he tells Eurimale to look forward to their reunion after death.

Shortly thereafter Eurimale is captured by a band of French sailors and taken to Paris, where she lives with the kind Captain. She never forgets Florello, however, and remains faithful to his memory. After the captain's death, she retreats to the tranquility of a country house near Montpellier belonging to one of the captain's relatives. Ten years after coming to France, Eurimale finally dies of sadness, highly admired by all who had known her.

Soirées de mélancolie

La Vision: This supernatural oriental tale set in 'Iraque Persienne' centres on two rich libertines, Naboul and Talmuch, who make a pact whereby the first to die will return to inform the survivor about the world of life after death. One night after Naboul's departure, Talmuch has a vision in which his friend appears to announce his death and warn Naboul to change his conduct. Talmuch finds Naboul's body where the vision described it to be and thereafter lives a virtuous life.

L'Innocence protégée: An oriental pastoral, this tale starts with the arrival of a mysterious stranger who is given shelter by the venerable

Mirven. The stranger reveals that she is Zara daughter of a virtuous shepherd. A few years ago she fell in love with a young shepherd, Zillem, but in the midst of their idyllic love, she was abducted by a villainous knight, Arinbal. After two years' captivity in Arinbal's tower, she has finally escaped. Zara returns to her village to discover that her father is dead but that Zillem still lives. Mirven advises them to leave this village since Arinbal might find them there. They settle down close to Mirven and live happily ever after.

Le Remords: In this prose poem, Mirza confesses his 'crimes' of debauchery, ambition, ingratitude, and 'vice'. He proclaims his feelings of despair and guilt, his longing for expiation and death, and his state of permanent melancholy.

Nisa: The shepherdess Nisa, heroine of this idyll, is greatly upset by the withering of a rose she has been tending as a symbol of her beauty and of Myrtil's love for her. Myrtil reassures her, however, that he loves her not so much for her physical beauty, which may fade, as for her 'belle âme' and virtuous actions.

Les Regrets: Zaruch and Noëma, the two lovers of this oriental tale, enjoy an idyllic romance until one day, innocent victim of a ferocious serpent, Noëma dies leaving Zaruch alone and desperate. After wandering aimlessly hoping for death, Zaruch comes by accident upon the *cabane* where he had lived with his beloved. There he dies happy to be on his way to reunion with Noëma.

Le Crime puni: This tale of terror and mystery takes place in a country churchyard. Three young 'débauchés' decide to desecrate a cemetery. They are terrified when the bones in the ossuary start to move. Two of the young men are literally frightened to death, while the third turns delirious. This 'miracle' was actually caused by a beggar who had been sleeping in the ossuary and aroused by the noise, acting practically as though he were the instrument of divine vengeance.

Le Songe: The narrator, who is in a troubled state, falls asleep in a wild forest and has an allegorical dream. Passing in succession are a child, a desperate old man, sensuous women, battle, a village, a naive young girl, and an old man who ascends into heaven. A wise man explains the dream as a remembrance of past misfortunes and a vision of future happiness. The narrator longs to return to the simplicity of country life where happiness is at least possible even if not assured.

L'Empire de la beauté: This 'sombre', mysterious tale takes place in the countryside of southern France. The narrator recounts how one night in the woods he came upon a strange man dressed in black kneeling before a *calvaire*. Local villagers identified the man as the 'revenant de la forêt'. The narrator's curiosity was so aroused that he returned to the spot and followed the figure to a cave. There in the second chamber was the 'revenant' lying face up in a rock hollowed out in the shape of a coffin. Eventually, the 'revenant' explained that he was doing self-imposed penance for having seduced a nun and causing her to commit suicide. The story had such an effect upon the narrator that when, shortly thereafter, he nearly seduced a 'bergère', he immediately re-gretted his precipitous action and vowed to remain faithful to his 'Julie' and to seek happiness only in marriage.

Le Vieux laboureur: In this oriental tale, an old labourer becomes dissatisfied with his tranquil existence when he sees the glorious and magnificent vizir Massoud passing through the countryside. But shortly thereafter, a stranger arrives to announce Massoud's death. His enemies at court had falsely accused Massoud. Although the sultan recognised his vizir's true loyalty and refused to act, eventually he was swayed by superstition to believe that recent calamaties were the fault of the vizir and that Massoud had therefore to die. The old labourer upon hearing this tale is very content to return to his simple but happy life.

A ma Julie: This *héroïde* is addressed to a former sweetheart. She alone among the author's family and former friends has remained faithful to him and consoled him after the wayward adventures of his youth.

Le Port: This prose poem expresses the author's happiness upon returning to his native province and receiving his parents' forgiveness for his unfortunate youthful adventures in Paris.

Valmore

A sentimental memoir novel of the 'frenetic' school, *Valmore* recounts the fast-moving adventures of two ill-fated young lovers, Valmore, the narrator, and Julie de Forhèle. Their fathers having for-bidden the match, Valmore decides rather than to perform his 'devoir' of joining his father's old regiment, that he will rescue 'la vertu per-sécutée'. The lovers elope, but when refused refuge with a relative, they wander off aimlessly into the countryside of their native Brittany overcome by guilt and remorse. Julie sneaks away to expiate her sins in a convent. Valmore is later caught by his father's men and returned home. Although he is eventually forgiven, he too runs away to expiate his sins. After ten years of hard fighting in the army, Valmore discovers Julie in Frankfurt, where she is performing the lead role in Racine's *Iphigénie*. Julie reveals, in a story within a story, that she had been befriended by a kindly actress right after the elopement and had never entered a convent at all. Valmore rails at Julie decrying her lowly status and apparent corruption, finally convincing her to mend her ways. The two are discovered in a compromising position by Valmore's commander, who arrives for a prearranged rendezvous with Julie. Valmore kills his commander and is thrown into jail. After a futile attempt at escape, Valmore is led off to the gallows only to have Julie throw herself before him and die causing the crowd to cry for mercy. A pardon is arranged, but Valmore is already emotionally and spiritually dead as he writes his memoirs and awaits his two-year sentence to run its course.

Valrose

This novel is a new version of *Ainsi finissent les grandes passions*. The narrative form has been shifted from letters to memoirs, and the names of characters and places (other than Paris) have been changed. Although the roles of the two rivals have been altered and expanded, the basic sentimental intrigue remains intact. Two melo-dramatic episodes have been added in the middle and a new, happy ending substituted for the original denouement. Many of the digressions have been omitted.

The central characters are the couple Valrose and Mme de Florac – the Chevalier de ... and Mme de V... of *Ainsi finissent*. One of the rivals, Dolbelle, retains certain attributes of the Vicomte de M... from *Ainsi finissent*, while the other rival, Monseigneur de Montaiglon, com-bines elements of both the Vicomte de M... and the Marquis de R.... The action takes place in Paris and Menerville (Gur... in *Ainsi finissent*).

The first of the added melodramatic episodes (tome second, chapitre 2) concerns the abduction of Mme de Florac by the rival Dolbelle and the pursuit and rescue by Valrose. The other episode, which follows immediately after the abduction, tells of the capture of the couple by a band of brigands and of their nearly successful attempts to ravish Mme de Florac as Valrose watches in horror chained to a rock. They are rescued thanks to the combined efforts of the two rivals, Montaiglon at the head of his regiment of *Dragons*, whose approach frightens off the brigands, and Dolbelle, who just happens by, repents, and sets the couple free.

According to the new denouement, Mme de Florac never gave in to the pleadings of the rival, Montaiglon, as he himself informs Valrose after the couple's breakup. Although she was severely tempted and distracted for a while from her feelings for Valrose, she was never unfaithful to him. Having been refused any hope of reconciliation with her lover, Mme de Florac is planning to enter a monastery. Valrose searches far and wide to find his beloved to persuade her to come back to him and to forgive him for his former doubts of her ultimate fidelity. Purely by chance, he witnesses her taking of the veil but faints at the moment of *reconnaissance*. His attempts to dissuade her taking the vows after the obligatory three month interval seem to no avail. However, one day an old friend invites him to his country estate, where Valrose suddenly finds Mme de Florac waiting for him at the altar of the chapel. They are married and seem destined to live happily ever after.

E

Descriptive summaries of the plays*

~~~~~~

Adélaïde de Bavière

Fifteenth-century Bavaria is the setting for this melodrama. The action takes place in the gardens and woods surrounding the Duke of Bavaria's castle.

Act I: In the castle garden the Duke's *piquer*, Olivier, discusses with Edmont, *écuyer* and confidant of the Duke, how sombre life at the castle has been during their lord's absence and how happy everyone will soon be when he returns. The Duchess Adélaïde arrives with Hildegarde, the Duke's sister, discussing plans for the welcoming celebration. Alone, the two women discuss the letter Adélaïde recently received from Count Adolphe, the Duke's favourite, in which the Count revealed his love for Adélaïde. Adélaïde fears the worst, although Hildegarde believes that the Duchess's refusal will put a stop to the affair. In the monologue which follows, Adolphe admits his culpability and regrets the change that love has wrought in his conduct toward the Duke, but he reveals himself powerless to resist his amorous desires. The Count's confidant, Rambaut, persuades Adolphe that, to save his own life, he must accuse Adélaïde before she can accuse him. Adolphe reluctantly agrees to let Rambaut proceed with the plan he has concocted to convince the Duke of Adélaïde's guilt. Adélaïde returns and repeats face to face her refusal to yield to Adolphe's desires. Adolphe is now firmly set to revenge his misfortunes.

Act II: Rambaut reveals to Adolphe a small keepsake container which Adélaïde had once prepared for the Duke, now filled with purported love notes from her to Adolphe – actually Adélaïde's translations of French novels – all prepared with the help of Adélaïde's unfaithful 'fille d'honneur'. Adolphe's resolve falters momentarily when Edmont announces the premature return of Duke Frédéric, but Rambaut spurs

* Summaries follow the revised versions.

214

him on. Olivier lends an awkward hand to the ladies as they decorate the 'trône champêtre' with flowers. The Duke enters triumphantly amidst much festivity and receives a crown of laurels from Adélaïde. Towards the end of the celebration, a messenger arrives with a letter for the Duke. Having dismissed everyone but Adolphe, the Duke orders the Count to read aloud the letter, which accuses Adélaïde of declaring her love. When confronted with the case of love notes, brought forth by Rambaut, Frédéric orders Edmont to execute Adélaïde near the forest chapel where they were married and then to announce her death with three strikes of the chapel bell. Adélaïde reappears and, without any explanation, the Duke has Edmont lead her away.

Act III: Edmont and Adélaïde stop momentarily in an opening in the forest on their way to the chapel. Adélaïde still does not understand what is happening to her but, as they leave, Edmont says he will explain everything when they arrive at the chapel. Olivier arrives wondering why he has been ordered by Edmont to accompany the Duchess's carriage and why all the secrecy concerning their actions. Hildegarde appears on her way to find Adélaïde but gets no information from Olivier. Olivier informs a group of villagers who are about to begin to celebrate the Duke's return that all celebrations have been forbidden by the Duke. They all leave at the sound of an approaching thunderstorm. Frédéric enters lamenting the situation and despairs upon hearing the bell sound three times announcing Adélaïde's death. Edmont reappears to recount the death scene. When Adélaïde's body is borne into the Duke's view, he orders it placed in the cenotaph at the end of his gardens.

Act IV: After a group of the Duchess's ladies finish performing the funeral rites around the cenotaph, Frédéric appears to contemplate the situation. Edmont arrives to tell the Duke of the great sadness that has spread among the people and throughout the court upon learning of Adélaïde's death, for which few yet know the true reason. Frédéric, saddened and burdened with guilt over his precipitous actions, expresses his desire to renounce his position and withdraw into an isolated retreat. At this moment Hildegarde arrives to reveal Adolphe's letter to Adélaïde whereupon Adolphe appears to confess his perfidy. Meanwhile the people are rioting demanding vengeance for Adélaïde's death. Frédéric renounces his authority before the assembled people and declares his intention to bring the guilty to justice. Just as he is about to commit suicide, Hildegarde rushes forward to restrain him, and Adélaïde steps out of the cenotaph. Adélaïde pardons Frédéric, and Hildegarde reveals that she had planned the simulated execution in order to teach Frédéric never again to pronounce judgement so precipitously at the risk of condemning innocence.

L'Amour arrange tout

This one act *comédie de mœurs*, which takes place in the Parisian bourgeois household of M. Dupuis, a retired merchant, centres on the marriage of his naive daughter Angélique. Believing that nobility is the only sure guarantee of the virtue she seeks in a husband, Angélique has opposed her father's wishes and refused to marry the bourgeois Monval, whose character she doubts, preferring instead the 'Marquis de Luzimore', who is in reality Laurens, a farmer's son, raised and educated by Monval's family. Monval has persuaded Laurens to repay his indebtedness to the family by entering into a scheme of vengeance: disguising himself as a noble, he is to seduce Angélique, marry her, and then be revealed as a common labourer's son. M. Dupuis consents to his daughter's choice since he finds the Marquis a most virtuous person. However, Laurens, who has fallen in love with Angélique, decides he cannot carry through with this cruel hoax and reveals his true identity to his beloved. Angélique castigates Monval for his deceitful actions and accepts Laurens as her future husband, having realised 'que l'éducation met de niveau tous les hommes & que la vraie noblesse est dans le cœur'.

La Bisarrerie de la fortune

The action of this *comédie de caractère et d'intrigue*, except for the second act, takes place in the village square in front of M. Champagne's inn and Mme Robert's house.

Act 1: A stranger has deposited with the local *notaire*, M. Dupré, a large sum of money destined for some local inhabitant as yet unidentified. M. Du Taillis, the worthy gamekeeper, informs his daughter, Rosette, that he must pass the night in the forest in hope of catching the bandits who have been preying on travellers. Rosette announces that she will never marry M. Champagne, the new innkeeper, and leaves as the latter approaches to discuss the marriage with Du Taillis. Georges, a labourer's son, has returned from a long voyage he made to satisfy the conditions set for their marriage by his beloved Mme Robert. Dutaillis warns Georges that Mme Robert is an 'avaricieuse' who will not be won over by the 'autres avantages' with which Georges has returned in place of the fortune she demanded. Mme Robert confirms the prediction when she refuses to let the *jeune philosophe* enter her house and claims to have forgotten her promise of marriage. Georges decides to forget Mme Robert, who is no longer worthy of him. When Champagne refuses to house and feed him on credit, Georges sets out to seek lodging but finally ends up in the forest.

Act II: While Georges is fast asleep under a tree in the forest, two robbers approach cautiously carrying a valise. When startled by shots from Du Taillis and his followers, who are in pursuit, they drop the valise and disappear. Georges, unaware of these happenings, awakens and is greeted by Rosette, who offers him the food she had brought for her father. Georges, alone again, discovers the valise, hesitates, but then decides not to open it. On his way to turn it over to the authorities, he is apprehended by a group of *gendarmes* and accused by a naturalist of having stolen the valise from him in the belief that it held the fortune rumoured to be on its way to a local inhabitant.

Act III: Although declared innocent, thanks to the testimony in his favour by Rosette and her father, Georges decides to leave this village and withdraw from the society which has treated him so cruelly. He and Rosette discover that they are in love, but without a penny to his name, Georges hesitates to think of marriage. As he debates his actions, Georges is notified that *he* is the surprise recipient of the money left by the naturalist with M. Dupré. Once in possession of his fortune, Georges contemplates his new-found happiness, the acts of generosity he can now perform, his marriage with Rosette now made possible, and 'la bisarrerie de la fortune'.

Act IV: To repay the kindness of Du Taillis, Rosette, and Dupré, Georges arranges a party at Champagne's inn. After he reveals to the assembled guests his recently acquired fortune, Mme Robert, who by chance was present during the announcement, attempts a reconciliation, but to no avail, since Georges announces his intention to wed Rosette. However, Champagne returns with the notaire Dupré to reveal that he is George's uncle and namesake and to claim that it is he for whom the money was actually destined. The Judge will have to choose the rightful recipient.

Act v: Champagne, having won the judgement, announces that he is abandoning his ignoble profession and starts to take on airs. He proposes marriage to Mme Robert, who accepts, and the two leave after making fun of Georges and Rosette, who are once again penniless. Georges believes he must now leave and renounce all plans for marriage. But in a *scène d'attendrissement*, Du Taillis persuades Georges to stay. The naturalist returns to declare unequivocally that Georges is, after all, the intended recipient of the fortune. Upon hearing this news, Mme Robert refuses to marry Champagne, and the two leave arguing over the payment of forfeiture for refusal to honour the marriage contract they have signed in the meantime. Georges and Rosette can now get married, and Georges's fortune will permit Du Taillis to retire.

Le Château du Diable

Action, spectacle, and suspense predominate in this *comédie héroïque* set in a fourteenth-century French village.

Act i: Robert, valet of Raoul, Comte de Salandrie, appears at the village inn seeking lodging for his master and Adélaïde de Ferraques, Raoul's wife of two years. They are on their way to a *manoir* Raoul has inherited. As a result of her marriage, Adélaïde has been disinherited and banished by her uncle, the Baron de Mongrigny. Robert learns that the Baron has taken up residence in a nearby château and is now Seigneur of the village. Adélaïde goes off to bed as soon as the couple arrives, but Raoul succumbs to the pleading of a local peasant to rid the community of some 'maudits lutins' who inhabit a local abandoned château, 'le château du diable', and are terrorising the villagers.

Act ii: Raoul and his valet search through the ruins of the château. Alone in the *salle basse*, Robert eases his fears with several glasses of wine. He is suddenly imparted a vigorous blow by a large, white arm which shoots up from the floor. Raoul returns and right in front of them appear first, a large tomb surrounded by life-sized statues of warriors, and then, a 'rouleau', which warns them to leave. As Raoul investigates the statues, they come to life and start to give battle. The warriors retire suddenly on signal from an Amazone, who now attempts to seduce Raoul. When he refuses her advances, Raoul is seized by the metal arms of a pyramid, which has in the meantime arisen just behind him. As Raoul and the pyramid sink into the floor, Robert faints, and all apparitions disappear in the distance. Adélaïde enters searching for her husband. She is thrown to the ground by six *démons*, who seek to block her passage, but after they disappear, she sets out to continue the search accompanied by the trembling Robert.

Act III. Raoul is seen chained to a rock in the rear of a lugubrious cave lit by a single suspended lamp. After proclaiming to one of his captors his duty as a *chevalier* to save the oppressed, Raoul is again tempted by the Amazone, still to no avail. Another prisoner, now a slave to his captors, alerts Raoul of an escape planned for two days hence. But the guards inform Raoul that the only way he can avoid immediate death is to renounce his marriage to Adélaïde and submit to the desires of the Amazone. Raoul pretends to accept these conditions, but when asked to kill the slave as proof of his intentions, he leaps supposedly to his death following the ritual that had been planned for his execution.

Act IV: Robert and Adélaïde, who are bemoaning the fate of Raoul, see rising from the floor of the *salle basse* a *trophée d'armes* identified by an inscription as Raoul's. When Robert bursts open a door at the rear of the room so they can flee, the entire wall collapses revealing a stake and executioners with torches in readiness for the execution of Adélaïde. She courageously mounts the stake, and the fire is started as Raoul is led in. He breaks away from his guards and whisks Adélaïde from the stake. The two flee up a tree to escape the encroaching flames but fall from sight, seemingly to their deaths, as the tree is consumed by fire. The stage goes dark and, when relit, reveals a beautiful garden decorated with garlands of flowers. Raoul recounts that he survived his leap to death by falling into a bed of leaves. A *pavillon* at the rear of the garden opens and out steps Mongrigny, who explains that he has concocted the whole series of events to test his niece and Raoul. Convinced of their worthiness, he now accepts them both into his family and makes them heirs to all his possessions.

Le Combat des Thermopyles

Revolutionary and republican rhetoric abound in this historical drama depicting the Spartan defence of the pass at Thermopylae against the army of Xerxes.

Act I: Léonidas awakens and surveys the encamped Spartan warriors, women, and old men as they still sleep. He contemplates the approaching battle with the Persians at Thermopylae and is stirred by patriotic sentiments. Léontiades, chief of the Thebans, is pessimistic about the chances of survival and less inspired to die in the service of his country. Alphée returns from an espionage mission in the camp of Xerxès to report on the massive army which will oppose the Greeks. Léonidas tells the assembled Greeks to take inspiration from the ceremony of reverence they have just witnessed before the tomb of three local warriors, since they too will soon be the objects of such admiration.

Act II: As Léonidas checks his defences after arriving at Thermopylae, Hydarnès, one of Xerxès' 'immortels', arrives bearing a message from the Persian king offering Léonidas all of Greece if he will surrender. Léonidas refuses, denouncing Xerxès' despotism and calling for revolution against all such tyrannical regimes. Word arrives that the Persians have discovered a hidden entrance to the pass and will have the Greeks surrounded by dawn. Léontiades has turned traitor and along with his Thebans has already defected to the enemy. Some of the Greek contingents decide now to leave, but the Spartans and the Thespians stay behind. Firm in their resolution to die in the name of liberty, the Spartans agree at Léonidas's suggestion to carry battle directly into the Persian camp during the night rather than await the arrival of the enemy.

Act III: Léonidas returns victorious after routing the Persians from their camp. He castigates at length Léontiades the traitor, who was captured in the enemy camp. As the Spartans suspend their battle trophies from an oak tree which they consecrate to the memory of their victory, word arrives that the Persians have penetrated the pass. Hydarnès is killed by Léonidas and borne away by his followers. Although outnumbered and all mortally wounded, the Spartans frighten the Persian army into retreat. Léonidas dies happy in the knowledge that liberty has been preserved.

La Fontaine merveilleuse

Dance, spectacle, and action abound in this *pantomime-féerie* set in an imaginary location on the shores of the Caspian sea.

Act I: In front of their simple house located in an idyllic seaside setting, Alahor and his wife Zobéïde lament the lack of recognition from the Sultan Moreddin for one of his most faithful and valiant officers. Zobéïde, left alone, is approached by two men who suddenly seize her and carry her away in their ship. Alahor, informed of the abduction seeks help from the Sultan, who happens to appear at that very moment. The Sultan, however, refuses to aid Alahor chiding him instead for the weakness demonstrated by his violent reaction to a woman's inconstancy. Alahor, greatly disturbed by the Sultan's lack of concern, vows to find Zobéïde himself. All of a sudden a large rock swings aside and the genie Kaled appears amidst rumblings and flames. He promises to aid Alahor in his efforts to rescue 'la vertu malheureuse'.

Act II: Zobéïde, a prisoner in the Sultan's palace apartment, refuses the advances of her captor, who is entranced by her distress. Altagis, chief of the eunuchs, proposes to Zobéïde that she pretend to consent to the Sultan's wishes but only on the condition that he first obtain for her water from the fountain of forgetfulness so that she might banish from her heart all feelings for her husband. This fountain, located on an inaccessible island in the Caspian sea is protected by a troop of 'mauvais génies', thus making the feat practically impossible to achieve. Zobéïde persuades the Sultan to abide by this wish. Later when he realises just how difficult it will be to obtain the magic water, Moreddin orders Alahor to perform the task promising him in the meantime to spare no efforts to find Zobéïde, whose whereabouts are still unknown to her husband. After the Sultan leaves, Altagis explains the entire situation to Alahor and arranges for a secret rendezvous between husband and wife. Alahor must still, however, carry out the quest for water from the fountain of forgetfulness, since he has given his word to the Sultan.

Act III: Alahor and Altagis await Zobéïde in the sumptuous *sérail* gardens. The couple is reunited at last but unable to separate in time to avoid discovery by the Sultan. When Alahor refuses to release Zobéïde from her marriage vows, the Sultan withdraws his offer of a pardon for the offence of entering the *sérail*. Altagis later persuades the Sultan that, rather than have Alahor executed, it would be wiser to carry on with the former plan of sending him to seek water from the fountain of forgetfulness since Zobéïde has exacted the Sultan's promise regarding this condition for granting her favours. Altagis, alone with Alahor, explains what has transpired, and Kaled reappears mounted atop a griffin to assure his protection during the venture.

Act IV: Having braved a series of perils and obstacles, Alahor has finally arrived in front of a gothic château-fort on the island of the fountain of forgetfulness. He is about to be defeated by a band of warriors when Assaïs, the 'fée secourable', arrives with her followers to call a halt to the fighting. Assaïs, actually one of the 'mauvais génies' of the island, attempts to seduce Alahor, but when she fails, she orders him to be killed and his body thrown to sea monsters. Alahor is saved when the earth opens and vomits forth flames which consume Assaïs and her band. A young dervish sent by Kaled arrives to instruct Alahor that he must open a tomb to find out how to proceed on his quest. Following the instructions he discovers therein, Alahor strikes a stone with a magic sword and suddenly the fountain of forgetfulness appears. A young nymph sitting beside the fountain trys to persuade Alahor to drink. After he refuses, the nymph announces that this was the final obstacle and orders a genie to transport Alahor back to the Sultan's palace.

Act v: Back in the palace, the Sultan is making plans to have Zobéïde declared Sultane. He contemplates her body as she sleeps and decides not to put off any longer the satisfaction of his passionate desires. All of a sudden an old man representing destiny appears carrying an open book wherein is written large 'malheur au parjure!' Altagis arrives to inform the frightened Sultan that Alahor has returned successful from his quest. In view of his assembled subjects, the Sultan drinks from the *flacon* brought back by Alahor, but the result is far from what he expected. He turns pale and jumps from his throne in agony only to be surrounded by three genies who disappear with him behind a blanket of flames. Kalad appears with Zobéïde and reunites the couple promising them as recompense for their virtue 'le bonheur pur de l'âge d'or'.

La Forêt périlleuse

The forest of Calabria is the setting for this brigand melodrama.

Act i: Colisan is searching for Camille, his betrothed, who disappeared a few days ago. He decides to pause for a moment's rest much to the delight of his valet, Fresco, who takes advantage of the occasion to partake of the food and drink they have brought with them. They hide when they see a group of armed men approach only to realise that this spot is the rendezvous point for a band of brigands. While waiting for other comrades to join them, the captain discusses their past exploits and the big adventure they are about to embark upon. Brisemont, one of the band, reveals a secret entrance to a cavern hideout, which he enters to bring out two more comrades. After the brigands leave, Colisan discovers that the door of the cave was accidentally left open. He enters taking with him the reluctant Fresco. Meanwhile, Brisemont has remembered that he forgot to close the door and returns to repair the oversight.

Act II: Inside the cave, Colisan and Fresco realise that they are trapped. As they discuss what to do next, they hear a female voice and discover that Camille is here imprisoned. She tells how she was abducted in the forest and brought here for the Captain's future pleasure. Colisan divises a plan for escape: Camille will pretend to give in to the Captain's desires and then, when alone with him, poison his wine, steal his keys, and free the three of them while the other robbers are getting drunk in the back of the cave. The band returns from their unsuccessful venture, and the plan is put into action. Camille is persuading the Captain of her change of mind when Fresco is discovered. He cleverly explains his presence and pleads so fearfully for his life that the Captain decides he is harmless and, rather than have him killed, makes him their cook. As Camille and the Captain leave hand-in-hand for a tour of the hideout, Colisan is convinced that his plan will work.

Act III: Following a ceremony during which the Captain presents Camille to the band of brigands as their queen, the two of them are left alone to feast on the dinner prepared by Fresco. Camille manages to slip the poison into the Captain's wine but not without the Captain's seeing her do so. Rather than confront her immediately, the Captain first switches goblets and invites Camille to drink. When she hesitates, he calls for Fresco and asks him to drink to their health. Fresco too hesitates, at which point Brisemont grabs the goblet, gulps the wine, and dies in a fit of convulsions. The angry Captain threatens Camille with his sword, Colisan reveals himself and flies to the rescue of his beloved. But other brigands reappear, and Colisan is taken captive and led off to be executed, much to the consternation of Camille. She faints when she hears the shots and then awakens to the sight of her lover's corpse, which the brigands have brought before her according to the Captain's orders. However, Colisan suddenly leaps up and embraces Camille explaining that the execution was only simulated. He resumes the posture of corpse just as the Captain returns. The Captain places his pistols on the table and is about to satisfy his passions before killing Camille when Colisan bounds forth, seizes the pistols, and shoots the Captain dead. It turns out that a handful of the brigands are actually agents of the law who had infiltrated the gang to discover all of their accomplices before finally arresting the whole lot.

Le Grand chasseur

The 'isle des palmiers', an island in the Caspian sea, is the setting for this melodrama, which pits Persians against 'Zélindiens', a people descended from the Tartars.

Act I: Ziska, a Zélindien warrior, tries without success to persuade the cowardly Taher to join the lion hunt now in progress in order to demonstrate his courage. Alone, Taher admits his fear and then, when the lion appears, desperately sounds his horn and quickly climbs a tree. Ziska reappears accompanied by Altinor, officer of the Zélindien guard, and with her javelin kills the lion. Taher descends from his refuge to the amusement of all assembled. Altinor takes Ziska aside to warn her of the capriciousness of her future husband, Palmar, 'le grand chasseur', chief of the Zélindiens. Altinor admits that he loves Ziska but has resigned himself to the fact of his chief's future marriage. As the Zélindiens prepare to serve dinner, they hear the voices of strangers and hide. Valoé, a young Persian emir, arrives with his beloved Florinde, a Georgian princesse, and his *écuyer*, Rustan. Rustan is delighted to find the food, of which he partakes, but is concerned upon seeing Palmar's flag, which reminds him of the Zélindien practice of burning all captured male Persians on the tomb of Hyllinos in retribution for past quarrels. Altinor and Taher emerge from hiding with the Zélindiens and take the Persians prisoner. When Palmar arrives, he is immediately struck by Florinde's beauty but refuses to yield to her pleas on behalf of Valoé and Rustan. As the two Persian men are led off to prison, Florinde is taken to Palmar's palace.

Act II: Inside his palace apartment, Palmar informs Altinor of his intentions to wed Florinde rather than Ziska, but Altinor warns of the consequences of Ziska's wrath. Ziska enters and confronts Palmar. When he steadfastly refuses to renounce his intentions to wed Florinde, Ziska swears vengeance as he departs, greatly troubling Palmar. Florinde appears and, after sending away Altinor and the entourage of female attendants, expresses her sorrow and affliction. Ziska emerges from hiding and confronts her rival, at first wanting to kill her. But when she learns that Florinde loves Valoé and not Palmar, Ziska vows to help by seeking to save the young Persian. When Florinde refuses Palmar's offer of marriage, the chief sends for the Persian captives and offers to spare Valoé if the Georgian princess will change her mind. This tactic fails, however, and Palmar sentences Valoé to execution. Ziska arrives at this moment with a band of Zélindiennes and rescues Valoé and Rustan from their captors.

Act III: In sight of Hyllinos's tomb, Ziska informs Rustan that, their first attempt at rescuing Valoé having ultimately failed, she now has a new plan already in action aided by the 'généreux Tiskan', an old Zélindien soldier. Palmar appears with his entourage and the captive Valoé, and preparations start for the sacrifice. As Valoé is finally led into the combustible *cabane* atop Hyllinos's tomb, an alarm is sounded. Taskan arrives in accordance with Ziska's plan, to announce that Persians have landed in search of Valoé and Florinde. Palmar departs with his warriors leaving Valoé behind under Altinor's guard. Ziska manages to lure Altinor away with all the guards except Taher. Rustan, pretending to be talking to some of the non-existent Persian contingent, frightens Taher into surrender and has him set Valoé free from the *cabane*. Palmar returns now knowing the alarm to have been false and sentences Tiskan to die with Valoé. When the *cabane* is opened, however, out steps Taher to announce Valoé's escape. Palmar, although upset by the escape, takes satisfaction in announcing that he has hidden Florinde where the Persians will never be able to find her. Altinor arrives with the news that a Persian rescue party has indeed landed and will be upon them before long. Valoé appears with the Persians, and a vigorous battle ensues, mirrored in the comic duel between Rustan and Taher. Two Zélindiennes are nearly overpowered by the Persians when Rustan suddenly recognises the voice of Ziska. The second Zélindienne turns out to be Florinde in disguise. Ziska's revenge is now complete. When Valoé asks how he can repay her help, she asks for Palmar's liberty. Valoé accords her wish on the condition that Palmar abolish the practice of sacrificing Persians to Hyllinos. Palmar agrees and there is a general reconciliation. Ziska, however, announces that she will henceforth dedicate herself to glory and renounce forever 'les chaînes de l'amour'.

Roland de Monglave

This melodrama of chivalry is set in fifteenth-century Swabia.

Act I: The valiant knight Roland tells his wife, Isaure, and *écuyer*, Dolin, that someday they will all return to the happy, carefree life of his country château but that for the present, his duty is to protect his lord, Milon, Duke of Swabia. Liziard, Roland's rival, with the help of his *écuyer*, Dinas, sets in motion a malicious scheme to discredit Roland and win the Duke's favour for himself. They send an anonymous letter to the Duke falsely accusing Roland of plotting to usurp the Duke's position, but the Duke refuses to believe the accusation suspecting it to be the product of Roland's enemies. When he hears that his son has been killed by a knight identified as Roland and that Roland's sword was left plunged into the son's body, the Duke is persuaded of Roland's guilt and has him arrested and thrown into the darkest dungeon to await a fitting punishment.

Act II: Isaure and Dolin attempt to rescue Roland from the Duke's citadel in the middle of the forest. They elicit the aid of Falker, the captain of the citadel guard, a venerable old soldier, whom they convince of Roland's innocence. He arranges for Roland to escape by a secret underground passageway, but the escape is discovered by the guards before the trio can get away. After extended combat, Roland is retaken prisoner, but Dolin manages to disappear into the forest carrying with him Isaure, who has fainted.

Act III: Roland is led in by guards as Liziard and Dinas prepare the *place publique* for a midnight execution. Liziard, who has been designated to officiate, has Dinas read the sentence aloud. The captain of Milon's guard arrives to interrupt the proceedings announcing that the Duke has ordered the execution delayed until daylight to achieve a more terrible and solemn effect. Rather than order Roland led back to the citadel, Liziard has him chained to a 'pyramide' and placed under continual guard. Dolin arrives in disguise, manages to get the guards drunk, and frees Roland. Dinas reappears, but Dolin disarms him and places him inside a gothic *tourelle*, after which Dolin and Roland depart. As the guards wake up and flee, Dinas appears at a window in the *tourelle* and manages to reach a bell cord hanging close by. The bell summons the guards and Liziard, who orders Roland found and returned dead or alive.

Act IV: Roland and Isaure are now in the Vallon de la Roche-Sauvage, a hiding place described to them by Falker, the old captain of the citadel guard. Dolin appears fighting furiously with Bolga, one of Liziard's followers. When Roland has Dolin spare the enemy soldier's life,

Bolga is won over to Roland's side and reveals the secrets of Liziard's scheme, including details of the murder of the Duke's son, the false testimony, and the planted evidence. Bolga leaves swearing not to reveal their whereabouts. Roland and Isaure settle into a comfortable hiding place as Dolin goes off promising to sound his horn when it is safe for the couple to reappear in public. When everyone has gone, Liziard appears deciding to rest for a moment. He takes refuge inside a cave as a thunderstorm approaches. Some of his soldiers show up next, and they too decide to rest for a few minutes. As they are about to leave, they spot the cave and decide to investigate it, but not without first firing several shots into it as a precaution. A man's voice crying out reveals that they have shot Liziard. As they drag out Liziard's body, Dolin returns and sounds his horn signalling to Roland and Isaure that they may reappear. Duke Milon joins the gathering for a reconciliation with Roland, who he now realises is innocent, thanks to Falker's pleadings and the revelations of Bolga, who has been recaptured by Dolin.

Le Vol par amour

This *comédie de caractère et d'intrigue* takes place in provincial post-revolutionary France.

Act I: Delmont, a prosperous farmer, and his daughter, Pauline, are standing in the village square discussing plans for her marriage. They are joined by Bertrand, a retired *procureur*, who acquired considerable wealth under the *ancien régime*. Pauline again makes known that she has no intention of complying with her father's wishes by marrying Bertrand, preferring instead her childhood friend Felix, who has been absent for five years. When Felix suddenly returns from his travels a rich man, Delmont is persuaded to accede to the young couple's desires and condones their marriage, much to the consternation of Bertrand. Bertrand schemes with Julien, his valet, to rob Felix of his portfolio of riches.

Act II: In the moonlight, Bertrand and Julien are seen burying the stolen portfolio somewhere in the woods near the spot where, in disguise, they ambushed Felix. No sooner do they leave than two robbers, Roc and Brulot, arrive to congratulate themselves on having stolen Bertrand's *bourse* containing all his fortune. Roc flees and Brulot hides in a tree taking the bourse with him as Felix arrives bemoaning the consequences of losing his recently acquired riches. He is joined by Pauline and then by Delmont, who decides to postpone the marriage until Felix somehow recovers his losses. After Delmont's departure, Felix discovers Brulot, who in his desire to escape arrest turns over Bertrand's *bourse* and escapes. Meanwhile, Bertrand, having discovered the theft, returns to recover Felix's money, with which he manages to win back Delmont's permission to wed Pauline. Bertrand believes his revenge complete when he accuses Felix as the thief who stole the *bourse*; however, the cowardly Julien has confessed all to the authorities. Delmont again awards Pauline's hand to Felix, having learned the dangers of too great a love for money.

Works consulted

A. Biographical sources

1. Archives

Archives départementales du Morbihan:

There are no 'Loaisel' family archives. Correspondence concerning genealogical research and a genealogy of the family is filed under 'Loaisel de Saulnays (famille de la région de Sérent), 385.T13'. The *régistres paroissiaux* conserved by the A. D. Morbihan provided all the *état civil* information. There is an incomplete inventory of the *régistres: Inventaire-sommaire des Archives départementales antérieures à 1790. Morbihan. Archives civiles. Série E, Supplément,* ed. M. Rosenzweig (Vannes 1881-1888). The inventory furnished a starting point, with additional leads being developed out of the documents themselves. There was insufficient time available for thorough research into other documents.

Service historique de l'Armée (Château de Vincennes):

There are three areas to be researched for information on individual officers:

1. Dossiers of individual officers classed alphabetically. There is a 'Loaisel' dossier, but it contains no documents other than correspondence from descendants requesting information on their ancestor. Included are letters from Loaisel's daughter, Angélique Eulalie, and records of the research undertaken.

2. Dossiers of beneficiaries of pensions from the Trésor Royal. There is no record of any pension for Loaisel.

3. *Contrôles du corps* (Séries YB, YC). The *contrôles* are listed in the following inventory: Ministère de la Guerre, *Inventaire des Archives conservées au Service historique de l'état-major de l'armée (Château de Vincennes) (Archives modernes)*, 2nd ed., rev. (1954). The *contrôles* are not indexed in any way and must be searched page by page for records of an individual officer.

Archives nationales, Minutier des notaires

Minutes were located by references from documents in the A. D. Seine and from within the minutes themselves. A very limited search was conducted in the *répertoires* of the minutes.

Archives départementales de la Seine

Information obtained concerned principally the *état civil*, for which is a complete system of card catalogues.

2. *Additional biographical sources*

Listed in this section are those works which yielded information used in researching and writing the biography. Many of the works listed below in sections B and C are potential sources of biography; however, if they are not listed also in this section, it is to be concluded that they contained no significant biographical information concerning Loaisel.

Arnault, Antoine Vincent *et al*, *Biographie nouvelle des contemporains*. Paris 1820-1825.

Baculard d'Arnaud, François-Thomas de, *Œuvres diverses et correspondance*. Bibliothèque nationale, Département des manuscrits, Nouvelles acquisitions françaises, no.14893.

Barroux, Robert, 'Loaisel de Tréogate', *Dictionnaire des lettres françaises: le XVIIIe siècle*. Paris 1960; ii.132.

Bousquet, Jacques, *Anthologie du dix-huitième siècle romantique*. Paris 1972.

Collas, Georges, 'Un préromantique breton: Loaisel de Tréogate: 1752-1812', *Mémoires de la Société d'histoire et d'archéologie de Bretagne* 14 (1933), pp.297-319.

Courcy, Pol Potier de, *Nobiliaire et armorial de Bretagne*, 3rd ed., rev. Rennes 1890.

Fabureau, Hubert, 'Loaisel de Tréogate', *Mercure de France* 314 (1952), pp.370-73.

Giffard, André, *Les Justices seigneuriales en Bretagne au XVIIe et au XVIIIe siècle* (1661-1791). Paris 1903.

Ginisty, Paul, *Le Mélodrame*. Paris [1910].

Hoefer, Jean Chrétien Ferdinand, *Nouvelle biographie générale*. Paris 1853-1866.

Isnard, P. Fr. d', *La Gendarmerie de la France: son origine, son rang, ses prérogatives et son service*. Paris 1781.

[Kerviler, René,] *Fiche* concerning Loaisel de Tréogat [*sic*]. Bibliothèque municipale de Nantes, Manuscript, Papiers Kerviler, Liasse 112 (113?). [This is the only original information on Loaisel de Tréogate in this collection of notes intended for the continuation of Kerviler's *Répertoire générale de bio-bibliographie bretonne*, which ceased publication after 17 volumes (Rennes 1886-1907) with the name 'Guépin'.]

La Chesnaye-Desbois, François Alexandre Aubert de, *Dictionnaire de noblesse*, 3rd ed., rev. Paris 1863-1876.

L'Estourbeillon de La Garnache, Régis Marie Joseph de, *Les Familles françaises à Jersey pendant la Révolution*. Nantes 1886.

Levot, Prosper Jean, *Biographie bretonne*. Vannes, Paris 1852-1857.

Loaisel de Saulnays, Henry, *Un méconnu: Loaisel de Tréogate (1752-1812), monographie littéraire*. Alger 1930.

Mention, Léon, *L'Armée de l'ancien régime de Louis XIV à la Révolution.* Paris s.d.

—, *Le Comte de Saint-Germain et ses réformes (1775-1777) d'après les archives du Dépot de la guerre.* Paris 1884.

Meyer, Jean, *La Noblesse bretonne au XVIIIe siècle.* Paris 1966.

[Michaud, Joseph François,] *Biographie universelle, ancienne et moderne.* Paris 1811-1828.

Milleville, Henry J.-G. de, *Armorial historique de la noblesse de France.* Paris 1845.

Quentin, Henri [pseudonym: Paul d'Estrée], *Le Théâtre sous la Terreur* (*théâtre de la peur*), *1793-1794.* Paris 1913.

Rabbe, Alphonse, *Biographie universelle et portative des contemporains.* Paris 1936.

Rosenzweig, M., *Dictionnaire topographique du Département du Morbihan comprenant les noms de lieu anciens et modernes.* Paris 1870.

Villar, Noel Gabriel Luce de, *Rapport et projet de décret présenté à la Convention nationale, dans la scéance du 18 fructidor (an III, 4 septembre 1795), au nom du comité d'instruction publique, sur les encouragemens destinés aux savans, gens de lettres et artistes.* Paris An III.

B. Bibliographical sources

In order to prevent duplication of the research already accomplished, a complete list is given below of all bibliographical sources consulted whether or not they produced any information of value. The following procedures govern the periodical entries: each periodical is listed only by the names – original and/or continuation – under which it was published during the period under consideration (1776-1812); dates represent the inclusive dates of publication of the periodical under the name listed; Gregorian (or Revolutionary) calendar equivalents are given only when they are printed as such; publishers and formats are specified only when needed for exact identification. Current bibliographies, such as the *Catalogue hebdomadaire*, are listed in section 1, since they were published as periodicals. Retrospective bibliographies are listed in section 2. Abbreviations and short titles used in citations are given in brackets after each work so cited.

1. Periodicals and literary correspondences

Affiches, annonces et avis divers, Paris 1761-1784, 4°; known also as *Affiches de province*; continued as *Journal général de France*, 1785-1797, 4°.

Affiches, annonces et avis divers ou Journal général de France, Paris 1783-1814, 8°: see *Annonces, affiches et avis divers*, Paris 1751-1782, 8°.

Affiches de Paris: see *Annonces, affiches et avis divers*, Paris 1751-1782, 8°.

Affiches de province: see *Affiches, annonces et avis divers*, Paris 1761-1784, 4°.

Almanach des muses, Paris 1765-1833.

Almanach des spectacles, Paris: Duchesne 1800: see *Almanach des spectacles de Paris*, Paris: Duchesne.

Almanach des spectacles de Paris, Paris: Duchesne 1752-1815; title varies: *Les Spectacles de Paris*, 1754-1791; *Les Spectacles de Paris et de toute la France*, 1792-1794; *Almanach des spectacles*, 1800; *Almanach des spectacles de Paris*, 1801 and 1815. Not published 1795-1799; 1802-1814.

Almanach des spectacles de Paris, pour l'an 1809, Paris: Léopold Collin 1809.

Almanach général de tous les spectacles de Paris et des provinces, Paris: Froullé 1791-1792.

Almanach littéraire ou étrennes d'Apollon, Paris 1777-1793.

Année littéraire, Amsterdam and Paris 1754-1790.

Année théâtrale, almanach pour l'An IX [-XII], Paris Du Pont, then Courcier, An IX [-XII].

Annonces, affiches et avis divers, Paris 1751-1782, 8°; known also as *Affiches de Paris* or *Petites affiches*; continued as *Affiches, annonces et avis divers ou Journal général de France*, 1783-1814, 8°.

Annuaire dramatique, ou étrennes théâtrales, Paris: Cavanagh 1805-1822.

[Bachaumont, Louis Petit de], *Mémoires secrets pour servir à l'histoire de la république des lettres*. London 1780-1789.

— G., J. [Jean Gay?], *Table alphabétique des auteurs et personnages cités dans les 'Mémoires secrets'*. Brussels 1866.

Bibliothèque française, Paris An VII-1808.

Bibliothèque universelle des romans, Paris 1775-1789; continued as *Nouvelle bibliotheque des romans*, 1798-1805.

Catalogue hebdomadaire, Paris 1763-1781; continued as *Journal de la librairie* 1782-1789.

Chronique de Paris, Paris 1789-1793.

Correspondance littéraire: see La Harpe.

Correspondance littéraire, philosophique et critique: see Grimm.

Courrier de l'Europe et des spectacles: see *Courrier des spectacles*.

Courrier des planètes: see *Lunes du Cousin Jacques*.

Courrier des spectacles, Paris 1797-1807; continued as *Courrier de l'Europe et des spectacles*, 1807-1811.

Cousin Jacques: see *Lunes du Cousin Jacques*.

Décade philosophique, Paris 1794-1804.

Etrennes de l'Institut national, Paris An VII-An VIII.

Feuille de correspondance du libraire, Paris 1791-1792.

Gazette nationale ou le moniteur universelle, Paris 1789-1810; continued as *Moniteur universelle*, 1811-1901.

Gentleman's magazine, London 1731-1907.

Grimm, Friedrich Melchior *et al*, *Correspondance littéraire, philosophique et critique*, ed. Maurice Tourneux. Paris 1877-1882.

Journal de la librairie: see *Catalogue hebdomadaire*.

Journal de lecture, Paris, Amsterdam 1775-1779.

Journal de l'Empire: see *Journal des débats*.

Journal de littérature, des sciences et des arts: see *Journal des sciences et des beaux-arts*.

Journal de Monsieur, Paris 1776-1783.

Journal de Paris, Paris 1777-1827.

Journal de Trévoux: see *Journal des sciences et des beaux-arts*.

Journal des débats, Paris 1789- ; entitled *Journal de l'Empire*, 1805-1815 (except 1 Apr 1814 - 20 Mar 1815).

Journal des sçavans, Paris 1665-1792.

Journal des sciences et des beaux-arts, Paris 1776-1778; continuation of *Journal de Trévoux*; continued as

Journal de littérature, des sciences et des arts, 1779-1783.

Journal des spectacles, Paris, 3 vendémiaire – 23 brumaire an III (24 septembre – 13 novembre 1794).

Journal des spectacles, contenant l'analyse des différentes pièces qu'on a représentées sur tous les théâtres de Paris, Paris, 1er juillet 1793 – 19 nivôse an II (8 janvier 1794).

Journal des théâtres, de littérature et des arts, rédigé par le citoyen Ducray-Duminil et autres gens-de-lettres, Paris, 10 frimaire – 30 floréal an VII (30 novembre 1798 – 19 mai 1799).

Journal des théâtres, et des fêtes nationales, Paris, 1er fructidor an II – 29 germinal an III (18 août 1794 – 18 avril 1795).

Journal encyclopédique, Liège, Bouillon, Brussels, 1756-1793.

Journal français, Paris 1777-1778.

Journal général de France, Paris 1785-1797, 4°: see *Affiches, annonces et avis divers,* Paris 1761-1784, 4°.

Journal général de la littérature de France, Paris and Strasbourg, 1798-1841.

Journal littéraire, Paris 1796-1797.

Journal typographique et bibliographique, Paris An VI-1810.

La Harpe, Jean-François de, *Correspondance littéraire.* Paris An XII [1804] – 1807.

Lunes du Cousin Jacques, Paris 1785-1787; continued as *Courrier des planètes,* 1788-1789; *Cousin Jacques,* 1790; *Nouvelles lunes du Cousin Jacques,* 1791.

Melpomène et Thalie vengées: see *Vérités à l'ordre du jour.*

Mémoires secrets: see Bachaumont.

Mémorial dramatique ou almanach théâtrale, Paris 1807-1819.

Mercure de France, Paris 1672-1820; title varies: *Mercure français,* 1791-1799; not published Sep 23 1799-May 21 1800.

Mercure français: see *Mercure de France.*

Moniteur universelle: see *Gazette nationale ou le moniteur universelle.*

Monthly review, London 1749-1844.

Nouvel almanach des muses pour l'an grégorien 1802 [*1803* and *1806*], Paris: Barba. [The three volumes noted were the only ones located; Grand-Carteret lists the set as containing 12 volumes, 1802-1813.]

Nouvelle bibliothèque des romans: see *Bibliothèque universelle des romans.*

Nouvelles lunes du Cousin Jacques: see *Lunes du Cousin Jacques.*

Observateur des spectacles, Paris 1802-1803.

Opinion du parterre, Paris, Martinet An XI-1813.

Petites affiches: see *Annonces, affiches et avis divers,* Paris 1751-1782, 8°.

Portefeuille français, Paris 1800-1813.

Publiciste, Paris 1797-1810.

Revue des théâtres: see *Vérités à l'ordre du jour.*

Spectacles de Paris: see *Almanach des spectacles de Paris,* Paris: Duchesne.

Spectacles de Paris et de toute la France: see *Almanach des spectacles de Paris,* Paris: Duchesne.

Spectateur national, Paris 1789-1792.

Vérités à l'ordre du jour, Paris An VI; continued as *Melpomène et Thalie vengées,* An VII; *Revue des théâtres,* An VIII.

2. *Bibliographies,* répertoires, *reference works, and sale catalogues*

Apollinaire, Guillaume, F. Fleuret, and L. Perceau, *L'Enfer de la Bibliothèque nationale, nouvelle édition.* Paris 1919. Reprint: Geneva 1970.

Arnault, Antoine Vincent *et al, Biographie nouvelle des contemporains.* Paris 1820-1825. [Arnault]

[Babault,] *Annales dramatiques; ou dictionnaire général des théâtres.* Paris 1809-1812. [Babault]

Barbier, Antoine Alexandre, *Dictionnaire des ouvrages anonymes,* 3rd ed., rev. Olivier Barbier, René and Paul Billard: vols iv-vii following *Les*

Supercheries littéraires dévoilées, by Joseph Marie Quérard, 2nd ed., rev. Gustave Brunet and Pierre Jannet. Paris 1872-1882. [Barbier]

Brunet, Gustave, *Dictionnaire des ouvrages anonymes* [de Barbier], supplement. Paris 1889. Reprint: Hildesheim 1963.

Celani, H., 'Additions et corrections au Dictionnaire des anonymes de Barbier', *Revue des bibliothèques* (1901). Reprint: Hildesheim 1963.

Barroux, Robert, 'Loaisel de Tréogate', *Dictionnaire des lettres françaises: le XVIIIe siècle*. Paris 1960, ii.132. [Barroux]

Bénézit, Emmanuel, *Dictionnaire critique et documentaire des peintres, sculpteurs, dessinateurs et graveurs*, new ed., rev. inheritors of E. Bénézit. Paris 1848-1855.

Bernard, C., 'Le Livre illustré en France à l'époque de la Révolution', *Bibliofilia* 30 (1928), pp.256-76.

[Beuchot, Andrieu J. Q.,] *Nouveau nécrologe français*. Paris 1812.

Block, Andrew, *The English novel, 1740-1850: a catalogue including prose romances, short stories and translations of foreign fiction*, new rev. ed. London, New York 1962.

Boissais, Maurice and Jacques Deleplanque, *Les Livres à gravures au XVIIIe siècle, suivi d'un essai de bibliographie*. Paris 1948.

Bond, Donald F. and George Havens (ed.), *The Eighteenth century*: vol.iv of *A critical bibliography of French literature*, ed. David C. Cabeen. Syracuse, New York 1951.

Brooks, Richard A., ed., *The Eighteenth century: supplement* to vol. iv of *A critical bibliography of French literature*, ed. David C. Cabeen. Syracuse, New York. 1968.

Bonnardot, Alfred, *Histoire artistique et archéologique de la gravure en France*. Paris 1849.

Bouchot, Henri, *Les Livres à vignettes du XVIe au XVIIIe siècle*. Paris 1891.

Bourcard, Gustave, *Dessins, gouaches, estampes et tableaux du XVIIIe siècle: guide de l'amateur*. Paris 1893.

—, *Les Estampes du XVIIIe siècle, école française: guide manuel de l'amateur*. Paris 1885.

Bousquet, Jacques, *Anthologie du dix-huitième siècle romantique*. Paris 1972. [Bousquet]

Brenner, Clarence D., *A bibliographical list of plays in the French language, 1700-1789*. Ann Arbor, Michigan 1947. [Brenner]

[Brissart-Binet, Charles,] *Cazin, sa vie et ses éditions par un cazinophile*. Cazinopolis [Chalons-sur-Marne] 1863.

Brooks, R.: see Bond.

Brunet, Charles: see Soleinne.

Brunet, Gustave, *Imprimeurs imaginaires et libraires supposés*. Paris 1866.

—: see also Barbier.

Brunet, Jacques Charles, *Manuel du libraire et de l'amateur de livres*, 5th ed., rev. Paris 1860-1865.

—, —, supplement. Paris 1878-1880.

Bure: see La Vallière.

Cabeen: see Bond.

Carteret, Leopold, *Le Trésor du bibliophile romantique et moderne, 1801-1875*. Paris 1924-1928.

Catalogue des pièces composant le théâtre révolutionnaire par ordre de représentation ou de publication, depuis l'année 1788. Bibliothèque de l'Arsenal, Manuscript, Rondel ms 349.

Celani: see Barbier.

Cioranescu, Alexandre, *Bibliographie de la littérature française du dix-huitième siècle*. Paris 1969. [Cioranescu, *Bibl*]

Cohen, Henry, *Guide de l'amateur de livres à gravures du XVIIIe siècle*, 6th ed., rev. Seymour de Ricci. Paris 1912. [Cohen, 6th ed]

—, —, 5th ed., rev. le baron Roger Portalis. Paris 1886. [Cohen, 5th ed]

—, *Guide de l'amateur de livres à vignettes (et à figures) du XVIIIe siècle*, 4th ed., rev. Charles Mehl. Paris 1880. [Cohen, 4th ed]

—, *Guide de l'amateur de livres à figures et à vignettes du XVIIIe siècle*, 3rd ed., rev. Charles Mehl. Paris 1876. [Cohen, 3rd ed]

—, *Guide de l'amateur de livres à vignettes du XVIIIe siècle,* 2nd ed., rev. Paris 1873.

Coroenne, A., *Bibliographie générale des petits-formats dits Cazins.* Paris 1877 1894.

Craufurd, Quentin, *Essais sur la littérature française écrits à l'usage d'une dame étrangère, compatriote de l'auteur.* n.p. 1803.

Delandine, Antoine François, *Bibliographie dramatique, ou, tablettes alphabétiques du théâtre des diverses nations.* Paris n.d. [Delandine]

[Delcro, Antoine Jacques,] *Dictionnaire universel littéraire et critique des romans imprimés ou manuscrits . . . depuis l'antiquité la plus reculée jusque et compris le 31 [décem]bre 1826,* 3rd manuscript ed. Bibliothèque nationale, Département des imprimés, Salle de la réserve, Rés gr Y². 2(1-3). [Delcro]

Desessarts, Nicolas Toussaint Lemoyne, *Nouveau dictionnaire bibliographique portatif,* 2nd. ed. Paris An XII-1804. [Desessarts, *Dict*]

—, *Les Siècles littéraires de la France.* Paris An VIII (1800) – An XI (1803). [Desessarts, *Siècles litts*]

Didier, Béatrice, *Littérature française;* tome xi: *Le XVIIIe siècle;* vol.iii: *1778-1820.* Paris 1976. [Didier]

Dighton, Basil Lewis and H. W. Lawrence, *French line engravers of the late XVIII century.* London 1910.

Dimier, Louis, *Les Peintres français du XVIIIe siècle: histoire des vies et catalogue des œuvres.* Paris 1929-1930.

[Douay, Georges,] *Répertoire général de toutes les pièces représentées sur les théâtres de Paris* [19—]. Bibliothèque de l'Arsenal, Manuscript, ms D 26. [Douay, *Rép Paris*] [Only vols vii-x (1780-1819) were consulted]

[Douay, Georges,] *Répertoire de toutes les pièces représentées sur les théâtres (scènes) de la province et de l'étranger*

[19—]. Bibliothèque de l'Arsenal, Manuscript, ms D 27. [Douay, *Rép prov*]

Dreher: see Thieme, Hugo.

Drevet: see Thieme, Hugo.

[Duclos, R. ?] *Dictionnaire bibliographique historique et critique des livres rares.* Paris 1802.

[Du Coudray, Alexandre Jacques], *Répertoire général de toutes les pièces de théâtre.* n.p. n.d.

Dufrenoy, Marie-Louise, *L'Orient romanesque en France, 1704-1789;* vol.ii: *Bibliographie générale.* Montréal 1947. [Dufrenoy, ii]

Du Peloux, Charles, *Répertoire biographique et bibliographique des artistes du XVIIIe siècle français.* Paris 1930-1941.

Duval, Henri, *Dictionnaire des ouvrages dramatiques depuis Jodelle jusqu'à nos jours.* Bibliothèque nationale, Département des manuscrits, Fonds français, nos 15048-15061. [Duval] [Vols. ii and iii (15049-50), *Comédies,* and vol.iv (15051), *Drames et mélodrames,* provide information on both performances and printed editions. Vol.xiii (15060), *Auteurs,* lists, under each author, play titles and years either of first performances or of published editions. The numerous inconsistencies and errors in vol.xiii render it practically useless except as an index.]

Ersch, Johann Samuel, *La France littéraire* [*sic*]*, contenant les auteurs français de 1771 à 1796.* Hamburg 1797-1798. [Ersch, *Fr lit*]

—, —, supplement. Hamburg 1802. [Ersch, *suppl*]

—, —, second supplement. Hamburg 1806. [Ersch, *sec suppl*]

Escoffier, Maurice, *Le Mouvement romantique, 1788-1850.* Paris 1934.

[Fantin Des Odoards, Antoine Etienne Nicolas,] *Tableau des écrivains français.* Paris 1809. [Fantin des Odoards]

'Fiches Lecomte': see Lecomte.

Filippi, Joseph de, *Essai d'une biblio-graphie générale du théâtre*. Paris 1861.

[Fleuriot, Jean-Marie-Jérôme,] *Paris littéraire, première partie*. Hamburg An VII.

Frautschi, Richard: see Martin.

Fromm, Hans, *Bibliographie des traduc-tions allemandes d'imprimés français, 1700-1948*. Baden-Baden 1950-1953. [Fromm]

Fuessli, Johann Rudolf, *Allegemeines Künstlerlexicon*. Zurich 1806-1821. [Volume ii is by H. H. Füssli.]

Füssli, H. H.: see Fuessli, Johann Rudolf.

[Gay, Jules,] *Bibliographie des ouvrages relatifs à l'amour, aux femmes, au mariage*, 4th ed., rev. J. Lemonnyer. Paris 1894-1900. [Gay]

Giraud, Jeanne, *Manuel de bibliographie littéraire pour les XVIe, XVIIe et XVIIIe siècles français, 1921-1935*. Paris 1939.

—, —, *1936-1945*. Paris 1956.

—, —, *1946-1965*. Paris 1970.

Giraud, Yves, *Bibliographie du roman épistolaire en France, des origines à 1842*. Fribourg 1977. [Y. Giraud]

[Girault de Saint-Fargeau, Pierre Augustin Eusèbe,] *Revue des romans: recueil d'analyses raisonnées des pro-ductions remarquables des plus célèbres romanciers français et étrangers*. Paris 1839.

Godenne, René, *Histoire de la nouvelle française aux XVIIe et XVIIIe siècles*. Geneva 1970. [Godenne, *Nouvelle*]

—, 'Supplément au répertoire par année des titres des nouvelles aux XVIIe et XVIIIe siècles', *French studies* 28 (1974), pp.146-58.

Goizet, J., *Dictionnaire universelle du théâtre en France et du théâtre français à l'étranger ... par J. Goizet, avec biographies de tous les auteurs et principaux artistes de toutes les époques, par A. Burtal*. Paris 1867. [Goizet, *Dict*] [Bibliography contains 'A' –

'Deux Avares'; biographies treat only 'A'.]

—, *Dictionnaire du théâtre, Lettres AB – AG (imprimées), K, Q, W, X, Y, Z (inédites)*, 1852, Bibliothèque de l'Arsenal, Manuscript, ms. 91619 bis. [Continuation of the *Dictionnaire universel*]

—: see also Soleinne.

Gove, Philip B., *The Imaginary voyage in prose fiction*. New York 1941.

Graesse, Johann Georg Theodor, *Trésor de livres rares et précieux*. Dresde 1859-1869.

Grieder, Josephine, 'English translations of French sentimental prose fiction, 1760-1800: a bibliography'. *Bulletin of bibliography* 29 (1972), pp.109-21, 125.

—, *Translations of French sentimental prose fiction in late eighteenth-century England: the history of a literary vogue*. Durham, N. C. 1975. [Grieder, *Trans*] [The bibliography published in this work supersedes the one published in the *Bulletin of biblio-graphy*.]

Guiot: see Laporte.

Hébrail: see Laporte.

Heinsius, Wilhelm, *Allgemeines Bücher-Lexikon, oder vollständiges alpha-betisches Verzeichnis der von 1700 bis zu ende 1827-1892 erschienenen Bücher*. Leipzig 1812-1894.

Heylli, Georges d': see Poinsot.

Hill, Frank P., *American plays printed 1714-1830: a bibliographical record*. Stanford University [1934]. [Hill]

Hoefer, Jean Chrétien Ferdinand, *Nouvelle biographie générale*. Paris 1853-1866. [Hoefer]

Horn-Monval, Madelaine, *Répertoire bibliographique des traductions et adaptations françaises du théâtre étran-ger du XVe siècle à nos jours*. Paris 1958-1967. [Horn-Monval]

Jacob, P. L., bibliophile: see Soleinne.

Jal, Auguste, *Dictionnaire critique de biographie et d'histoire, errata et supplément pour tous les dictionnaires historiques d'après des documents authentiques inédits*. Paris 1867.

Kayser, Christian Gottlob, *Vollständiges Bücher-Lexikon, 1750-1910*. Leipzig 1834-1911.

[Lablée, Jacques,] *Tableau de nos poètes vivans, par ordre alphabétique*, Année 1789. London 1789.

Lacroix, Paul: see Pixerécourt and Soleinne.

Lanson, Gustave, *Manuel bibliographique de la littérature française moderne, 1500-1900 (XVIe, XVIIe, XVIIIe et XIXe siècles)*, new ed. Paris 1921.

[Laporte, Joseph de and Jacques Hébrail,] *La France littéraire*. Paris 1769.

[Laporte,] *Supplément à La France littéraire*, tome troisième. Paris 1778. [Laporte, *Suppl*]

[—:] [Guiot, Joseph André,] *Nouveau supplément à la France littéraire, tome quatrième*. Paris 1784. [Laporte, *Nouv suppl*]

La Vallière:

Bure, Guillaume de, *Catalogue des livres de la bibliothèque de feu m. le duc de La Vallière*, 1ère partie. Paris 1783.

Nyon, Jean-Luc, l'aîné. *Catalogue des livres de la bibliothèque de feu m. le duc de La Vallière, seconde partie*. Paris 1784. [Nyon, *Cat La Vallière*]

[Lecomte, Louis Henry,] 'Les Fiches Lecomte'. Bibliothèque de l'Arsenal. ['fiches Lecomte'] [A collection of manuscript *fiches* listing plays performed up until 1900 giving 'avec précision les auteurs, la scène et la date, avec une bibliographie sommaire de chaque pièce qui mentionne si elle n'a pas été représentée ou imprimée' (Rondel, *Catalogue analytique*, p.29)]

Lefilleul:

Catalogue mensuel des livres neufs et d'occasion, rares et curieux, anciens et modernes de la librairie L. Lefilleul, 27 boulevard Poissonière, Paris. Mars 1877. [Lefilleul]

—. Décembre 1878.

Le Petit, Jules, *Bibliographie des principales éditions originales d'écrivains français du XVe au XVIIIe siècle*. Paris 1888.

Levot, Prosper Jean, *Biographie bretonne*. Vannes, Paris 1852-1857. [Levot]

Lewine, J., *Bibliography of eighteenth-century art and illustrated books*. London 1898. [Lewine]

Loaisel de Saulnays, Henry, *Un méconnu: Loaisel de Tréogate (1752-1812), monographie littéraire*. Alger 1930. [Saulnays]

Lorenz, Otto et al, *Le Catalogue général de la librairie française*. Paris 1867-1945. [Lorenz]

[Marc, A.,] *Dictionnaire des romans anciens et modernes*. Paris 1819. [Marc]

Martin, Angus, 'A first listing of new French prose fiction 1780-1783', in his 'Towards a checklist of French prose fiction 1751-1788', *Australian journal of French studies* 3 (1966), pp. 356-69.

—, 'A first listing of new French prose fiction 1784-1788', *Australian journal of French studies* 4 (1967), pp.109-31. [Martin, 'First listing, 1784-1788']

—, 'A first listing of new French prose fiction 1780-1788: addenda and corrigenda', *Australian journal of French studies* 6 (1969), pp.131-37.

—, Vivienne Mylne, and Richard Frautschi, *Bibliographie du genre romanesque français, 1751-1800*. London, Paris 1977. [MMF] [This work supersedes Martin's 'First listings']

[Michaud, Joseph François,] *Biographie universelle, ancienne et moderne*. Paris 1811-1828. [Michaud]

Monglond, André, *La France révolutionnaire et impériale: annales de la bibliographie méthodique et description des livres illustrés*. Grenoble, 1930-1963. [Monglond, *Fr rév*]

—, *Index de la France révolutionnaire et impériale (1789-1812)*. Geneva 1978.

Morabito, Pasquale, *Uno scrittore sconosciuto: Joseph-Marie Loaisel de Tréogate*. Reggio Calabria 1975. [Morabito]

Mornet, Daniel, 'Bibliographie des romans, iie partie, Romans publiés de 1761 à 1780', in his 'Introduction' to *La Nouvelle Héloïse*, by Jean-Jacques Rousseau, 'Les grands écrivains de la France'. Paris 1925, i.358-85. [Mornet ed. *Nouvelle Héloïse*, i]

Mylne, Vivienne: see Martin.

Nicoll, Allardyce, *A history of English drama, 1660-1900*. Cambridge 1952-1967.

Nodier: see Pixerécourt.

Nyon: see La Vallière.

Paris, Bibliothèque nationale, *La Gravure originale en France au XVIIIe siècle*, ed. Yves Bruand. Paris 1960.

Peignot, Gabriel, *Dictionnaire critique, littéraire et bibliographique des principaux livres condamnés au feu, supprimés ou censurés*. Paris 1806.

Pigoreau, Alexandre Nicolas, *Petite bibliographie biographico-romancière, ou dictionnaire des romanciers*. Paris 1821. Reprint: Geneva 1968. [Pigoreau]

Pixerécourt, René Charles Guilbert de, 'Tableau chronologique de mes pièces', in his *Théâtre choisi*, ed. Charles Nodier. Paris 1841, vol.i, pp.xliv-lxxvii. [Pixerécourt, 'Tableau chronologique']

—:

    Lacroix, Paul et Charles Nodier, *Bibliothèque de m. G. de Pixerécourt, avec des notes littéraires et bibliographiques*, Paris 1838. [Lacroix, *Bibl Pixerécourt*] [References to Loaisel's works are contained in the section entitled 'Révolution française . . .', pp.343-414. Not all copies of the catalogue contain these pages. The copy examined was BN call number Δ 10003 (1-3).]

    Bibliothèque de m. G. de Pixerécourt, suite, autographes et manuscrits de m. G. de Pixerécourt . . . dont la vente aura lieu le mercredi 4 novembre 1840. Paris 1840.

    Catalogue de livres, manuscrits, autographes, provenant de la bibliothèque de feu m. G. de Pixerécourt, dont la vente aura lieu le mardi 27 novembre 1849. Paris 1849.

—:

    Virely, André, *René Charles Guilbert Pixerécourt (1773-1844)*. Paris 1909. [Virely]

Place, Joseph and Hector Talvart, *Bibliographie des auteurs modernes de la langue française*. Paris 1928- .

Poinsot, Edmond Antoine [pseudonym: Georges d'Heylli], *Dictionnaire des pseudonymes*, 3rd ed. Paris 1887.

Poirier, Roger, *La Bibliothèque universelle des romans: rédacteurs, textes, public*. Geneva 1976.

Portalis, Roger, *Les Dessinateurs d'illustrations au XVIIIe siècle*. Paris 1877.

Portalis, Roger and Henri Béraldi, *Les Graveurs du XVIIIe siècle*. Paris 1880-1882.

Quérard, Joseph Marie, *La France littéraire*. Paris 1827-1864. [Quérard, *Fr litt*]

—, *La Littérature française contemporaine, 1827-1849 . . ., dictionnaire bibliographique*. Paris 1840-1857.

—, *Les Supercheries littéraires dévoilées*, 2nd ed., rev. Gustave Brunet and Pierre Jannet. Paris 1869-1870. [Quérard, *Supercheries*]

Rabbe, Alphonse, *Biographie universelle et portative des contemporains*. Paris 1836. [Rabbe]

Renouvier, Jules, *Histoire de l'art pendant la Révolution, considérée principalement dans les estampes*. Paris 1863.

Roden, Robert F. *Later American plays, 1831-1900*. New York 1900.

Sabin, Joseph, *Bibliotheca americana: a dictionary of books relating to America, from its discovery to the present time*. New York 1868-1936. [Sabin]

Sander, Max, *Les Livres illustrés français du dix-huitième siècle*. Stuttgart 1926.

Saulnays: see Loaisel de Saulnays.

Séguin, J. A. R., *French works in English translation (1731-1799): a bibliographical catalogue*. Jersey City 1965-1970.

Slatkine:
Librairie M. Slatkine et fils, 5, rue des Chaudronniers, Geneva, *Livres anciens et d'occasion: histoire littéraire de la France, dix-huitième siècle*, deuxième partie, C-M, Catalogue no.274. Printemps 1968. [Slatkine]

Soleinne:
Lacroix, Paul [pseudonym: P. L. Jacob, bibliophile], *Bibliothèque dramatique de monsieur de Soleinne.* Paris 1843-1845. Reprint: New York [1966]. [Lacroix, *Bibl Soleinne*]

Goizet, J., *Table générale du catalogue de la bibliothèque dramatique de m. de Soleinne.* Paris 1845. Reprint: New York [1966].

Brunet, Charles, *Table des pièces de théâtre décrites dans le catalogue de m. de Soleinne.* Paris 1914. Reprint: New York [1966].

Summers, Montague, *A gothic bibliography.* London [1941]. [Summers]

Taylor, Isidore-Justin-Séverin, baron:
Bibliographie théâtrale ou catalogue des pièces de théâtre de la collection de m. le baron Taylor [18—]. Bibliothèque de l'Opéra, Manuscript, Rés. 652 (1-2). [Taylor, *Bibl* ms]
Catalogue de la bibliothèque dramatique de feu le baron de Taylor . . . dont la vente aura lieu du lundi 27 novembre au mercredi 13 décembre 1893. Paris 1893.

Talvart: see Place.

Tchemerzine, Avenir, *Bibliographie d'éditions originales et rares d'auteurs français des XVe, XVIe, XVIIe et XVIIIe siècles.* Paris 1927-1934.

Thieme, Hugo P., *Bibliographie de la littérature française de 1800 à 1930.* Paris 1933.
Dreher, S. and M. Rolli, *Bibliographie de la littérature française, 1930-39; complément à la bibliographie de H. P. Thieme.* Lille, Geneva 1948.

Drevet, Marguerite L, *Bibliographie de la littérature française, 1940-49; complément à la bibliographie de H. P. Thieme.* Lille, Geneva 1955.

Thieme, Ulrich and Felix Becker, *Allgemeines Lexikon der bildenden Künstler von der Antike bis zur Gegenwart.* Leipzig 1907-1950. [Thieme-Becker]

Tourneux, Maurice, *Bibliographie de l'histoire de Paris pendant la Révolution française.* Paris 1890-1913. [Tourneux]

Travers, Seymour, *Catalogue of nineteenth-century French theatrical parodies (1789-1914).* New York 1941.

Versini, Laurent, 'Romans épistolaires parus de 1700 à 1800', in his *Laclos et la tradition: essai sur les sources et la technique des 'Liaisons dangeureuses'.* Paris 1968, pp.650-64. [Versini]

Virely: see Pixerécourt.

Wegelin, Oscar, *Early American plays, 1714-1830,* 2nd ed., rev. New York 1905. Reprint: New York 1968. [Wegelin]

Weller, Emil, *Dictionnaire des ouvrages français portant de fausses indications des lieux d'impression et des imprimeurs, depuis le XVIe siècle jusqu'aux temps modernes*: vol.ii of his *Die falschen und fingierten Druckorte.* Leipzig 1864. [Weller]

Wicks, Charles B. and Jerome W. Schweitzer, *The Parisian stage: alphabetical indexes of plays and authors.* University, Alabama 1950-1967. [Wicks and Schweitzer]

Worp, Jacob A., *Geschiedenis van het drama en van het tooneel in Nederland.* Groningen 1904-1908. [Worp]

Zambon, Maria Rose, *Bibliographie du roman français en Italie au XVIIIe siècle: traductions.* Florence, Paris 1962.
—, *Les Romans français dans les journaux littéraires italiens du XVIIIe siècle.* Florence, Paris 1971.

3. *Library catalogues*

Arras, Bibliothèque communale de la ville d'Arras, *Catalogue méthodique de la Bibliothèque communale de la ville d'Arras*, ed. August Wicquet. Arras 1885-1889. [Arras, *Cat*]

France, Direction des bibliothèques de France, *Catalogue général des manuscrits des bibliothèques publiques de France*. Paris 1885- .

—, Ministère de l'instruction publique et des beaux-arts. *Catalogue général des manuscrits des bibliothèques publiques des départements*. Paris 1849-1885.

—, —, *Catalogue des manuscrits conservés aux Archives nationales*. Paris 1892.

German Democratic Republic:
Französische Drücke des 18. Jahrhunderts in den Bibliotheken der Deutschen Demokratischen Republik; Bibliographie, ed. Werner Krauss and Martin Fontius. Berlin 1970. [Krauss and Fontius]

Krauss and Fontius: see German Democratic Republic.

Le Mans, Bibliothèque municipale, *Catalogue de la Bibliothèque de la ville du Mans, Belles-lettres*. Le Mans 1880. [Le Mans, *Cat*]

London, British Museum, Department of printed books, *General catalogue of printed books*, Photolithographic edition of 1955. London 1959-1966. [BL, *Cat*]

Paris, Bibliothèque de l'Arsenal, Ancien fonds, *Belles lettres*. Manuscript catalogue arranged alphabetically by author. [Ars, *BL*]

—, —, —, *Romans*. Manuscript catalogue arranged alphabetically by title.

—, —, Fonds Rondel, *Théâtre français, Révolution 2*: vol.xi of *Catalogue mss. de la Bibliothèque Rondel*. Manuscript catalogue arranged alphabetically by author within each volume; volumes arranged by period. [Ars, *Rondel*]

—, —, *Catalogue des manuscrits de la Bibliothèque de l'Arsenal*, ed. Henri Martin. Paris 1885-1899.

—, —, —, supplement: vol.xliii of *Catalogue général des manuscrits des bibliothèques publiques de France*. Paris 1904.

—, —, —, second supplement: vol.xlv of *Catalogue général des manuscrits des bibliothèques publiques de France*. Paris 1915.

—, —, *supplément au Catalogue général des manuscrits, 9404-9616 bis* [fonds Douay]. Typescript.

Paris, Bibliothèque nationale, Département des estampes, *Inventaire du Fonds français: gravures du dix-huitième siècle*, ed. Marcel Roux. Paris 1930- .

—, —, Département des imprimés, *Catalogue général des livres imprimés de la Bibliothèque nationale: auteurs*. Paris 1897- . [BN, *Cat*]

—, —, —, *Catalogue général des livres imprimés: auteurs – collectivités – auteurs – anonymes: 1960-1964*. Paris 1965-1967.

—, —, Département des manuscrits, *Catalogue général des manuscrits français*. Paris 1868-1918.

—, —, —, —, *Table générale alphabétique*. Paris 1913-1948.

Troyes, Bibliothèque de la ville de Troyes. *Catalogue de la Bibliothèque de la ville de Troyes*, ed. Emile Socard. Troyes 1883. [Troyes, *Cat*]

United States, Library of Congress, *The National union catalog of manuscript collections*. Washington 1959- .

—, *The National union catalog: pre-1956 imprints*. London 1968- . [*NUC*]

C. Other works

Many of the sources listed above yielded information in addition to biography and bibliography, strictly speaking. For the sake of economy, they have not been listed again below. Abbreviations and short titles used in citations are given in brackets after each work so cited.

Assézat-Tourneux: see Diderot.

Baldensperger, Fernand, 'Un prédécesseur de René en Amérique', *Revue de philologie française* 15 (1901), pp.229-34.

Barquissau, Raphael, *Les Poètes créoles du XVIIIe siècle*. Paris 1949.

Barroux, Robert *et al*. *Dictionnaire des lettres françaises: le XVIIIe siècle*. Paris 1960.

Belin, J.-P., *Le Commerce des livres prohibés à Paris de 1750 à 1789*. Paris 1913. Reprint: New York n.d.

Bellanger, Claude *et al*, *Histoire générale de la presse française*. Paris 1969-1972.

Bellen, Eise Carel van, *Les Origines du mélodrame*. Utrecht 1927.

Besterman, Theodore, *A world bibliography of bibliographies*, 4th ed. Lausanne 1965-1966.

Bonno, Gabriel, 'Liste chronologique des périodiques de langue française du XVIIIe siècle', *Modern language quarterly* 5 (1944), pp.3-25.

Bowers, Fredson, *Principles of bibliographical description*. Princeton 1949. Re-issue: New York 1962.

Brazier, Nicolas, *Histoire des petits théâtres de Paris depuis leur origine*, new ed. Paris 1838.

—, *Chronique des petits théâtres de Paris*, ed. Edmond Antoine Poinsot [pseudonym: Georges d'Heylli]. Paris 1883.

Brooks, Peter, *The Melodramatic imagination: Balzac, Henry James, melodrama, and the mode of excess*. New Haven, London 1976.

Carlson, Marvin A., *The Theater of the French Revolution*. Ithaca, New York 1966.

Cazin, Paul, *Le Prince-évêque de Varmie, Ignace Krasicki, 1735-1801*. Paris 1940.

Chinard, Gilbert, *L'Amérique et le rêve exotique dans la littérature française au XVIIe et au XVIIIe siècle*. Paris 1913.

—, *L'Exotisme américain dans l'œuvre de Chateaubriand*. Paris 1918.

Ciorancescu, Alexandre, 'Notes sur la *Bibliographie littéraire du XVIIIe siècle*', *Dix-huitième siècle* 3 (1971), pp.361-70.

Contes des génies ou les charmantes leçons d'Horan, fils d'Asmar: vol.xxx of *Le Cabinet des fées*. Genève, Paris 1786.

Coulet, Henri, *Le Roman jusqu'à la Révolution*. Paris 1967-1968.

Darnton, Robert, 'Reading, writing, and publishing in eighteenth-century France: a case study in sociology of literature', *Daedalus* 100 (1971), pp. 214-56.

Dawson, Robert L., *Baculard d'Arnaud: life and prose fiction*. Studies on Voltaire 141-42. Banbury 1976.

Delon, Michel, 'Vision du monde "préromantique" dans *Dolbreuse* de Loaisel de Tréogate', in *La Bretagne littéraire au XVIIIe siècle*, Colloque Duclos, 6-8 avril 1973, Rennes, *Annales de Bretagne et des pays de l'ouest* 83 (1976), pp.829-38.

Diderot, Denis, *Œuvres complètes*, ed. J. Assézat and M. Tourneux. Paris 1875-1877. [Assézat-Tourneux]

Estève, Edmond, 'Dix-huitième siècle et romantisme', *Revue d'histoire littéraire de la France* 19 (1912), pp.75-84.

Estivals, Robert, *La Statistique biblio-graphique de la France sous la mo-narchie au XVIIIe siècle*. Paris, La Haye 1965.

Etienne, Servais, *Le Genre romanesque en France depuis l'apparition de la 'Nouvelle Héloïse' jusqu'aux approches de la Révolution*. Bruxelles 1922. [Etienne]

Etude des périodiques anciens: colloque d'Utrecht, 9-10 janvier 1970. Paris 1972.

Fargher, Richard, 'Victor Hugo's first melodrama', in *Balzac and the nine-teenth century: studies in French literature presented to Herbert J. Hunt by pupils, colleagues and friends*, ed. D. G. Charlton, J. Gaudon, and Anthony R. Pugh. Leicester 1972.

Fauchery, Pierre, *La Destinée féminine dans le roman européen du dix-huitième siècle, 1713-1807: essai de gyné-comythie romanesque*. Paris 1972.

Favre, Robert, *La Mort dans la littérature et la pensée françaises au siècle des lumières*. Lyon 1978.

Folies sentimentales, ou l'égarement de l'esprit par le cœur. Paris: Royez 1786. *Nouvelles folies sentimentales, ou folies par amour*. Paris: Royez 1786.

Frantz, Pierre, 'L'espace dramatique de *La Brouette du Vinaigrier* à *Coelina*', *Revue des sciences humaines* 41 (1976), pp.151-62.

Frautschi, Richard L. and J. Moreland, 'Toward a list of French prose fiction', *Romance notes* 9 (1968), pp. 341-43.

Gaskell, Philip, *A new introduction to bibliography*. Oxford 1972.

Godenne, René, 'Loaisel de Tréogate et Chateaubriand', In *La Bretagne littéraire au XVIIIe siècle*, Colloque Duclos, 6-8 avril 1973, Rennes, *Annales de Bretagne et des pays de l'ouest* 83 (1976), pp.839-45.

Grand-Carteret, John, *Les Almanachs français (1600-1895)*, Paris 1896.

Hartog, Willie G., *Guilbert de Pixeré-court: sa vie, son mélodrame, sa technique et son influence*. Paris 1913.

Hatin, Eugène, *Histoire politique et littéraire de la presse en France*. Paris 1859-1861.

Henriot, Emile, 'Loaisel de Tréogate ou le précuseur oublié', in his *Romanes-ques et romantiques*. Paris 1930.

Hoog, Armand, 'L'âme préromantique et les instincts de mort', *Bulletin de la Faculté des lettres de Strasbourg* 21 (1952), pp.123-33, 149-60.

—, 'Un cas d'angoisse préromantique', *Revue des sciences humaines* 17 (1952), pp.181-97.

—, 'The Romantic spirit and the American "elsewhere"', *Yale French studies* 10 [1952], pp.14-28.

Hugo, Victor, *Théâtre complet*. Biblio-thèque de la Pléiade. Paris 1963-1964.

Inklaar, Derk, *François-Thomas Bacu-lard d'Arnaud, ses imitateurs en Holland et dans d'autres pays*. Paris 1925.

Kavaliunas, Jolita, 'Passions and the search for happiness: the concepts of passions and guilt in their relationship to happiness, as manifested in certain French novels of the eighteenth century', Ph.D. Dissertation. Case Western Reserve University 1972.

Killen, Alice M., *Le Roman terrifiant ou roman noir de Walpole à Anne Radcliffe et son influence sur la littérature française jusqu'en 1840*. Paris 1923.

Kirsop, Wallace, *Bibliographie matérielle et critique textuelle: vers une collabo-ration*. Paris 1970.

Krauss, Werner, 'L'étude des écrivains obscurs du siècle des lumières', *Studies on Voltaire* 26 (1963), pp. 1019-24.

Laquiante, A., *Un hiver à Paris sous le Consulat – 1802-1803 – d'après les lettres de J.-F. Reichardt*. Paris 1896.

Laufer, Roger, *Introduction à la texto-logie*. Paris 1972.

—, 'La bibliographie matérielle dans ses rapports avec la critique textuelle, l'histoire littéraire et la formalisation', *Revue d'histoire littéraire de la France* 70 (1970), pp.776-83.

Lecomte, Louis Henry, *Le Théâtre de la Cité, 1792-1907*: vol.ix of his *Histoire des théâtres de Paris*. Paris 1910.

Lély, Gilbert, *Vie du marquis de Sade*: vols i-ii to Lély's edition of *Œuvres complètes* of Sade. Paris 1972.

Lettres de tendresse et d'amour. Amathonte, Paris n.d.

Lévy, Maurice, *Le Roman 'gothique' anglais, 1764-1824*. Toulouse 1968.

Louw, Guilbert van de, *Baculard d'Arnaud, romancier ou vulgarisateur: essai de sociologie littéraire*. Paris 1972.

Maclès, Louise Noelle, *Les Sources du travail bibliographique*. Geneva 1950-1958.

Martin, Angus, 'Baculard d'Arnaud et la vogue des séries de nouvelles en France au xviiie siècle', *Revue d'histoire littéraire de la France* 73 (1973), pp.982-92.

—, 'Romans et romanciers à succès de 1751 à la Révolution d'après les rééditions', *Revue des sciences humaines* 35 (1970), pp.383-89.

Masson, Pierre-Maurice, *La Religion de Jean-Jacques Rousseau*. Paris 1916. Reprint: Geneva 1960.

Mauzi, Robert, *L'Idée du bonheur dans la littérature et la pensée françaises au XVIIIe siècle*. Paris 1960.

—, 'Les maladies de l'âme au xviiie siècle', *Revue des sciences humaines* 25 (1960), pp.459-93.

McGhee, Dorothy M., *The Cult of the 'conte moral': the moral tale in France — its emergence and progress*. Menasha 1960.

McKerrow, Ronald B., *An introduction to bibliography for literary students*. Oxford 1927.

Mélodrame, Le, special issue of *Revue des sciences humaines*, no.162: avril-juin 1976.

Mercier de Compiègne, Claude-François-Xavier, *Azoline ou la rose d'amour, nouvelle turque; suivi des Albigeoises*. Chypre, Paris 1791.

Monglond, André, *Le Préromantisme français*, new ed. Paris 1965-1966.

Monselet, Charles, *Les Oubliés et les dédaignés: figures littéraires de la fin du XVIIIe siècle*. Paris 1859.

—, —, new ed. Paris 1876.

Montargis, Jean, 'La première et la dernière œuvre dramatique de Victor Hugo: *Le Château du diable* (1812) – *Le Suicide* (1878)', *Nouvelle revue française* 52 (1939), pp.456-65.

Mornet, Daniel, 'Les enseignements des bibliothèques privées (1750-1780)', *Revue d'histoire littéraire de la France* 17 (1910), pp.449-96.

—, 'L'influence de Jean-Jacques Rousseau au xviiie siècle', *Annales de la Société Jean-Jacques Rousseau* 8 (1912), pp.33-67.

—, 'L'influence de la *Nouvelle Héloïse* sur le roman français de 1761 à 1787', *Revue universitaire* 14 (1905), pp.306-18.

—, 'Introduction' to his edition of *La Nouvelle Héloïse*, by Jean-Jacques Rousseau, 'Les Grands écrivains de la France'. Paris 1925, i. [Mornet ed. *Nouvelle Héloïse*, i]

—, 'Un 'préromantique': les *Soirées de mélancolie* de Loaisel de Tréogate', *Revue d'histoire littéraire de la France* 16 (1909), pp.491-500.

—, *Le Romantisme en France au XVIIIe siècle*, 2nd ed. Paris 1925. Reprint: New York 1971.

—, *Le Sentiment de la nature en France de J.-J. Rousseau à Bernardin de Saint-Pierre: essai sur les rapports de la littérature et des mœurs*. Paris 1907. Reprint: New York 1971.

Mortet, Charles, 'Le format des livres: notions historiques et pratiques', *Revue des bibliothèques* 3 (1893), pp. 305-25. Reprint: Paris 1894.

Nouvelles folies sentimentales: see *Folies sentimentales*.

Paris, Bibliothèque nationale, Département des imprimés, *Catalogue de l'histoire de la révolution française*, ed. André Martin and Gérard Walter: vol.v, *Ecrits de la période révolutionnaire: journaux et almanachs*. Paris 1943.

—, —, Département des périodiques, *Catalogue collectif des périodiques du début du XVIIIe siècle à 1939 conservés dans les bibliothèques de Paris et dans les bibliothèques universitaires des départements.* Paris 1967-1977.

Picard, Louis B., *Les Marionnettes, ou un jeu de la fortune,* in vol.v of his *Théâtre.* Paris 1812.

Piszczkowski, Mieczyslaw, *Ignacy Krasicki: monografia litteracka.* Krakow 1969.

Pitou, Alexis, 'Les origines du mélodrame française à la fin du XVIIIe siècle', *Revue d'histoire littéraire de la France* 18 (1911), pp.256-96.

Pougin, Arthur, 'Le théâtre révolutionnaire en 1791: le Théâtre Molière', *Bulletin de la société de l'histoire du théâtre* (1903), 2e année, no.6, pp.3-30.

Préromantisme: hypothèque ou hypothèse?, Colloque, 29-30 juin 1972, Clermont-Ferrand, ed. Paul Viallaneix. Paris 1975.

Rabany, Charles, *Kotzebue: sa vie, son temps, ses œuvres dramatiques.* Paris, Nancy 1893. [Rabany]

Rahill, Frank, *The World of melodrama.* University Park, Pennsylvania and London 1967.

Rondel, Auguste, *Catalogue analytique sommaire de la collection théâtrale Rondel, suivi d'un guide pratique à travers la bibliographie théâtrale et d'une chronologie des ouvrages d'information et de critique théâtrales.* Paris 1932.

—, 'Conférence sur la bibliographie dramatique et sur les collections théâtrales', *Bulletin de la société d'histoire du théâtre* (janvier-mars 1913). Reprint: Lille 1913. [Rondel,

'Conférence bibliographie dramatique']

Rossard, Janine, *Une clef du romantisme: la pudeur.* Paris 1974.

Rousseau, Jean-Jacques, *Œuvres complètes,* Bibliothèque de la Pléiade. Paris 1959, i.

Sage, Pierre, *Le 'Bon prêtre' dans la littérature française d'"Amadis de Gaule' au 'Génie du Christianisme'.* Geneva, Lille 1951.

Le Théâtre de la Révolution et de l'Empire, 132 pièces de théâtre sélectionnées et présentées par Marc Régaldo, Microéditions Hachette. Paris 1975.

Thomasseau, Jean-Marie, *Le Mélodrame sur les scènes parisiennes de 'Coelina' à 'l'Auberge des Adrets' (1800-1823).* Lille 1973.

Trahard, Pierre, *Les Maîtres de la sensibilité française au XVIIIe siècle (1715-1789).* Paris 1931-1933.

Ubersfeld, Anne, 'Les bons et les méchants', *Revue des sciences humaines* 41 (1976), pp.193-203.

—, *Le Roi et le bouffon: étude sur le théâtre de Hugo de 1830-1839.* Paris 1974.

Van Tieghem, Paul. *Le Préromantisme: études d'histoire littéraire européenne.* Paris 1930, ii.

—, *Le Sentiment de la nature dans le préromantisme européen.* Paris 1960.

Vier, Jacques, *Histoire de la littérature française: XVIIIe siècle.* Paris 1965-1970.

Wais, Kurt, *Das Antiphilosophische Weltbild des französischen Sturm und Drang, 1760-1789.* Berlin 1934.

Young, Edward, *Les Nuits d'Young,* traduites de l'Anglois par m. Le Tourneur. Amsterdam: Changuion; Paris: LeJay 1769.

Index

References in italics are to entry numbers in the annotated listing.

Adélaïde de Bavière, drame en quatre actes, en prose, à spectacle (Loaisel de Tréogate), 87, 96, 148, 194, 197, 214-16; *44-45*

Affiches de Paris and *Affiches de province:* see *Annonces, affiches et avis divers* and *Journal général de France*

Ainsi finissent les grandes passions; ou les dernières amours du Chevalier de . . . . (Loaisel de Tréogate), 24, 27, 51, 54, 65, 75, 77-79, 81-86, 92-97, 112, 189, 193, 196, 201-204; *1-4, 35, 86*

Allgemeines Lexikon der bildenden Künstler, 239; *32*

Almanach des muses, 105, 152-53, 160, 177, 180, 232; *50, 58, 61*

Almanach des spectacles, 150, 153, 160, 162, 164-65, 179-84, 232

Almanach des spectacles de Paris, 232

Almanach des spectacles de Paris, pour l'an 1809, 148, 165, 232

Almanach général de tous les spectacles de Paris et des provinces, 86, 179, 182-83, 232; *46*

Almanach littéraire ou étrennes d'Apollon, 59, 65, 72, 80-81, 85-86, 104, 232; *3, 6, 13, 33, 35, 37*

Amans siciliens, ou les apparences trompeuses, comédie en deux actes et en prose, Les (Loaisel de Tréogate), 87, 91, 149-50, 194

Ambigu-Comique, Théâtre de l', 90-92, 96, 148, 163, 165, 175-77, 180, 183-84, 194; *67-68, 70*

American Antiquarian Society, Worchester, Massachusetts, 109; *64*

Amis des Arts, et des Elèves de l'Opéra-Comique, Théâtre des, 149

'A M. Le Chevalier de Parny, après avoir lu ses *Poésies érotiques*' (Loaisel de Tréogate), 5, 54, 74-75, 188, 193, 195, 198, 200; *93*

Amour arrange tout, comédie en un acte et en prose, L' (Loaisel de Tréogate), 47, 86-88, 150, 193, 196, 216; *46*

Année littéraire, 59, 72, 80-81, 85, 104, 232; *3, 13, 29, 33, 35, 37*

Année théâtrale, 232

Annonces, affiches et avis divers, 68-71, 73, 105, 232; *6*

Annuaire dramatique, ou étrennes théâtrales, 148, 150, 152, 160, 162, 165, 175, 177, 179-80, 182-84, 232

Apollinaire, Guillaume, 233

Archives nationales, 230, 240

Armée, Service historique de l', 25, 36, 38-40, 45, 229

Arnault, Antoine Vincent, 14, 24-25, 106, 116, 187-88, 230, 233; *29, 32, 37, 42-43*

Arras, Bibliothèque communale, 240; *16*

Arsenal, Bibliothèque de l', 16, 101, 108-10, 184, 240; *6-7, 13, 21, 29, 33, 37, 44, 46, 50-51, 54, 58, 60, 61-64, 67-69, 77-78, 85-88, 90, 92-93, 95*

Assézat, J., 241; *21, 24-26*

Augan, 35

Aux âmes sensibles, élégie (Loaisel de Tréogate), 22, 27, 51, 68, 70, 73-74, 193, 196; *94-95*

Babault, 148, 152, 165, 175, 233; *50*

Bachaumont, Louis Petit de, *Mémoires secrets pour servir à l'histoire de la république des lettres,* 53, 72, 106, 232

Baculard d'Arnaud, François-Thomas de, 13, 15-16, 19, 22, 53-55, 63-64, 67, 71-72, 103; *Les Amans malheureux,* 67; *Epreuves du sentiment,* 45, 63; *29; Euphémie,* 67; *Favel,* 67; *Germeuil,* 19; *Œuvres diverses et correspondance,* 53-54, 230

Baer, G., *57*

Baldensperger, Fernand, 13, 15, 19-20, 241

Balzac, Jean-Louis Guez de, 55

Barbier, Antoine Alexandre, 233; *7, 33, 35, 46, 86*

Barquissau, Raphael, 74, 241

Barroux, Robert, 21, 24-25, 102-103, 108, 148, 150, 152-53, 160, 162, 164-65, 175, 180, 183-84, 230, 234, 241; *3, 6, 8-9, 12-13, 16, 19, 29, 31, 33, 35, 37-38, 41, 43-44, 46, 48, 50, 52, 54, 55-56, 58, 61-63, 67, 71, 74, 85, 88, 90, 92, 94*

Bastille, 81

Beaujolais, Théâtre des, 88, 150, 179, 193-94

Becker, Felix, 239; *32*

Belin, J.-P., 241; *33*

Bellanger, Claude, 59-60, 241

Bellen, Eise Carel van, 20, 241

Belzors (attributed to Loaisel de Tréogate), 151-52

Bénézit, Emmanuel, 234

Béraldi, Henri, 238

Bernard, C., 234

Besterman, Theodore, 102, 241

Beuchot, Andrieu J. Q., 234

Bibliographie de la littérature française, 1930-39, 239

Bibliographie des auteurs modernes de la langue française, 238

Bibliographie du genre romanesque français, 1751-1800, 14, 26, 103, 107, 110, 237; *2-4, 6-7, 9-11, 13, 15-16, 18-21, 23-26, 28-29, 33, 35-37, 41, 43*

Bibliographie théâtrale ou catalogue des pièces de théâtre de la collection de m. le baron Taylor, 108, 239

Bibliothèque de m. G. de Pixerécourt, 108, 238

Bibliothèque française, 105, 232; *32, 43*

Bibliothèque nationale, 22, 101, 107-109, 116, 187, 238, 240; *2-3, 6-7, 9, 13, 19, 21, 23, 35, 41, 46, 54-55, 58, 61, 62, 67, 71, 74, 77, 85-86, 88, 90, 94*

Bibliothèque universelle des romans, 79-80, 84, 97, 232; *13-14*

Binet, 93; *43*

Biographie nouvelle des contemporains, 14, 24-25, 106, 116, 187-88, 230, 233; *29, 32, 37, 42-43*

Bisarrerie de la fortune, ou le jeune philosophe, comédie en cinq actes et en prose, La (Loaisel de Tréogate), 49, 87-91, 98, 152-53, 194, 196-98, 216-18; *47-57, 60*

Block Andrew, 234; *8*

Boileau-Despréaux, Nicolas, 55

Boissais, Maurice, 234

Bond, Donald F., 102, 234

Bonin, Jan René, 37

Bonnardot, Alfred, 234

Bonno, Gabriel, 102, 241

Boston Public Library, 109; *69*

Boston Theatre, *65, 69*

Boston University, Library of, *65*

Bouchot, Henri, 234

Bourcard, Gustave, 234

Bourdaloue, Louis, 55

Bousquet, Jacques, 22, 24, 26-27, 108, 116, 148, 150, 152-53, 160, 162, 164-65, 175, 180, 183, 230, 234; *3, 6, 9, 12-13, 16, 19, 29, 31, 33, 35, 37, 41, 43-46, 50, 58, 61-63, 67, 71, 74, 85, 88, 90, 92, 94*

Bovrel, Château de, 34-35

Bowers, Fredson, 110-12, 241

Brazier, Nicolas, 241; *57*

Brenner, Clarence D., 107, 234; *46*

Bretagne, 16, 33-38, 43; *86*

Breteuil, baron de, *1*

Brionne, 49

Brissart-Binet, Charles, 234

British Library, 101, 109-10, 116, 240; *29, 35, 37, 44-46, 52, 54, 58, 61-63, 77, 79, 81-82, 85, 88, 92*

Brooks, Peter, 14, 23, 241

Brooks, Richard A., 102, 234

Brown University, Library of, 109; *69, 81*

Brunet, Charles, 239; *86*

Brunet, Gustave, 234; *33*

Brunet, Jacques Charles, 234

Bure, Guillaume de, *Catalogue des livres de la bibliothèque de feu m. le duc de La Vallière*, 1ère partie, 108, 237; *7*

Cabeen, David C., 102, 234

Cabinet des fées, Le: see *Les Contes des génies*

California at Los Angeles, Library of University of, 109; *15*

Carlson, Marvin A., 89, 241

Carteret, Leopold, 234

Case Western Reserve University, Library of, 109; *15*

Castries, Armand Charles Augustin, duc de, 41-42, 44

Catalogue collectif des périodiques du début du XVIIIe siècle à 1939, 103, 244

Catalogue de la bibliothèque dramatique de feu le baron de Taylor, 108, 239; *50*

Catalogue de l'histoire de la Révolution française, 102, 243

Catalogue des pièces composant le théâtre révolutionnaire par ordre de représentation ou de publication, depuis l'année 1788, 234

Catalogue général de la librairie française, Le, 237

Catalogue hebdomadaire, 105, 231, 232; *6, 29, 33, 37*

Cazin, Paul, 241; *57*

Celani, H., 234

Chapelain, Jean, 55

Charlier, G., *23*

Chateaubriand, François-René de, 13, 15, 18, 20, 23

Château du Diable, comédie héroïque, en quatre actes et en prose, Le (Loaisel de Tréogate), 19-20, 22-23, 87-91, 159-60, 194, 196, 198, 218-19; *58-60*

Chaulieu, Guillaume Amfrye de, 55

Chazel, 150

Chicago, Library of University of, 109; *6, 37, 69*

Chinard, Gilbert, 15, 241

Chronique de Paris, 88, 152, 160, 179, 182-83, 232

Cioranescu, Alexandre, 25-26, 102, 106, 108, 116, 234, 241; *3, 6, 9, 12-13, 29, 31, 33, 35, 37, 41, 43-44, 46, 50, 54, 58, 61-63, 67-68, 85, 88, 92, 94*

Cité, Théâtre de la, 90, 153, 162, 164-65, 180, 184; *64, 67-68, 77*

Cité-Variétés, Théâtre de la, 162, 194

Cohen, Henry, 107-108, 116, 234-35; *12-13, 19, 26, 32, 37, 43*

Coll, m., 40

Collas, Georges, 20-21, 24, 33, 230

Columbia University, Library of, 109; *3, 9, 13, 41*

Combat des Thermopyles, ou l'école des guerriers, fait historique en trois actes et en prose, Le (Loaisel de Tréogate), 87, 89-90, 96, 194, 197, 219-20

Comédie-Française, 89

Comtesse d'Alibre, ou le cri du sentiment, anecdote françoise, La (Loaisel de Tréogate), 27, 47, 51, 55, 58, 60, 66-73, 75, 77, 81, 85, 89, 92, 97-98, 193, 196-98, 204-205; *5-11*

Contes des génies, Les, 92, 241

Cornell University, Library of, 109; *74*

Coroenne, A., 235

Correspondance littéraire: see La Harpe

Correspondance littéraire, philosophique et critique, 53, 106, 232; *35*

Correspondance littéraire secrète, 60, 106

Coulet, Henri, 22, 241

Cour, Anne Marie de La, 33, 193

Courcy, Pol Potier de, 230

Courrier de l'Europe et des spectacles, 104-105, 165, 177, 232

Courrier des planètes, 232

Courrier des spectacles, 88, 90, 96, 104-105, 148-49, 152-53, 160, 163-65, 175, 177, 180-81, 232; *64*

Cousin Jacques, 232

Craufurd, Quentin, 235

Crébillon, Prosper Jolyot de, 55, 69; *Atrée et Thyeste*, 69

Cubières-Palmezeaux, Michel de, 49; *35*

Darnton, Robert, 28, 241; *3*

Dawson, Robert L., 53-54, 63, 103, 241

Décade philosophique, 105, 152, 232; *43*

Delandine, Antoine François, 235; *44, 54, 62-63, 85*

Delaville, Jeanne Sophie, 36, 48-49, 195

Delcro, Antoine Jacques, 107, 235; *3, 5, 9, 13, 18, 24, 29, 32-33, 37, 43*

Delille, Jacques, *Les Jardins*, 55

Delisle de Sales, Jean-Baptiste-Claude Izouard, *dit*, 45, 75; *Histoire des hommes*, 45, 75, 187

Delon, Michel, 23-24, 78-79, 241

Denis, Alphonse, *57*

Desessarts, Nicolas Toussaint Lemoyne, 106, 116, 150, 152, 160, 162, 164-65,

179-80, 182-83, 188, 235; *3, 6, 8-10, 13, 19, 29, 31, 33, 35, 37, 39, 43, 46, 94*

Deutsche Staatsbibliothek, 110; *38, 48*

Dey, Achille, 48

Dictionnaire des lettres françaises: le XVIIIe siècle, 21, 24-25, 102-103, 241

Diderot, Denis, *21, 23-27; Œuvres complètes*, 241; *21, 24-26*

Didier, Béatrice, 13-14, 22, 116, 235; *6, 12, 33, 43*

Dighton, Basil Lewis, 235

Dimier, Louis, 235

Dinan, Alain de, 38

Dolbreuse, ou l'homme du siècle, ramené à la vérité par le sentiment et par la raison, histoire philosophique (Loaisel de Tréogate), 13-14, 16, 18-19, 21-24, 27, 44, 51, 54-55, 65, 75-82, 84-86, 89, 97, 110, 188, 193, 196-97, 205-208; *12-20*

Dorat, Claude-Joseph, 15-16, 22

Douay, Georges, 107, 148, 150, 152-53, 160, 162, 164-65, 175, 177, 179, 180, 182-84, 235; *59, 91*

Dreher, S., 239

Drevet, Marguerite L., 239

Duclos, R., 235

Du Coudray, Alexandre Jacques, *Répertoire général de toutes les pièces de théâtre*, 235

Dufrenoy, Marie-Louise, 235; *29, 41*

Dufresny, Charles, *La Coquette du village, ou le lot supposé*, 49

Du Paty, seigneur: see Vincent Joseph Loaisel

Du Paty, sieur: see Alexandre Marie Loaisel

Du Peloux, Charles, 235

Duval, Henri, 107, 148, 150, 152, 160, 162, 165, 175, 177, 179-80, 182-84, 235; *44, 46, 50, 57-58, 61, 71, 85-86, 88, 92*

The Eighteenth century: supplement to vol. iv of *A Critical bibliography of French literature*, 102, 234

The Eighteenth century: vol. iv of *A critical bibliography of French literature*, 102, 234

Emulation, Théâtre de l', 88, 160

Encyclopédie, L', 84

Enfer de la Bibliothèque nationale, L', 233

Englemann, M. G., *66, 89*

Ermenonville, *12*

Ersch, Johann Samuel, *La France littéraire*, 106, 116, 187-88, 235; *4, 6, 8-9, 13, 17-18, 29-30, 32, 34, 37-38, 41, 43-44, 48, 50, 53, 58, 85, 94*

Escoffier, Maurice, 235

Estève, Edmond, 16-17, 241

Estivals, Robert, 102, 242

Etienne, Servais, 17-19, 22, 242; *35*

Etrennes de l'Institut national, Les, 232

Etude des périodiques anciens: colloque d'Utrecht, L', 102, 242

Fabureau, Hubert, 21, 24, 230

Fantin Des Odoards, Antoine Etienne Nicolas, 116, 235; *3, 13, 29, 33, 58, 63, 85*

Fargher, Richard, 23, 88, 242

Fauchery, Pierre, 21, 242

Fauchet (abbé), *1*

Favre, Robert, 21, 242

Fénelon, François de Salignac de La Mothe, 55

Feuille de correspondance du libraire, 232; *23*

'Fiches Lecomte', les: see Lecomte

Filippi, Joseph de, 236

Fils naturel, Le (attributed to Loaisel de Tréogate), 21; *21-27*

Fleuret, F., 233

Fleuriot, Jean-Marie-Jérôme, *Paris littéraire*, 236

Florello, histoire méridionale (Loaisel de Tréogate), 13, 15, 19-21, 23, 25, 27, 40, 42-43, 51, 52, 56-65, 67, 74-75, 77, 89, 107, 193, 196-98, 208-209; *28-31, 35, 39, 40-42*

Florida, Library of University of, 109; *13*

Folies sentimentales, Les, 242; *35*

Folle de Saint-Joseph, La, 54; *1-2, 35*

Fontaine merveilleuse, ou les époux musulmans, pantomime-féerie en cinq actes, à grand spectacle, mêlée de dialogue, de combats, chants et danses, La (Loaisel de Tréogate), 87, 92, 163-64, 194, 197, 220-22; *62*

Fonteney, 73

Index

Fontenoy, 39

Fontius, Martin, 240; *29, 32, 37, 41*

Forêt périlleuse ou les brigands de la Calabre, drame en trois actes, en prose, La (Loaisel de Tréogate), 19-20, 22-23, 27, 47, 87-88, 90, 92, 98, 164-65, 194, 197-99, 222-24; *63-84*

France littéraire, La, 106, 237; *29, 33, 37, 94*

Frantz, Pierre, 23, 242

Französische Drücke des 18. Jahrhunderts in den Bibliotheken der Deutschen Demokratischen Republik; Bibliographie, 240; *29, 32, 37, 41*

Frautschi, Richard L., 14, 26, 103, 107, 110, 237, 242; *2-4, 6-7, 9-11, 13, 15-16, 18-21, 23-26, 28-29, 33, 35-37, 41, 43*

French line engravers of the late 18th century, 235

Freneuse, Château de, 49

Freneuse-sur-Risle, 49

Fréron (père), Elie-Catherine, 59

Fréron (fils), Louis Marie Stanislas, 72, 81

Fromm, Hans, 110, 116, 236; *17, 38, 48, 52-53, 56*

Fuessli, Johann Rudolf, 236

Füssli, H. H., 236

Gaîté, Théâtre de la, 153, 160, 181

Gaskell, Philip, 110, 242

Gay, Jules, 86, 107, 236; *1, 3-4, 6, 21, 25, 32, 43, 92*

Gazette nationale ou le moniteur universelle, 232

Gentleman's magazine, 232; *8*

Geoffroy, Julien-Louis, 81

Gessner, Salomon, 74

Giffard, André, 33-34, 230

Ginisty, Paul, 13, 19-20, 47, 230

Giraud, Jeanne, 236

Giraud, Yves, 236; *3-4, 6*

Girault de Saint-Fargeau, Pierre Augustin Eusèbe, 236

Godenne, René, 21, 23, 24, 64, 116, 236, 242; *29, 37, 41*

Goethe, Johann Wolfgang von, *Die Leiden des jungen Werthers*, 74

Goizet, J., 107, 148, 150, 152-53, 160, 162, 236, 239; *44, 46, 50-51, 54, 58, 60-61*

Göttingen, Niedersächsischen Staats- und Universitätsobiliothek, *38*

Gove, Philip B., 236

Graesse, Johann Georg Theodor, 236

Grand-Carteret, John, 103, 242

Grand Chasseur, ou l'isle des palmiers, Le (Loaisel de Tréogate), 54, 87, 96, 175, 195, 198, 224-25; *85*

Grave, Pierre Marie, marquis de, *35*

Graveurs du XVIIIe siècle, Les, 238

Gravure originale en France au XVIIIe siècle, La, 238

Grecian Saloon, *79*

Grecourt, Jean-Baptiste-Joseph Willart de, 55

Grieder, Josephine, 116, 236; *8, 21-22, 24-25, 27*

Grimm, Friedrich Melchior, 53, 106, 232; *35*

Grosier, Jean Baptiste Gabriel Alexandre, 72

Guiot, Joseph André, *Nouveau supplément à la France littéraire*, 237; *6, 13*

Hartog, Willie G., 96, 103, 242

Harvard University, Library of, 109; *3, 6, 9, 13, 41, 50, 58, 69, 85-86, 94*

Hatin, Eugène, 60, 72-73, 81, 242

Havens, George, 102, 234

Hébrail, Jacques, *La France littéraire*, 106, 237; *29, 33, 37, 94*

Heinsius, Wilhelm, 236

Héloïse et Abeilard, ou les victimes de l'amour, roman historique, galant et moral (Loaisel de Tréogate), 96, 108, 195, 198; *32*

Henriot, Emile, 19-20, 242

Hervé, Gabriel Alexandre Marie Gobrien, *35*

Hervé, Joseph François, 37

Hervey, James, 55

Heylli, Georges d': see Poinsot

Hill, Frank P., 236; *65, 69, 72-73, 75*

Histoire générale de la presse française, 59-60, 241

Hoefer, Jean Chrétien Ferdinand, 14, 24-25, 106, 116, 230, 236; *3, 6, 8-11, 13, 29, 31-33, 35, 37, 43, 46, 50, 57, 61, 64*

Hoog, Armand, 21, 242

Horace, 54

Horn-Monval, Madelaine, 236; *57*
Hugo, Victor, 13, 17, 23, 88, 242
Huot, François, *32*

Ille et Vilaine, Archives départementales de l', 37
Imbert, Guillaume, *Correspondance littéraire secrète*, 60, 106
Indiana University, Bloomington, Library of, 109; *61*
Inklaar, Derk, 19, 242
Iowa, Library of University of, 109; *44-45, 58, 61*
Isnard, P. Fr. d', *La Gendarmerie de la France: son origine, son rang, ses prérogatives et son service*, 39, 41, 44, 230

Jacob, P. L., bibliophile: see Lacroix
Jal, Auguste, 236
Jersey, 37
Jeunes Artistes, Théâtre des, 150, 183
Jeunes-Elèves, Théâtre des, 152
Journal de la librairie, 105, 232; *13*
Journal de lecture, 232
Journal de l'Empire, 105, 165, 175, 177, 232
Journal de littérature, des sciences et des arts, 72, 79-80, 104, 232; *13*
Journal de Monsieur, 80-81, 232; *13*
Journal de Paris, 66, 72, 80, 85, 89, 92, 104-105, 152, 232; *3, 6, 9, 12-13, 19, 21, 32-33, 43*
Journal de Trévoux: see *Journal des sciences et des beaux-arts* and *Journal de littérature, des sciences et des arts*
Journal des débats, 232
Journal des sçavans, 59, 232; *29, 37*
Journal des sciences et des beaux-arts, 60, 65, 104, 232; *29, 33, 37*
Journal des spectacles, 233; *50*
Journal des spectacles, contenant l'analyse des différentes pièces qu'on a réprésentées sur tous les théâtres de Paris, 233
Journal des théâtres, de littérature et des arts, 91, 149-50, 180, 233
Journal des théâtres, et des fêtes nationales, 152-53, 233
Journal encyclopédique, 59, 65, 71-72, 80, 104, 106, 188, 233; *6, 13, 29, 33, 37*

Journal français, 233
Journal général de France, 84-85, 104, 233; *3, 35*
Journal général de la littérature de France, 105, 233; *43, 63*
Journal littéraire, 233
Journal typographique et bibliographique, 105, 233; *32, 43*
Jules et Sophie: see *Le Fils naturel*

Kavaliunas, Jolita, 23, 242
Kayser, Christian Gottlob, 237
Kerviler, René, 38-39, 45, 230
Killen, Alice M., 73, 242
Kirsop, Wallace, 242
Kotzebue, August von, 88, 91; *59*
Krasicki, Ignace, *57*
Krauss, Werner, 14, 240, 242; *29, 32, 37, 41*

Lablée, Jacques, *Tableau de nos poètes vivans, par ordre alphabétique*, 237
La Chesnaye-Desbois, François Alexandre Aubert de, 38, 230
Laclos, Pierre-Ambroise-François Choderlos de, 15
Lacroix, Paul, 108, 238-39; *44, 46, 50, 54, 57-58, 61-62, 64, 85-86, 88, 92*
La Glehenaye, 177; *86*
La Harpe, Jean-François de, 53, 106, 233
Lamartine, Alphonse de, 13, 16-17
Lane, W. E., *81, 82*
Lanson, Gustave, 237
Laporte, Joseph de, *La France littéraire*, 106, 237; *29, 33, 37, 94*
Laquiante, A., 91, 242
Laufer, Roger, 28, 242
La Vallière, 108, 237; *6-7, 29, 33, 37*
Lawrence, H. W., 235
Lecomte, Louis Henry, 107, 150, 152, 177, 180, 182-84, 237, 243; *86-87*
Lefilleul, catalogue, 107, 237; *32*
Leipzig, Universitätsbibliothek, *29, 37, 41*
Lély, Gilbert, 81, 243
Le Mans, Bibliothèque municipale, 240; *24*
Léonard, Nicolas-Germain, 15-16; *Lettres de deux amants habitants de Lyon*, 18
Lepan, Édouard-Marie-Joseph, 90, 96

Le Petit, Jules, 237
L'Estourbeillon de La Garnache, Régis Marie Joseph de, 37, 230
Le Tourneur, Pierre, 57-58, 244
Lettres de tendresse et d'amour, 243
Levot, Prosper Jean, 14, 24-25, 107, 116, 150, 153, 179, 182, 187-88, 230, 237; *3, 6, 9, 13, 18, 29, 32-33, 37, 43-44, 46, 50, 58, 61-62, 64, 67, 74, 85, 92, 94*
Lévy, Maurice, 73, 243
Lewine, J., 107-108, 116, 237; *12-13, 19, 21, 25-26, 32, 37, 43*
Library of Congress, 109; *63, 69*
Liège, Bibliothèque générale de l'Université de, 108; *2-3*
Loaisel, Alexandre Marie, 33, 35, 37-38, 193
Loaisel, Anselm, 33
Loaisel, Emilie Judith, 33-35, 37-38, 46-47, 193
Loaisel, Françoise Mathurine Maire, 33, 37, 193
Loaisel, Gobrien Mathurin Joseph, 33, 37, 39, 193
Loaisel, Jean, 38
Loaisel, Julien Alexandre, 37
Loaisel, Vincent Joseph, 33-35, 37, 193
Loaisel de Saulnays (famille), 25, 33, 37-38, 229
Loaisel de Saulnays, Henry, 20, 22, 24-25, 34-35, 38, 47, 49, 103, 108, 116, 150, 152, 165, 175, 179, 182, 187-88, 230, 237; *3, 5-6, 8-16, 18-20, 28-29, 31, 33, 35-37, 39, 41, 43-44, 46, 50-51, 54, 58, 60-62, 64, 67, 74, 77, 85-86, 88, 90, 92, 94*
Loaisel de Saulnays, Jean David, 49
Loaisel Tréogate, Alexandre Prosper, 34, 36-37, 46, 194
Loaisel Tréogate, Angélique Eulalie, 36, 46, 194
Loaysel, Robin de, 38
Locke, John, 61
Loi singulière, ou malheur et constance, La (attributed to Loaisel de Tréogate), 176-77; *86-87*
Lorenz, Otto, 237; *77*
Louis le Débonnaire, 75
Louw, Guilbert Van de, 103, 243

Lucile et Dercourt, comédie en prose et en deux actes (Loaisel de Tréogate), 86-87, 179, 194; *46*
Lucile et Milcourt: see *La Comtesse d'Alibre*
Lunes du Cousin Jacques, 233
Lunéville, Château de, 39, 43

Maclès, Louise Noelle, 102, 243
Malestroit, 33, 37
Mante, Ed., *8*
Manuscrits des bibliothèques publiques de France, Catalogue général des, 240
Manuscrits des bibliothèques publiques des départements, Catalogue général des, 240
Marais, Théâtre du, 88, 152, 160, 194
Marc, A., 237; *3, 6, 9, 13, 29, 32, 35, 43*
Marie-Antoinette, 73, 81; *6*
Marmontel, Jean-François, 55; *Contes moraux*, 64
Marseille, *64*
Martin, André, 102, 243
Martin, Angus, 14, 16, 26, 28, 63, 103, 107, 110, 237, 243; *1-4, 6-7, 9-11, 13, 15-16, 18-21, 23-26, 28-29, 33, 35-37, 41, 43*
Martin, Théâtre de la rue, 153, 160
Masson, Pierre-Maurice, 19, 243
Mauzi, Robert, 21, 243
McGhee, Dorothy M., 21, 243
McKerrow, Ronald B., 110, 112, 243
Mélodrame, Le (*Revue des sciences humaines*), 14, 243
Melpomène et Thalie vengées, 233
Mémoires secrets: see Bachaumont
Mémorial dramatique ou almanach théâtrale, 177, 233
Ménage, Gilles, 55
Mention, Léon, 39, 44, 231
Mercier de Compiègne, Claude-François-Xavier, *Azoline ou la rose d'amour, nouvelle turque; suivi des Albigeoises*, 243; *35*; *Les Trois nouvelles*, 35
Mercure de France, 60, 65-66, 70-71, 80-81, 92, 104, 106, 150, 164, 180, 187-88, 233; *6, 13, 21, 29, 33, 37*
Mercure français, 88, 91, 152, 233; *35*
Métra, François, *Correspondance littéraire secrète*, 60, 106

Meyer, Jean, 35, 231
Michaud, Joseph François, 14, 22, 24-25, 106, 116, 187-88, 231, 237; *4-6, 9, 13, 18, 29, 31-32, 37, 39, 41-43, 94*
Michigan, Ann Arbor, Library of University of, 109; *11, 50, 60, 67, 87, 90*
Milleville, Henry J.-B. de, 49, 231
Minutier des notaires, Archives nationales, 25, 35-36, 48-49, 230
Miramont, Pierre Marie Louis Antidore, 34
Molac, 33
Molière, Théâtre de, 88, 159-60, 179-81, 194; *58*
Monglond, André, 19, 22, 153, 237, 243; *6, 9, 19, 21, 23-26, 31, 35, 41, 43-44, 50, 54, 58, 61-63, 71, 85-86, 88, 90, 92*
Moniteur universelle, 233
Monselet, Charles, 13-14, 243
Montargis, Jean, 243
Monthly review, 233; *8, 22, 27*
Morabito, Pasquale, 22, 26-27, 108, 116, 237; *3, 6, 9, 13, 19, 29, 31, 33, 37, 41, 43-44, 46, 54-55, 61-62, 67, 71, 74, 77, 83, 85, 88, 90, 92, 94-95*
Morbihan, Archives départementales du, 25, 33, 35, 37-38, 46, 229
Moreland, J., 110, 242
Mornet, Daniel, 13, 15-20, 22, 24, 28, 62, 238, 243; *3, 6-7, 13, 15-16, 21, 29, 33, 37*
Mortet, Charles, 110-11, 243
Mouhy, Charles de Fieux, chevalier de, 22
Mowinskiego, Michala, *57*
Mowinsky: see Mowinskiego, Michala
Mylne, Vivienne, 14, 26, 103, 107, 110, 237; *2-4, 6-7, 9-11, 13, 15-16, 18-21, 23-26, 28-29, 33, 35-37, 41, 43*

Nancy, 53
Nantes, Bibliothèque municipale de, 38
Nation, Théâtre de la, 98
National union catalog of manuscript collections, 240
National union catalog: pre-1956 imprints, 102, 109, 115-16, 240; *35, 81*
Newberry Library, Chicago, 109; *13*

New York Public Library, 109; *45, 54, 69, 88*
Nicoll, Allardyce, 238; *76, 79*
Nodier, Charles, 108, 238; *54, 61*
Noël, C. F., *32*
Northwestern University, Library of, 109; *94*
Nouvel almanach des muses pour l'an grégorien . . ., 74, 105, 195, 233; *93*
Nouvelle bibliothèque des romans, 233; *32*
Nouvelles folies sentimentales: see *Folies sentimentales*
Nouvelles lunes du Cousin Jacques, 233
Nyon, Jean-Luc (l'aîné), *Catalogue des livres de la bibliothèque de feu m. le duc de La Vallière, seconde partie*, 108, 237; *6-7, 29, 33, 37*

Oberlin College, Library of, 109
Observateur des spectacles, 233
Opéra, Bibliothèque de l'(Paris), 109; *50*
Opinion du parterre, 177, 233
Orléans, Louis-Philippe, duc d', *1*
Oron, Bibliothèque du château d', *3*
Ovid, 54

Paris, 16, 24, 35, 43, 45-50, 53-54, 89, 175, 180; *1*
Parisian stage, 107, 148, 152, 175, 177, 239; *86*
Parny, Evariste-Désiré Desforges de, 54, 74-75; *Poésies érotiques*, 55, 74; *Réponse aux vers précédens*, 54, 74-75, 201
Pascal, Blaise, 55
Patrie, Théâtre de la (Berlin), 88; *59*
Peignot, Gabriel, 238
Pennsylvania, Philadelphia, Library of University of, 109; *35, 54, 63, 64, 69, 85*
Perceau, L., 233
Petites affiches: see *Annonces, affiches et avis divers* and *Affiches, annonces et avis divers ou Journal général de France*
Philip II of Spain, 75
Picard, Louis B., *Les Marionnettes*, 49-50, 244
Pigoreau, Alexandre Nicolas, 238; *4, 9, 13, 19, 24, 32, 40, 43*
Piszczkowski, Mieczyslaw, 244; *57*

Pitou, Alexis, 19-20, 244
Pixerécourt, René Charles Guilbert de, 54, 96, 103, 108, 175, 238; *54, 61, 85*
Place, Joseph, 238
Pliny, 54
Ploermel, 33, 35
Poinsot, Edmond Antoine, 238; *86*
Poirer, Roger, 238
Portalis, Roger, 238
Portefeuille français, 148, 233
Porte Saint-Martin, Théâtre de la, 91, 181
Pougin, Arthur, 150, 244
Préromantisme: hypothèque ou hypothèse?, Le, 13, 244
Princeton University, Library of, *35*
Projet de discipline militaire (Loaisel de Tréogate), 188
Prout, Marie Opportune, 24, 35-36, 47-48, 193-94
Publiciste, 233

Quentin, Henri, 47, 231
Quérard, Joseph Marie, 102, 106-107, 116, 187-88, 238; *3, 6-7, 9, 13, 18, 29, 32-33, 35, 37, 41, 43-44, 46, 50, 57-58, 61-63, 67, 74, 85-86, 88, 92*
Querlon, Anne-Gabriel Meusnier de, 60, 73
Quimper, 35

Rabany, Charles, 244; *59*
Rabbe, Alphonse, 14, 22, 24-25, 49, 106-107, 116, 150, 153, 160, 162, 164-65, 175, 179-80, 182-83, 187-88, 231, 238; *4-5, 9, 13, 18, 29, 31-33, 37, 39, 41-43, 94*
Rahill, Frank, 23, 244
Raoul de Montfort (attributed to Loaisel de Tréogate), 179-80
Redon, 37
Reeve, Clara, *The Old English baron*, 73
Reichart, Frederick, 88, 91; *59*
Rennes, Bibliothèque universitaire de, 109; *16*
Renouvier, Jules, 238
République, Théâtre de la, 89, 152, 194; *53*
Restif de La Bretonne, Nicolas-Edme, 93
Revue des théâtres, 150, 164, 180, 233
Richardson, Samuel, 55

Risle, 49
Robespierre, Maximilien de, 89-90
Roden, Robert F., 238
Roland de Monglave, drame en quatre actes (Loaisel de Tréogate), 19, 87, 90-92, 180-81, 194, 197-98, 225-27; *88-90*
Rolli, M., 239
Rondel, Auguste, 103, 244; *50*
Rosenzweig, M., 35, 231
Rossard, Janine, 23, 244
Rousseau, Jean-Jacques, 13, 15, 18-19, 55, 75, 81, 95; *12*; *Les Confessions*, 95; *La Nouvelle Héloïse*, 15, 18, 63, 75, 78, 81; *Œuvres complètes*, 244
Royou, Thomas-Marie, 81

Sabin, Joseph, 116, 238; *65, 69, 72-73, 75*
Sachsische Landesbibliothek, *32*
Sade, Donatien-Alphonse-François, marquis de, 81
Sage, Pierre, 21, 244
Sainte Geneviève, Bibliothèque (Paris), 109; *13*
Saint-Germain, Claude-Louis, comte de, 44
Saint Guyomard, 33-34, 193
Saint-Lambert, Jean-François, marquis de, 55
Saint-Pierre, Jacques-Henri Bernardin de, 15
Sallier Dupin, Jacques-Yves de, 38
Saltykov-Shchedrin State Public Library, Leningrad, 109; *43*
Sander, Max, 238
Saulnays: see Loaisel de Saulnays
Schweitzer, Jerome W., 107, 148, 152, 175, 177, 239; *86*
Séguin, J. A. R., 238; *8*
Seine, Archives départementales de la, 24-25, 34-37, 45, 47-50, 230
Sérent, 33
Sgard, Jean, 102
Slatkine, catalogue, 239; *4*
Soirées de mélancolie (Loaisel de Tréogate), 16-17, 19-21, 25, 41-47, 51, 59-67, 74, 84-85, 89, 107, 193, 196-97, 209-11; *33-35*
Soleinne, 108, 239; *44, 46, 50, 54, 57-58, 61-62, 64, 85-86, 88, 92*

Sorbière, Samuel-Joseph, 55
Spectacles de Paris, 160, 233
Spectacles de Paris et de toute la France, 152, 233
Spectateur national, 233
Summers, Montague, 239; *22, 27*
Suter, William E., *76, 79-81*

Talvart, Hector, 238
Taylor, Isidore-Justin-Séverin, baron, 108, 239; *50*
Tchemerzine, Avenir, 239
Théâtre de la Révolution et de l'Empire, 132 pièces de théâtre sélectionnées et présentées par Marc Régaldo, Le, 23, 244; *84*
Théâtre Français comique et lyrique, 182-83, 194
Thieme, Hugo P., 239
Thieme, Ulrich, 239; *32*
Thierville, Château de, 49
Thomasseau, Jean-Marie, 14
Tibullus, 54
Tourneux, Maurice, 102, 107, 239, 241; *21, 24-26, 44, 50, 58, 61, 64, 71, 88, 92*
Trahard, Pierre, 20, 244
Travers, Seymour, 103, 239
Tréogat, 35
Tréogate (famille), 34-35, 47
Troyes, Bibliothèque, 16, 240; *33, 54*
Tulane University, Library of, 109
Turnbull, John D., *65, 69, 72, 73*

Ubersfeld, Anne, 23, 244
Ussieux, Louis d', *Le Décaméron français*, 63

Vadé, Jean-Joseph, 55
Valkelt, Johann Gottlieb, *38*
Vallée-Sainte-Anne, 35
Valmore, anecdote françoise (Loaisel de Tréogate), 17, 19, 51, 55, 58-60, 63-65, 74-75, 89, 107, 193, 196-98, 211-12; *17, 28, 30-31, 35, 36-42*
Valrose, ou les orages de l'amour (Loaisel de Tréogate), 25, 42-43, 46-47, 77-78, 84, 86, 92-98, 107, 112, 189, 194, 197, 212-13; *4, 32, 43*
Van Tieghem, Paul, 21-22, 57, 74, 244
Variétés nationales et étrangères, Théâtre des, 160
Vassar College, Library of, 109; *15*
Vaud, Bibliothèque cantonale et universitaire du canton du, *16*
Vérités à l'ordre du jour, 165, 233
Versini, Laurent, 21, 239; *3*
Victoires nationales, Théâtre des, 165
Vier, Jacques, 22, 244
Vigny, Victor-Alfred de, 17
Villar, Noël Gabriel Luce de, *Rapport et projet de décret présenté à la Convention nationale, dans la scéance du 18 fructidor . . .*, 48, 89, 231
Vincennes, Château de (see also Armée), *1*
Virely, André, 238; *85*
Virgil, 54
Virginie, drame en prose et en trois actes (Loaisel de Tréogate), 86-87, 182-83, 194; *91*
Vol par amour, comédie en deux actes, en prose, Le (Loaisel de Tréogate), 87, 90-91, 183-84, 194, 197, 227-28; *92*

Wais, Kurt, 20-21, 244
Walpole, Horace, *The Castle of Otranto*, 73
Walter, Gérard, 102, 243
Wegelin, Oscar, 239; *65, 69, 72-73, 75*
Weller, Emil, 239; *33*
Wéris, Jean, 24
Wicks, Charles B., 107, 148, 152, 175, 177, 239; *86*
Worp, Jacob A., 116, 239; *45, 55, 66, 89*

Yale University, Library of, 109; *14, 25, 35, 44-45, 54, 57, 59, 67, 79-80, 90, 93*
Young, Edward, 13, 55, 57-58, 61-62; *Les Nuits d'Young*, 57-58, 244

Zambon, Maria Rose, 239